THE
CRASH
COURSE

REVISED EDITION

CHRIS MARTENSON, PhD

THE CRASH COURSE

REVISED EDITION

AN
HONEST APPROACH
TO FACING THE

FUTURE OF
OUR ECONOMY,
ENERGY, AND
ENVIRONMENT

WILEY

Published by John Wiley & Sons, Inc., Hoboken, New Jersey.
Published simultaneously in Canada.

For general information on our other products and services or for technical support, please contact our Customer Care Department within the United States at (800) 762-2974, outside the United States at (317) 572-3993 or fax (317) 572-4002.

Wiley also publishes its books in a variety of electronic formats. Some content that appears in print may not be available in electronic formats. For more information about Wiley products, visit our web site at **www.wiley.com**.

Library of Congress Cataloging-in-Publication Data is Available:

ISBN 9781394168866 (cloth)
ISBN 9781394168873 (ePub)
ISBN 9781394168880 (ePDF)

Cover Design: Wiley
Cover Images: © Harvepino/iStock/Getty Images, © alexsl/iStock/Getty Images

SKY10041283_011623

Contents

Part V　Environment　199

Part VI　Convergence　233

Part VII　What Should I Do?　247

Acknowledgments

This book is dedicated to Evie Botelho, without whom my life would be far less vibrant and who has been teaching me about the healing nature of love. And to my children, Erica, Simon, and Grace, who provide me with all the reasons any father could want to leave behind a better world. I love them all dearly.

I'd also like to recognize and thank my entire team at Peak Prosperity, who are as dedicated and as tireless a team as any: Aaron McKeon, Michael Congero, and Ryan Tiefen, with a very special shout-out to Morgan Stewart for his copyediting and "proofing under pressure."

I would also like to acknowledge a few of the people who have helped me get through these past few years with my energy and soul intact: Jeff Hanson for being a great ally and friend, Paul Marik and Pierre Kory for their incredible and inspiring integrity, and Joyce Kamen and Kelly Bauman for their unwavering focus on helping people. Dan Edwards for helping out around the farm while I was otherwise occupied, and Jason Yost for holding down a huge project. Dave Pare and Pete Smith for endless hours of talking as we puzzled through all the subjects herein and many more besides. Jason Feldman for being a fantastic friend and critical mind who helped enormously with our special Brookside project and for bringing incredible subjects to my attention. Ted Cleary for levity, good food, puzzling out the world, and making us all laugh.

Finally, a huge and boisterous shout-out goes to my many followers and supporters, many of whom have been with me every step of the way over the years, been faithful advocates for truth, and who contribute daily to making Peak Prosperity what it is. None of it could have or would have been possible without you. My instinct is to list the hundreds of deserving names here, but space won't allow it and I fear accidentally leaving someone out. This book is for each and every one of you. Thank you from the bottom of my heart for allowing me to do what I do best—be your faithful information scout.

Introduction

We are at peak prosperity—a golden moment in human history when human creativity, industrial systems and know-how, and abundant energy supplies have happily coincided to create the highest standards of living for the most people in all of history. It's all coming to an end. But that's not necessarily a bad thing and for those who are prepared, the future could be even more fulfilling and entertaining than the past.

This book will help you foresee the future, but not by invoking spooky divinations. It simply provides a framework for seeing the world as it actually is, not as we might wish it to be. It offers a view usually relegated to the dusty edges of inquiry, where a few wild-haired professors and rebel intellectuals have gathered for years. One that dares to suggest that limits exist and that humans are not actually all that different from any other organism on the planet when it comes to exploiting resources. Over here on the fringe, it's a lot less lonely than it used to be as millions of people are waking up to the many troubles we face and are beginning to ask the right questions.

My perspective comes from being a devoted outsider after being a deep insider. My PhD in Pathology from Duke, my MBA from Cornell, and my successful stints working in a couple of Fortune 300 companies mean I understand the current game and how it's played. But over the past 15 years, I have been a deep outsider, too. I've spent years in relative isolation thinking and researching and writing and then researching some more. I inhabit all corners of the internet, from the mainstream to quirky intellectual outposts. Psychology tests indicate that my highest personal values are freedom of thought, intellectual curiosity, and integrity. In other words, I am not afraid to run against the crowd and come to unpopular conclusions.

Where has all that fiercely independent research brought me? To this one big insight: Our entire way of life is completely and hopelessly unsustainable. It's nothing personal, it's just basic math. Our monetary system and our economic model are both based on perpetual exponential growth, which are impossibilities on a finite planet. Fashioned at a time when the world seemed bountiful without end, those ideas are now completely due for a top-to-bottom overhaul. If we don't do it at this time, the end is easily predicted; we'll carry on until some sort of a massive calamity brings it all to a sudden and painful crash. This book is written with the hope that there's still time to grab the steering wheel and wrestle this car safely to the side of the road. In that sense, it is optimistic.

Digging a bit deeper into the *why*, virtually all of our economic abundance and growth were fueled, quite literally, by fossil fuels, oil in particular. And they still are; the only problem is that the end of the age of oil is now staring us squarely in the face. Worse, our ecosystems on planet Earth are flashing urgent warning signals, yet our global leadership seems unable to do more than fly themselves in private jets to fancy locations to present PowerPoint slide decks to each other and then tell the rest of us that maybe we should take cold showers and entertain the idea of eating crickets.

Which means the time has come for all of us to undertake the project of becoming more resilient. There's no white knight riding to the rescue, and realistically there's nothing that can be done at this late stage besides brace for the inevitable and jarring changes that are on the way.

The good news? I truly believe that this is a necessary transition for humanity and that a better future awaits. One where our relationships to each other and the earth are once again back on solid (not Facebook) footings, and where our jobs and lives are filled with purpose and meaning. At its heart, this is actually a very optimistic book, because I believe in people; I believe in you and your ability to decide what's best for you and your loved ones, and I know that humanity has managed to perform some heroic feats when it's got a big idea lodged in its cultural soul. The pyramids of Cheops, the Temple at Angkor Wat, and the Cathedral of Chartres come to mind.

We're between stories and that is an uncomfortable place to be. The old story of endless growth on a finite planet is winding down, while the new story has not yet been written so nobody yet knows what it is. Will that new story be one of prosperity and abundance? Or will it be some dystopian nightmare created by psychotic leaders unable or unwilling to engage with reality? The outcome is both in doubt and up to us.

But the data we have says that the easy times are over, and things generally get a bit harder from here on out. Ever-increasing quantities of oil brought us extremely rapid and comprehensive complexity and abundance. As that process winds down, we'll experience the opposite of it, hopefully gradually and slowly, because a sudden loss of complexity means a collapse of our economy and its many support systems. It may be many years or even decades before things truly settle into a new equilibrium (of sorts—there really isn't any such thing in this ever-changing universe).

Because I steep myself daily in being a guide to this unknown territory, I am acutely aware of the degree to which people are already frazzled by it all. Covid really sucked a lot of energy from everybody and regrettably diverted much-needed time and attention away from critical projects. Worst of all, it frayed and even destroyed many people's trust in government institutions and so-called experts, and really dented the reputation of my much-beloved arena of science. Trust is something we need more of, not less, but it was lost in spades because truly the wrong people were allowed to get their hands on the reins of power.

Yet despite those negatives, there's much to be positive about. There is much that can be done that will contribute to a more resilient future for you and the world. But first we have to know where we are. To orient properly, you must be aware of the idea that the Age of Growth is over. It's a new era. Our task now is to settle into a very different existence—one that will be filled both with fewer things and less stuff, but also with more meaning and legitimately worthy challenges. If we approach things correctly, that is.

These challenges are ones that may well rescue you from a dull life of passing the time while waiting for . . . something.

Like any good adventure, a little danger will be involved. But nothing quite so profoundly dangerous as wasting your entire life on trivial pursuits. This book is an invitation—and hopefully an encouragement—to join the millions of people who are no longer content to live in the old story and have begun to quietly, and sometimes noisily, push off in new directions.

Whether you end up planting a garden or banging a pot on the streets of Buenos Aries in protest or helping people become healthier by employing evidence-based approaches, or doing any of a thousand other things in support of resilience and change, you will be in great company.

It is my sincere hope that this book helps in some small way to encourage you to begin or advance your contributions to creating a world worth inheriting.

Let's write that new story together. It all begins by having a clear view of the actual world in which we live and the true drivers of our predicaments, and comes into being with every new seed planted in the ground and every new idea brought up and considered.

The Crash Course

PART I

How to Approach the Next Twenty Years

CHAPTER 1

The Coming Storm

In 2008 and 2009, economic activity in the United States and most other developed nations tumbled off a cliff. At several points, there was real panic in the air. Stock markets around the world fell to levels that wiped out more than a decade of gains. Trillions evaporated in the housing market, and global trade plummeted.

In 2020, Covid struck and suddenly everything seemed to become chaotic all at once. Supply chains broke down and only very slowly recovered; central banks printed up roughly 20 trillion new dollars and distributed them into economies that were hardly growing, unleashing massive inflation not seen on the world stage for a half a century and a profound wealth gap without any historical parallel.

Later, in 2022, Europe was plunged into a historically unique energy crisis. Never before had a continent of 400 million people and complex manufacturing and supply chains been starved for energy. A lot of history is being made these days.

Why did these things happen—and will they happen again?

In truth, we face many predicaments that run far deeper than even these recent, disquieting economic events might suggest. It's time to face the facts: A dangerous convergence of unsustainable trends in the economy, energy, and the environment will make the next few years and decades the most challenging for the most people ever.

The Crash Course offers a framework for understanding this predicament and provides sufficient context to support the idea that it is well past time to begin preparing for a very different future.

Everybody in power either believes or pretends to believe the future will simply be like the present, only bigger and with better technology. *The Crash Course* asks the question *What if this assumption is untrue?* and provides both data and ideas to support the conclusion that the economic status quo cannot be taken for granted, at least not in the form to which we've become accustomed.

The big story is this: The world has physical limits we are already encountering, but our economy operates as if no physical limits exist. Our economy requires growth. I don't mean that growth is "required" as if it's written in a legal document somewhere, but it is "required" in the sense that our economy only functions well when it's growing. With growth, jobs are created and debts can be serviced. Without growth, jobs, opportunities, and the ability to repay past debts simply and mysteriously disappear, causing economic pain and confusion.

In the near future, humanity as a species will have to grapple with a condition that it has never faced before: less and less energy available each year. In the past, there was always another continent brimming with energy resources to tap; another well that could be drilled; more hydrocarbon wealth that could be brought up from the depths. We have always had access to increased resources when we wanted them, and during that long run of history, we have fashioned an enormously complicated society and global economic model around the idea that there always would be more. This was a bad assumption, and it should have been more rigorously challenged and kept front and center of our national and global attention. It was mostly forgotten, when it wasn't being actively ridiculed.

Along the way, we moved from burning wood to burning coal, then to whale oil, and then to petroleum. The unanswered question is this: *After oil, what comes next?* What *is* the next *source* of energy? Nobody has a truly viable answer as we cross the threshold of Peak Oil, a geological concept that represents the moment after which slightly less and less oil comes up out of the ground no matter how much money we spend or how hard we try.

Many hold out hope that technology will ride to the rescue, perhaps in the form of nuclear power, natural gas, or alternative sources of energy. But the issues of time, scale, and cost loom large, because we have taken too long to finally recognize the imminence and severity of the petroleum predicament. Every analysis that looks into the resource issue concludes there isn't enough left in the ground to build out the clean energy future so many are hoping for.

With a peak in energy extraction, a host of environmental issues suddenly come into play. Agricultural soils that were forced to produce higher yields via the continuous application of fertilizers derived from fossil fuels will turn out to have been fundamentally depleted. Minerals of increasingly dilute concentrations that require more and more energy to produce will suddenly cost exponentially more each year to extract and process. Where markets once allocated our energy resources according to ability to pay, true scarcity will soon form the dividing line between economic progress and decline for the world's various nations. How soon will all of this happen? If not this year, then within 10–20 years, which is the blink of an eye given the scale and scope of the potential disruptions implied by this structural shift.

It is only when we assemble the challenges we find in the economy, energy, and the environment—what I call "the three Es"—into one spot that we can fully appreciate the true dimensions of our predicament. The next 20 years are going to be shaped by fundamental resource scarcity in ways we never experienced in history. The developed world is entering this race economically handicapped, with no one to blame but itself.

Once I truly understood the role of net energy in delivering all of the miraculous abundance I see and experience, and I then familiarized myself with the inevitable decline of fossil fuels, I came to a startling conclusion: ***These are the good old days***.

This is it. Today, things are as easy and wonderful as they've ever been for the average human on earth over the past few thousand years, and someday we'll look back on today and reminisce about just how great we had it.

> *"Remember when you could just hop on a plane and go anywhere in the world for the cost of just a day or two of your income?"*

> *"Or how about walking into a grocery store, any time of the year, and buying whatever fresh veggies you wanted at any time of the day or night, without regard to season? Remember that?"*

The daily miracle of life is insanely good. Simply click a mouse button and a day or two later the big, brown truck of happiness rolls up your driveway delivering goodies. Or, get knocked out for a painless surgical procedure. Maybe use GPS to navigate the worst Boston commute as you smoothly glide in a well-engineered personal chariot with 150 horses under the hood.

In truth, you have it better than true royalty did just 100 years ago. And it won't last. It can't. The flows of energy required to maintain the complexity of our current system simply aren't there.

> *Happiness is not having what you want, it is wanting what you have.*
> —Sheryl Crow

Having gratitude for what you do have is infinitely better for your mental well-being than worrying about what you don't, or won't, have. When I fly somewhere I am grateful for the magical speed and ease of the technology. When I fill up my gas tank on my car, I am grateful for the incredibly complex supply chains and financial systems in place for that to happen.

But none of this can last. The energy systems that make it all possible are still 80.4% reliant on fossil fuels, and alternative energy systems are mined, refined, built and installed using fossil fuels. There are exactly zero full-cycle alternative energy systems that can be rebuilt using their own energy output. As the prolific and incredibly insightful energy and systems author Nate Hagens wisely says, they are not renewable energy systems, they are rebuildable energy systems.

We could and we should be doing things very differently here at this moment in human history, but we're acting like we always have: ignoring problems until they cannot be ignored any longer. This was a workable approach during most of human history, but it's simply insane here with nearly eight billion people, heading towards 10 billion, and no comprehensive plan for weaning ourselves off of fossil fuels.

Heck, there's no plan at all that I have seen.

The primary question is whether we want our future to be shaped by disaster or by design. The set of predicaments and problems we now face are very different from the conditions of the past 20 years, and therefore present a solid challenge to the existing status quo. Those currently wielding power and influence are most likely to defend the status quo, raising the risk that our future will consist more of disaster than design.

Further, abrupt changes have the unfortunate tendency of escaping notice by the majority of people, who have been conditioned to expect that the future will resemble the past. This is a perfectly valid assumption for ordinary moments, but it is a liability during extraordinary times.

From time to time, it may seem that this book is delivering a doom-and-gloom message. But truthfully, I consider myself to be an optimist. The spirit and intent of *The Crash Course* 2.0 are to help you see the options and opportunities in this story of change. I have created a better life for myself and my family through the insights developed from this work. You can, too.

There's a storm coming, and it's time to batten down the hatches.

CHAPTER 2

The Lens

How to See the Future

I would like to share with you the method of thinking that led me to buy an irresponsible quantity of gold and silver in 2001, allowed me to skirt the worst of the 2008 financial crisis, and why I now live on a farm in rural Massachusetts. When I am not working at my desk to serve the community assembled at **PeakProsperity.com**, my partner Evie and I work daily to increase our resilience so that we cannot just survive the coming years and decades, but *thrive* while we help others do the same.

This method is a "lens" through which the world can be viewed. It combines the economy, energy, and the environment—which I introduced in Chapter 1 (*The Coming Storm*) as the three Es—into a single, comprehensive whole. It is a systems-level approach, but one founded on common sense instead of complicated math. If you want to make any sense of the world at all, then the deep expertise of the narrow specialists dominating the mainstream media must be set aside in favor of a generalist's panoramic view. If you find it compelling, then it might change your life and how you see the world, as it has for thousands of other people. If it's not your cup of tea, then that's perfectly fine, too; we need lots of different viewpoints to get through these next few trying years.

The first E, the **economy**, is founded on a workable understanding of how our money system *actually* operates, as well as basic economic information about debt, savings, and inflation. Not too much information; just enough to allow you to assess the sustainability of our current trajectory so you can undertake new actions and make new decisions.

Much of this analysis springs from the observation that our particular style of economy is hooked on growth. It *needs* growth the way some sharks must keep swimming because without constant movement, they'll die. Our financial system isn't addicted to just any kind of growth, but perpetual *exponential* growth, which is a peculiar thing because that's an impossibility; nothing grows exponentially forever. Or even for all that long.

As you may have noticed, world events seem to be speeding up and becoming ever more chaotic, if not urgent. I believe a thorough understanding of exponential growth helps to explain what's happening. If you are interested in peering into the future with the intent of predicting how it will unfold, you *must* learn this concept, and how and why it relates to our system of money and, by extension, economy.

Even if we were to limit ourselves to examining just the economy while completely ignoring energy and the environment (as most professional economists do), I could make a compelling case that after the past 50 years our accumulated debts and fiscal mismanagement now comprise the most daunting structural challenges ever in history. As well, there are demographic issues to factor (such as aging populations cashing in and checking out) that make the whole thing look like a rather poorly designed pyramid scheme. The developed world made a collective and colossal bet that the future economy will be a lot larger to pay it all back. But will it?

That's a good question. When we bring in the second E, **energy**, the story quickly falls apart. Our economy is dependent on growth, and petroleum—**oil**—is the undisputed king of fuels that drives economic expansion. It has no substitutes, no replacements waiting in the wings, and it is indisputably depleting. As of this writing, there are simply zero credible plans for how alternative or "clean" energy will move from interesting side shows to being the main act. The European natural gas crisis of 2022 revealed that for all of Germany's hundreds of billions of dollars of investments in wind and solar, those technologies were not even remotely close to being able to power the country.

Further, there is growing alignment between various government and private institutions on when Peak Oil will arrive, after which the irreversible decline in oil production will start and last . . . forever. This does not mean we'll "run out of oil" all at once; it means that despite our best and even heroic efforts, gradually less and less oil will be extracted each year, at higher and higher costs. If oil is depleting but our debt loads and economic system require more oil to fund more growth in order to avoid collapsing, then how does this "pencil out," as they say? It doesn't. And that's why I wrote this book: to alert you to a quite obvious, but little appreciated, systems-level impossibility.

Oil is not the only critical resource that will be in shorter-than-hoped-for supply in the future.

Literally dozens of essential minerals and other natural resources found in the third E, the **environment** (such as silver, copper, cobalt, lithium, and phosphorus) will peak right alongside oil. Many hold out hope that perhaps Elon Musk's electric cars will help save the day, but even the most rudimentary of calculations reveal that getting enough cobalt—an irreplaceable battery component—will be a huge problem. The known reserves simply don't exist.

Again, this is not a story of "running out;" this is a story of resources not being available in sufficient reserves or remaining concentrations to simply step in and take over all the heavy lifting oil provides so perfectly. We'll have to make other arrangements. That's not necessarily a bad thing, but if all your retirement dreams and hopes for your offspring are rooted in the idea that things will carry on as they have, you will be unpleasantly surprised by what the future holds. Forewarned is forearmed.

As fewer and fewer resources are wrested out of the earth to sustain the economy, it will begin to shudder and then shrink.

Will all economic activity cease with the depletion of a few key elements? No, of course not. But neither can our economy continue to operate in precisely the same way that it did when demand alone dictated supply—a system that was based on exponential growth. When *that* stops, our debt-based financial system will cease to function as it has for the past few hundred years. Perhaps it won't operate at all and, to be honest, nobody really knows for sure what's going to happen.

It's a really big change and I'm not at all confident anybody in power has any sort of a workable plan. The fact that so many of them have built bunker properties on island nations of late should tell you they don't have full confidence in their plans either.

More worryingly, we are in the midst of several ecosystem collapses and species losses happening with staggering speed. The insect apocalypse is terrifying, with bees and butterflies getting a lot of the attention, but countless smaller and less flashy insect species are also in steep declines. We're busily overseeing the dismantling of a 450-million-year-old food chain, and nobody has the slightest clue what the impacts might be. Worst of all, practically nobody seems to know the cause and even fewer are trying to figure out what it might be.

Droughts and floods now plague our living and agricultural areas with increasing frequency and intensity, raising fears that we might be entering a new era of climate chaos.

A wealth of data suggests a period of profound change is already upon us that warrants the attention of every serious long-term investor and prudent adult with an eye on the future. We can no longer constrain our thinking to just one E, the **economy**; we must include the other two Es, **energy** and the **environment**. Each of the three Es depends on the other two. They are utterly intertwined and interdependent, and that's why we need to consider them together, all at once.

For far too long, economists behaved as if the economy was an independent system. It is not. It is a subset of the larger world. I attribute all of my success at predicting the unfolding events to the fact that I hold this larger, more complete, and therefore more useful and even predictive view of the world.

To understand the economy, we have to understand energy and the environment. Once we see the role of energy in promoting economic growth and complexity (which we'll get into in some detail later) we will be in a position to assess future prospects that might inhibit or reverse the growth.

When we do, we are using what I call "the lens." The critical insight achieved from using this tool brings the understanding that continued economic growth is absolutely essential for our financial system to avoid collapsing, but is also an impossibility. This is the primary tension of our times. The implications are both profound and numerous.

Once I adopted this lens, I found myself unable to put it completely aside. It shapes my thinking and my decisions and is the primary means by which I make sense of new information when it becomes available.

As a scientist, I have constantly sought evidence that this view, this lens, might be wrong, but the data continues to pile up in its favor.

Of course, if new information comes along and proves this lens to be mistaken or misleading I would change my thinking. But as the information has rolled in over the past several years, the validity of this view has only been confirmed and reinforced.

My big picture conclusion: The next few years and decades will be shaped by Resource Wars.

In 2008, when the video from of *The Crash Course* first was freely offered to the world, I said *the next 20 years are going to be completely unlike the last 20 years*. When a sharp corner lies ahead, you have to know it's coming and then steer carefully through the bend. How will the world look in 2030? What will change and why? The lens of the three Es offers some answers and hopefully some comfort, because not knowing why something is happening is its own source of anxiety.

CHAPTER 3

A World Worth Inheriting

My mission, and the mission of my company and team, is to create a world worth inheriting. I have three children, and every expectation of having grandchildren someday. I fervently wish to leave them a world as good as the one I was born into. I want them to have the same opportunities that I enjoyed.

This mission extends well beyond my own small clan. I want *your* children and grandchildren to have access to an abundant world filled with interesting critters, meaningful relationships, purposeful activities, and ample career choices where they can apply their gifts and talents. I believe a world in which everyone enjoys a good measure of prosperity enriches us all.

I am concerned, however, that our current path and trajectory will deliver the exact opposite of these hopes and dreams. My worry is that the cultural inertia of those in power will guide us toward a series of wasted efforts to sustain the unsustainable. The social forces always conspire to keep the status quo chugging along but it is that very trajectory that will deliver us into a future of completely avoidable crisis and shortages. If we allow this to happen, what we will face is a future of scarcity, conflict, and diminished opportunities.

I cannot accept those outcomes and so I have spent nearly every day of the past 15 years building and operating the website **PeakProsperity.com**. Beyond being a repository of articles, videos, and data, Peak Prosperity is a vibrant community of people such as yourself who are curious, open-minded, and care deeply about the world they are leaving behind. They understand it's time to begin making arrangements for a very different world than the one they were born into.

To meet the future, as with any great undertaking, we begin by educating ourselves. This means steeling ourselves to take an unflinching look at our many predicaments and facing them squarely and bravely. No more kicking the can down the road for the next generation to deal with, and no more pretending that somehow someone will think of something and fix the unfixable. Education is our first step, taking action comprise the second step, and finding and building community is the third step.

The measure of any generation is what it does with what it has. Luckily, we still have abundant natural resources, and we have all the information we need to make a better future. But our window of opportunity is closing rapidly. Solutions are becoming fewer, and the more time we waste the fewer the options will remain. Someday our windows of opportunity will close entirely; our proactive options will have been permanently squandered. We will be left to choose among an unpleasant palette of meager choices. That's grim, right? So, let's not do that and decide to take a different path.

A world worth inheriting is one whose citizens are living within their economic and natural budgets. It's a place of clean air and clear water, packed with birds and insects and animals living in lush bioregions rooted in vibrant soils. It is a stable world where people and businesses can plan for the future because they know what will be there when it arrives. It is a world in which the brittle architecture of our just-in-time food systems and businesses are replaced by robust, sustainable, locally-focused operations. In this world worth inheriting, communities take on more responsibility for their destinies, and stronger and more fulfilling relationships develop among neighbors.

Right now, sadly, we cannot even count on our money, the sacred contract that binds us all, to be managed well. Perhaps it will be worth less; perhaps it will be worthless. These are both possible and even likely outcomes given our current economic trajectory, and both are unacceptable.

If we humans cannot even manage something as simple as not creating too much money, which is a very simple thing to do by comparison, what hope do we have of figuring out which combination of the 500,000 environmental chemical contaminants we've released are causing insect populations to collapse? The answer is "none."

I know we can do better and, frankly, we deserve better.

What will it take to do better? The answer I have is both simple and devilishly hard: We have to change the stories we tell ourselves. We're an oral species. Stories and mythologies actually run the show, as those are hooked straight into our emotions and systems of belief. The narratives that we run at the individual, national, and even global levels define the actions we take and what we prioritize. Therefore, the stories *are* destiny. This is basic brainwashing, when you get down to it. The more we tell ourselves we are A or B, the more we believe it.

Here is an example: Up until about 2006, the entire developed world perpetuated an ongoing story that went like this: *Houses always go up in price.*

As we all know, the tale was not true, but it was a deeply embedded belief that shaped individual decisions and led even the most sophisticated investors in the world astray. That's the power of a story.

The right narrative can save the world, while the wrong one can lead us straight to personal and/or collective hell. This means we should take the time to examine our current stories and assess whether they are truly the right ones for our era and our set of circumstances.

Some of the stories we might want to reevaluate include:

- Economic growth is essential (and good).
- The rest of the world needs the United States more than the United States needs the rest of the world.
- Technology will always meet our energy needs.
- Alternative energy can easily replace fossil fuels.
- The experts know best and are both competent and have our best interests in mind.

There is a very strong chance that some or all of these stories (and many more) will prove to be wrong, and, like any false narrative, highly destructive to hopes, dreams, and prosperity.

We are at an absolutely unique time in humanity's history, where the steps we take, or don't take, today are going to have incredibly lasting impacts on the future. Which means we'd better be sure we have the right data in hand and the right stories steering the ship. We need to locate any false stories and change them, while at the same time supplanting them with realistic, positive visions that will guide the transformations that we need to see.

In most stories of change, there are winners and losers. I want to give you the opportunity to be among the winners. I also want to set the stage for building a more prosperous future for everyone. I believe it can be done. We don't need new technologies, or revolutions, or dramatic breakthroughs in thoughts or ideas; we already have everything we need, save one thing: political will.

But that, too, can be overcome. It begins here between us, in this book, starting with a proper and honest assessment of the situation in which we find ourselves.

I am confident that together we can indeed create a world worth inheriting.

CHAPTER 4

Trust Yourself

To enhance your use of the lens described in Chapter 2, I invite you to adopt the technique of *trusting yourself*. Somehow, in some countries, the idea of *doing your own research* has been demonized in some circles. Related to that would be the derivative of *forming your own opinions* or trusting yourself. I think you should do all of these things.

If the recent past has taught us anything, it's that many so-called experts cannot be trusted. Far too many are blinded by their investment in a given school of thought, dogma or ideology, while others are compromised by conflicts of interest.

I now go through a process of vetting every expert and have them on probation from the get-go, requiring them to prove themselves first before I will absorb their data or ideas.

Like many others, my faith in nearly all major public institutions has been eroded, and in some cases it's gone. The Federal Reserve lost it when its leaders kept talking about "price stability" and "full employment" but their actions only ever did one thing reliably: widen the wealth gap.

The Centers for Disease Control (CDC) proved during the Covid pandemic that its leaders made decisions about public health only after it had first aligned with political and pharmaceutical interests. Often this meant public health never really influenced the decisions and the United States suffered many more unnecessary deaths than in other countries, such as Sweden and India.

The U.S. Food and Drug Administration (FDA) similarly seems to be completely owned by pharmaceutical interests, while the U.S. Energy Information Administration (EIA) has still never managed to publicly mention or explore the concept of Peak Oil. How is this even possible?

Each of these represents a profound individual failure of mission (and other countries have eerily parallel stories to tell about their own equivalent public entities). Collectively, they clearly say something very close to *"You're on your own!"*

So, the invitation being made here is to give yourself permission to rely on your own intuition, research, and experience regarding what is best for you and your family. Go with what you just *know* to be right. Trust your gut. Trust yourself.

If something doesn't seem right, it probably isn't. If you wait for authorities, even trusted professionals, to offer a clear signal that it's time to take different actions and make different decisions, you will almost certainly be late to the game and disappointed with the results. It may not sound easy, but if you learn to trust yourself first and foremost, it will greatly improve your chances of future success.

It took me a while to come to this realization, but I finally figured out that my interests were only accidentally and occasionally aligned with those of Wall Street and the numerous purveyors of their products. Ditto for the FDA, whose conflicts of interest are transparently tilted in favor of pharmaceutical companies. Same for the Federal Reserve, which cares a lot more about "the financial system" and bank profitability than it does the welfare of the general public.

Conflicts of Interest

Conflicts of interest are a part of life (and always have been), but today they are usually carefully hidden, so it's important to remember to bring them consciously to mind.

Once the conflicts of interest are worked out, one conclusion that emerges is that it often makes sense to do the exact *opposite* of what Wall Street recommends. Wall Street can be 100% counted on to always seek to make a profit for itself. That's all it cares about, that's all it does, and it does it really well. If there aren't sufficient options for both itself and its many customers to earn a profit, then Wall Street will ensure that it is the winner.

Similarly, politicians deal in a form of profits, too, but their currency is power. It took me a while to see the game for what it was, but I now know that waiting for the political class to inform us about any issues of real or pressing urgency is not wise, especially when the issues do not have any clear political advantage. Take Peak Oil (discussed in Chapter 17), for example—there's no "win" in that story for any politician in office, which results in nothing being said at all. They simply don't talk about it . . . publicly, anyway. They will speak earnestly if not endlessly about climate change but not do anything about it except possibly tinker with the tax code at the margins or spend more money they haven't got, effectively stealing from the future. Buckle down and ask people to sacrifice today (via higher taxes and/or lower economic growth) to carry out a well-considered plan for the future? It hasn't happened once in the 15 years I've been closely tracking the issue.

Where Wall Street has misinformed us and politicians have chosen not to inform us at all, the mainstream media has also dropped the ball, failing to counteract these transgressions by failing to provide necessary oversight and essential context. The media, our "fourth pillar of democracy," has largely failed in its investigative duties, and now mainly provides interesting but generally unhelpful post-mortems on accidents after they've happened. And that's on a good day. Mainstream media is now mostly in the business of reinforcing the main narratives of the political and financial power structures. They are indisputably the greatest purveyors of misinformation.

You Are the Ultimate Truth-Teller

The way to counteract these conflicts of interest is to simply trust yourself, decide for yourself what makes sense, and act accordingly. When it comes to great moments in history, where enormous departures from "how things were" violently swerve off the road and into new territory, early movers have the biggest advantage.

Do not wait to read about a looming issue in your local newspaper or hear about it on television from a politician, because by then it will be too late.

In a nutshell, if something seems wrong, it probably is. I have lost count of the number of people who have told me that they "knew something wasn't right" as their portfolios shed 40% or more in 2008 and 2009. Many did not fully trust the placating explanations offered by their stockbrokers, but they didn't act on those feelings, and they subsequently lost money.

The critical thing about trusting yourself is that it often means acting on incomplete information, relying on what you might call a "gut hunch" or intuition. Our bodies will often "know" something is wrong well before our minds can fully process the situation.

In the future that I anticipate, where colliding trends in the economy, energy, and the environment are going to deliver extremely large and fast-paced changes, the ability to make rapid decisions will be essential. This is the sort of landscape where trusting yourself becomes a vital skill.

Instincts Can Save You

A second aspect of trusting yourself is that quite often your instincts will lead you to do what very few other people seem to be doing. Surprisingly often, your gut sense will tell you to buck the conventional wisdom, ignore your broker, or override a past decision. I am now extremely glad I trust myself to make decisions that run counter to conventional wisdom and sometimes cut across the social grain.

I benefited greatly from trusting my gut feelings that led to responses such as buying gold when it was generally reviled as an investment back in 2003, selling my house before the housing collapse, and dumping all of my stocks before the big rundown into 2008. I fought my broker and withstood smirks from knowing friends and even some family members who were sure that I was making enormous mistakes. After all, nobody else seemed to be doing these things, so how could they make any sense?

In 2019, my Spidey senses were jangling, and my fiancée and I went on an urgent search for a house in the country with land. We got lucky and found a perfect property with an artesian well, running surface water on two boundaries, safe from flooding, and with great soil and good southern exposure for solar and growing food.

We secured the deal in November 2019 and closed on January 28, 2020. Then, Covid hit and such properties were no longer available as they all got snapped up by worried city folks with far larger budgets than we had. Pure intuition guided this move, as there wasn't any possible way I could have known that Covid was on the way.

Today, these look like genius moves, but they were actually obvious decisions. All that was required to make them was taking a good, hard look at the data and then trusting my gut—head and heart working together; both equally important.

To be fair, while some of the decisions I made led to financial gains, and some led to improvements in my quality of life, not *all* of them did. The important thing here is that trusting my intuition ensured that I was not paralyzed. There is a time to reflect deeply and accumulate as much information as you can before making a decision, but during less certain or fast-moving times, you just have to go with what you know to be true on some other level. In a time of crisis, taking action is more important than making perfect decisions.

So, how can you arrive at the best decisions quickly and efficiently?

My solution is to ask you to trust yourself. Feeling secure in your intuition is the quickest way to navigate uncertainty to arrive at a good decision.

Head and Heart

Here is a short list of things that were concerning me way back in 2003 when my broker, family, and friends all assured me I was off my rocker and making a set of very bad decisions:

- I was stumped by how an economic system predicated on continual expansion of credit could continue on like that forever.
- I didn't understand how people making $50,000 per year could buy $500,000 houses with no money down and have any hope of paying it back.

- The concept of Wall Street somehow transforming subprime loans into higher-grade securities, while extracting money every step of the way, puzzled me deeply.
- It didn't seem possible to me that money and debt could continue to expand faster than the economy without some sort of inflationary outcome or eventual financial crisis.

On January 23, 2020, I very publicly alerted the world and my many followers that a new pandemic was on the way from China. Again, I simply knew this to be the case based on all the available evidence and my own common sense. At the time the World Health Organization (WHO) was busily downplaying the data and labeling anybody promoting the idea of stopping flights from Wuhan as racists.

Meanwhile, the U.S. press was busy telling people influenza was worse. I told people to stock up on N95 masks and toilet paper. I did so because I was following the evidence, sparse though it was. Mainly, I doubted the Chinese would cripple one of their largest economic centers unless things were far worse than they let on initially. I was right; the major institutions were publicly and demonstrably very wrong.

So, while I readily admit to rooting around in masses of complicated data during such periods, this habit was the key neither to my recent investing success nor to my other life-altering decisions. Instead, I found that asking a few very simple questions provided the answers I needed, such as:

- Does what's happening make sense?
- What conflicts of interest exist in those crafting the messages?
- Are these practices sustainable?
- If these things can't go on forever, what impact would I experience if they stopped?
- How much do I trust the authorities here to either tell me the truth or to do the right thing?

The most important lesson that I have learned—especially when things are uncertain—is that you should trust yourself and act accordingly. The "experts" almost universally have a vested interest in things remaining as they are. They will tell a calming tale that usually boils down to (1) don't do anything new or different and (2) you should continue to place your trust in them.

If you have significant doubts about the sustainability of your country's current trajectory, or the stock market, or where food comes from, or a brand-new drug brought to market, then those doubts are worth listening to and acting on. There is a time to trust professionals, and there is a time to trust yourself. *Now is the time to trust yourself.*

We are about to embark on a series of chapters in which I will present evidence indicating numerous current but unsustainable trends that will not only someday stop (as all unsustainable things must do) but will collide synergistically, magnifying their impact. These trends are complex, nonlinear, and intertwined. While their specific impact cannot be predicted (as we'll discuss in the chapter on complex systems), they can be appreciated and understood in ways that illuminate the future.

Just as we don't have to understand molecular biology in order to "know" about the process of aging, we can assess the trends in the economy, energy, and environment to determine where this is all heading without having to know every detail. Much of what I am going to present is really just a common-sense connection of dots, combined with a researcher's ability to extract relevant information and an educator's desire to make it all interesting and understandable.

As we step through the material, I am going to invite you to recall the simple questions mentioned earlier, particularly *"Is this sustainable?"* At the end of it all, if you find you agree with me that we are collectively on a highly unsustainable path, the decisions you then need to make for a more prosperous, safe, and purpose-filled future will become clear.

It begins by trusting yourself.

PART II

Foundation

CHAPTER 5

Dangerous Exponentials

Compound interest is the eighth wonder of the world. He who understands it, earns it; he who doesn't, pays it.

—Albert Einstein

In this book, we will explore a few key concepts to help you gain a better understanding of what lies ahead. None of them is more important than exponential growth. **Exponential growth** holds the honorary position as the "fourth E" in this story alongside the economy, energy, and the environment.

Understanding the ways in which our lives are shaped by exponential growth is foundational. Once you see it, you'll see it everywhere. Want to be able to foresee the future and anticipate what's happening right now? Then you'll want to spend some time on exponential growth.

So what are we talking about, exactly? When a government official comes on the television and says our highest priority is "returning the economy to a path of growth," what they are really saying is that our top priority is returning the economy to a path of *exponential* growth.

That's because anything growing by some percentage over time is growing exponentially. Even something as seemingly tame as "1% per decade" is still a measure of exponential growth because it's a percentage of growth over time. This is because any future growth is itself based off of all past growth. That is, the growth *compounds* upon itself.

Examples of exponential growth in our lives extend well beyond the economy. We are literally surrounded by examples of exponential growth. The human population has been growing exponentially for thousands of years; consequently, so has humans' use of resources.

This decade there will be exponentially more retail outlets built, reams of paper produced, cars on the road, units of energy burned, money created, and food consumed than last decade.

Exponential growth dominates and defines everything that is happening—and that will happen—regarding the economy, energy, and resources of all kinds, which is why you should pay particular attention to this chapter. As soon as you understand exponential growth and can connect it to the other three Es, then you, too, will appreciate why the future will be radically different from the past.

If exponential growth is so ubiquitous and surrounds us at every turn, why is it not completely obvious to everyone? Why do we need to discuss it at all? The reason is that we're all accustomed to thinking linearly, and exponential growth is nonlinear. We think in straight lines, but exponentials are curved. Here is an example: Suppose I gave you two chalkboard erasers, and asked you to hold them at arm's length and then move them together at a constant (linear) rate of speed. You would do pretty well at this task, as would most people.

Now let's repeat the same experiment, but this time we'll replace the erasers with two powerful magnets. As you move them together, the first part of the journey will progress in a nice, constant fashion, just like with the erasers. But at a certain point—BANG!—the magnets will suddenly draw themselves together and wreck your deliberately even speed. (Let's hope you kept your fingers out of the way.)

You could repeat this experiment a hundred times and the outcome would always be the same. BANG! Those magnets would slam together.

You would never be able to get your body to achieve the same even pace of approach with the magnets as you could with the erasers. Nobody could. Our human brains and bodies are wired to process *linear* forces, and magnets do not exert a constant (or linear) force over distance. Their force of attraction increases *exponentially* as they get closer.

Despite our natural affinity for straight lines and constant forces, we *can* still achieve a useful understanding of exponential growth and why it is important. It's what we're going to do in this chapter.

Exponential growth is not unnatural, but the idea of *perpetual* exponential growth is. We have no models of perpetual exponential growth in the physical world to which we can turn for observation and study. For example, microorganisms in a culture will increase exponentially, but only until an essential nutrient is exhausted, and at that point, the population crashes. Viruses will reproduce and then spread exponentially throughout a population, but they will eventually burn out as their hosts either develop immunity or die off.

While we are surrounded by examples of exponential growth, one thing that we lack here on earth, however, is an example of something growing exponentially *forever*. Exponential growth is always a self-limiting event and one that is usually relatively short in duration. Nothing can grow forever, yet for some very poorly explained reason, that's exactly what most of us are led to believe *and* it's exactly what our poorly-designed monetary system requires. We'll explore more about the nuts and bolts of why that is in later chapters.

More on the Concept of Exponential Growth

What do we mean when we say that something is "growing exponentially"?

To begin with, let's define "growth." When we say that something is growing, we're saying that it's getting larger. Children grow by eating and adding mass, equities grow in price, and the economy grows by producing and consuming more goods. Ponds get deeper, trees grow taller, and profits expand. Within these examples of growth, we can identify two types.

The first type is what we would call "linear growth." *Linear* means adding (or subtracting) the same amount each time. The sequence 1, 2, 3, 4, 5, 6, 7 is an example of linear (or arithmetic) growth in which the same number is reliably added to the series at every step. If we add 1 each time, or 5, or 42, or even a million, it won't change the fact that this kind of growth is linear. If the amount being added is constant, then it represents linear growth. Drawn on a graph, it looks like a straight line heading up and to the right.

The other type of growth is known as "geometric" or exponential growth, and it is notable for constantly *increasing* the amount of whatever is being added during each unit of time in the series. One example is the sequence 1, 2, 4, 8, 16, 32, 64, in which the last number in the series is multiplied by 2 (or increased by 100%) at every step.

The amount that gets added in each period is both dependent upon *and* is added to the prior amount. In the sequence example given, we see a case where the growth rate is 100%, or a full doubling each time. Which means that 2 becomes 4, and 4 becomes 8, and so on. But something doesn't have to grow by 100% to be exponential; it could be any other constant percentage over any unit of time and it would still fit the definition.

Now let's take a closer look at exponential growth so that we can all be clear about what it is and how it relates to our collective future. Figure 5.1 illustrates exponential growth—a chart pattern that is often called a "hockey stick."

In Figure 5.1, we're graphing an amount of something over time. It could be the number of yeast cells growing in a flask of freshly squeezed grape juice every 10 minutes, or it could be the number of McDonald's hamburgers sold each year. It doesn't really matter what it is or what's driving the growth; all that is required to create a line on a graph that looks like the curve seen in Figure 5.1 is that whatever is being measured must grow by some percentage

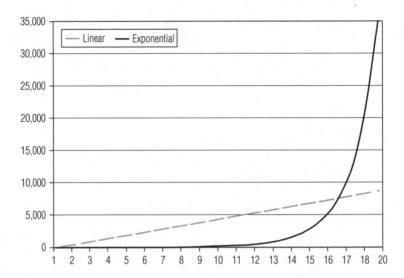

FIGURE 5.1 Linear Growth Compared to Exponential Growth

Linear growth is the dotted line; exponential growth is the solid line. The units on both axes are arbitrary; amount is on the vertical (or *y*) axis and time is on the horizontal (or *x*) axis.

over each increment of time. That's it. Any percentage will do: 50%, 25%, 10%, 1%, or even 0.001%. It doesn't matter what is being measured, either: 10% more yeast cells per hour, 5% more hamburgers per year, and 0.25% interest on your savings account will all eventually result in a line on a chart that looks like a hockey stick. The higher the percentage rate of growth, the shorter the amount of time necessary to create that hockey stick.

Looking at the figure a bit more closely, we observe that the curved line on the chart begins on the left with a flat part, seems to turn a corner (at what we might call the elbow), and then has a steep part.

A more subtle interpretation of Figure 5.1 reveals that once an exponential function "turns the corner," even though the *percentage rate* of growth might remain constant (and low!), the *amounts* do not. They pile up faster and faster. This is because they are growing based on all of the prior growth combined. One percent of 100 is 1, while 1% of 1 trillion is 10 billion.

Here's an example: Imagine a long-ago ancestor of yours put a single penny into an interest-bearing bank account some 2,000 years ago and it earned just 2% interest per year the whole time. The difference in your account balance between years zero and one would be just two one-hundredths of a cent. Two thousand years later, your account balance would have grown to more than $1.5 quadrillion (more than 20 times all the money in the world in 2010) and the difference in your account between the years 1999 and 2000 alone would have been more than $31 trillion. Where the amount added was two one-hundredths of a cent at the beginning, it was roughly equivalent to half of all the money in the entire world at the end. That's a rather dramatic demonstration of how the *amounts* vary over time even as the rate of interest remains constant, and relatively small.

Now, let's look at an exponential chart of something with which you are intimately familiar that has historically grown at roughly 1% per year. Figure 5.2 is a chart of world population.

Again, I want to draw your attention to the fact that the chart has a flat part, then a corner that gets turned, and then a steep part. By now, it is quite possible that any mathematicians reading this are hopping up and down because of what they detect to be an enormous rookie error.

A first point of departure is that where mathematicians have been trained to define exponential growth in terms of the *rate* of change, we're going to concentrate here on the *amount* of change. Both are valid, it's just that *rates* are easier to express as a formula and *amounts* are easier for most people like us to intuitively grasp. So, we're going to focus on amounts, even though this is not where classical mathematicians would train their logical eyes.

Unlike the *rate* of change, the *amount* of change is not constant in exponential growth; it grows larger and larger with every passing unit of time. For our purposes, it is more important that we appreciate what exponential

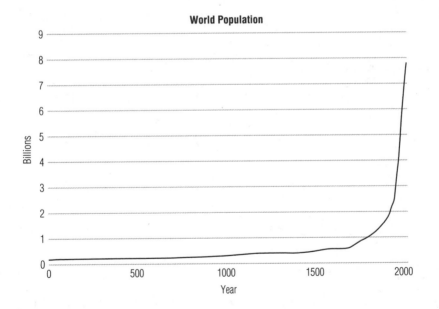

FIGURE 5.2   World Population

World population is soon to exceed 8 billion. Currently at 7.8 billion in 2022.

Source: https://ourworldindata.org/world-population-growth.

growth demands in terms of physical amounts than whatever intellectual gems are contained within the rate of growth.

A second point of contention I expect most mathematicians would vigorously dispute is the idea that there's a turn-the-corner stage in an exponential chart. In fact, they're right. It turns out that the point where an exponential chart appears to turn the corner is an artifact of how we draw the left-hand scale. An exponential chart is indeed turning the corner at any and every point along its trajectory. Where that point happens to *appear* on our charts is simply a function of how we scale the vertical or *y*-axis.

For example, if we take our population chart in Figure 5.2, and instead of setting the left axis at 10 billion, we set it at 1 billion (Figure 5.3), we see that the line disappears entirely off the chart somewhere around 1850. We can't see the part after that because it is now way above the top of the chart frame, but in this version of the chart we note that the turn-the-corner event appears to happen around 1900. Instead of having this conversation about turning the corner with population growth right now, it appears as though we really should have had it back in 1900.

Similarly, if we scale our left axis to, say, one trillion (Figure 5.4), the corner disappears entirely, and the entire line becomes flat. We can't see its curve anymore. But it is still there; it has just been suppressed by our management of the left axis. No more population problem! Right?

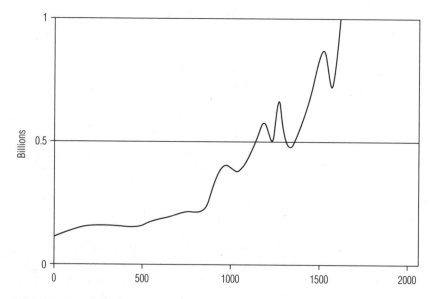

FIGURE 5.3 World Population

Same world population chart as Figure 5.2, but with left axis set at 1 billion.

Source: U.S. Census Bureau Historical Estimates.

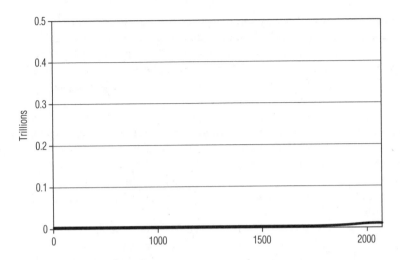

FIGURE 5.4   World Population

Same world population chart as Figure 5.2, but expressed in trillions.

Source: U.S. Census Bureau Historical Estimates.

So, the turn-the-corner moment is really just a product of how we draw our chart. Does it mean the turn-the-corner stage is a worthless artifact and we can forget all about it? Is it math sleight-of-hand that could even be seen as dishonest? No, this turn-the-corner phenomenon is very real and vitally important. Let me explain.

Where the turn-the-corner stage becomes enormously meaningful and important is when we can reasonably set a boundary—that is, *fix* the left axis to a defined limit—because then it matters a lot *where* you are in the story. When we can fix the axis against some known limit, the shape of the chart then tells you important things about how much time you have left and how the future will unfold.

For example, if we were studying yeast growth, we might start with a flask holding one liter of grape juice, which can ultimately support the growth of only so many yeast cells. With this defined limit, we can accurately calculate when an introduced population of yeast will crest and then crash.

Similarly, if we happen to know the carrying capacity of the earth for human beings, then we can "fix the left axis" and make some important observations about what the future might bring (and how much time remains to get our affairs in order). Without fossil fuels to assist with agricultural production, the total carrying capacity of the earth for humans is thought to be somewhat less than the current 7.8 billion and possibly as low as one billion.[1]

In the other direction—where reverse compounding takes over—we might be in a situation where we are drawing on savings to support ourselves in retirement. If our money supply is fixed but our expenses are growing with inflation, then our supply of money will deplete exponentially. Again, it's the growth of something, in this case expenses, by some percentage (the rate of inflation) over a unit of time. Instead of a hockey stick chart, we'd face what looks like a waterfall chart, where our savings would head faster and faster toward zero over time.

Back to the population story; even if these carrying-capacity calculations prove to be pessimistic and we could set the left axis for sustainable human population at 10 billion (although I've not read any scientific analyses supporting such a number), we would still discover that population has "turned the corner" and we're now all on the steep portion of the curve. Which means we (the global "we") have got to make some pretty serious adjustments and decisions soon.

In summary, you and I live in a very different world with entirely different challenges and opportunities than any of the people who came before us. The next few decades will see what I hope is a peaceful transition of the human population from expanding to not expanding. The alternative to a thoughtful and peaceful transition is overshoot and collapse, mirroring the experience of yeast in a flask.

Speeding Up

A critical concept I want you to take away from this discussion about exponential growth is that of "speeding up." It's the most important effect of exponential growth in a finite space: the exceptionally rapid way that the end speeds into view like a rocket powering toward a viewer.

It doesn't matter how you prefer to approach this concept. You can either think of speeding up in terms of how the amounts accelerate in size over each unit of time, *or* you can think about how the amount of time shrinks between each fixed amount that is added.

It's either more stuff with each unit of time or less time between each unit of stuff. Either way you prefer to think of it, you will be left with the idea of speeding up.

To illustrate this idea using population, if we started with one million people on the planet and set the growth rate to a relatively tame rate of 1% per year (it is actually just slightly higher than that at present), we would find that it would take 694 years for world population to grow from one million to one billion people (see Figure 5.5).

But we would reach a world population of two billion people after only 100 more years, while the third billion would require just 41 years. Then 29 years, then 22, and then finally only 18 years, to bring us to a total of six billion people. Each additional billion-people mark on our graph took a shorter and

Population Growth
Start: *1 million*
Growth Rate: *1% per year*

Time between each additional billion	
694 years = 1 billion	***Speeding Up***
70 years = 2 billion	
41 years = 3 billion	
29 years = 4 billion	
22 years = 5 billion	
18 years = 6 billion	
12 years = 7 billion	

FIGURE 5.5   Population Growth Example

Note how time "speeds up" by shrinking between each new billion people added to the total population.

shorter amount of time to achieve. The time between each billion shrank each time, meaning that each billion came sooner and sooner, faster and faster. That's what I mean by speeding up.

Speeding up is a critical feature of exponential growth—things just go faster and faster, *especially toward the end, where limits exist.*

Making It Real

Using an example loosely adapted from a magnificent paper by Dr. Albert Bartlett,[2] let's see if we can bring the power of compounding to life for you.

Here's a thought experiment. Suppose I had a magic eye dropper and I placed a single drop of water in the middle of your left hand. The magic part is that this drop of water will double in size every minute. At first nothing seems to be happening, but by the end of a minute, that tiny drop is now the size of two tiny drops. After another minute, you now have a little pool of water sitting in your hand that is slightly smaller in diameter than a dime. After six minutes, you have a blob of water that would fill a thimble. Hold that rate of growth in your mind.

Next, imagine that you're in the largest stadium you've ever seen or been in—perhaps Fenway Park, the Astrodome, or Wembley Stadium. Something that holds 70,000 or maybe even 90,000 people. Now, park yourself in one of the highest rows of bleacher seats.

I'm a tiny speck down on the field and at 12:00 p.m. in the afternoon, I place a magic drop in the middle of the field.

To make this even more interesting, let's assume two more things: first, that the park is watertight, and second, that you're handcuffed to your seat.

My question to you is this: *How long do you have to escape from your hand-cuffs?* When would the park be completely filled? Based on your sense of how quickly the water expanded in your hand over those first six minutes, is your sense that you have days? Weeks? Hours? Minutes? Months? Years? How long do you think you have before the park will be overflowing?

The answer is, you have until exactly 12:50 p.m. *on that same day*—just 50 minutes—to figure out how you're going to escape from your handcuffs. In only 50 minutes, our modest little drop of water has managed to completely fill the stadium. But wait, you say, how can I be sure which stadium you picked? Perhaps the one you picked is 100% larger than the one I used to calculate this example (Fenway Park). Wouldn't that completely change the answer? Yes, it would—by one minute. That's because every minute, our magic water *doubles*, so even if you selected a stadium 100% larger (or 50% smaller) than the one I used to calculate these answers, the outcome only shifts by a single minute.

Now let me ask you the most important question: *At what time of the day would your stadium still be 97% empty space (and how many of you would realize the severity of your predicament)?* Go on, take a guess.

The answer is that at 12:45 p.m.—just five minutes before the park is engulfed—it is only 3% full of water and 97% remains completely free of water. If at 12:45, you were still handcuffed to your bleacher seat patiently waiting for help to arrive, you might be mistakenly confident that plenty of time remained for rescue to arrive. After all, the field is only covered with about four feet of water and you are 120 feet above it, so what's the big deal? Because of how exponential functions speed up at the end, and because our park is a fixed volume (limit), you would actually have been in a very dire situation with just five minutes to go.

And that right there illustrates one of the key features of compound growth and one of the principal things that I want you to take away from this chapter. With exponential growth in a fixed container, events progress much more rapidly toward the end than they do at the beginning. We sat in our seats for 45 minutes and nothing much seemed to be happening. But then, over the course of five minutes—*glurb!*—the whole place was full of water. Forty-five minutes to fill 3% but just five more minutes to fill the remaining 97%.

It took every year of human history from the dawn of time until 1960 to reach a world population of three billion people, and only 40 additional years to add the next three billion people.

Because human population has been compounding for millennia, and because humans such as myself want things like houses, cars, and food on demand, we are literally surrounded by examples of resources being demanded and consumed in exponentially larger quantities.

With this understanding, you will begin to understand the urgency I feel—there's simply not a lot of maneuvering room once you hop on the vertical portion of a compound graph. Time gets short. We are well past the "final five minutes" of our stadium story. We're in the last minute. Better get that hacksaw working overtime on those handcuffs!

Surrounded by Exponentials

Dr. Albert Bartlett once said that "the greatest shortcoming of the human race is the inability to understand the exponential function."[3]

He is absolutely right. We are literally surrounded by examples of exponential growth we created for ourselves, yet very few people recognize this or understand the implications. You now know one implication: speeding up.

Figure 5.6 shows total global energy consumption over the past 200 years. It is plainly obvious that energy use has been growing nonlinearly; the line on the chart looks suspiciously like one of our hockey stick charts. Most of that energy, by far, is in the form of depleting, nonrenewable fossil fuels.

Can we really safely assume energy consumption can grow exponentially forever, or might we be safer imagining there is some sort of a limit, a defined capacity to our energy stadium as it were, that would cause us to fix the left axis on this chart?

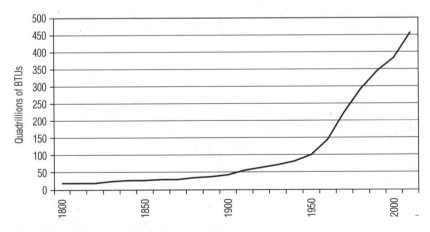

FIGURE 5.6   Total Energy Consumption

This chart includes energy from all sources: hydrocarbons, nuclear, biomass, and hydroelectric.

Source: Vaclav Smil, *Energy Transitions.*

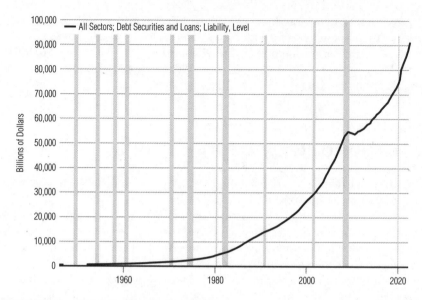

FIGURE 5.7 Total Credit Market Debt

This is a measure of all debt in the U.S. system. It includes household debt, corporate, state, and federal debt. It excludes unfunded liabilities such as Social Security and Medicare.

Source: Federal Reserve.

As we'll see later on, not only should we immediately grapple with the idea that fossil fuels are a one-time gift of natural circumstances, but we can also draw a good bead on just how much is left.

Figure 5.7 is another exponential chart, that of the total level of debt in the United States, which has been compounding at the incredible rate of 8.3% per year between 1950 and 2022.

Can we safely assume that money and debt can simply grow into infinity? What if that's not the case? What risks do we face?

These are just a few examples. We could spend the rest of the book reviewing hundreds of separate nonlinear charts of things as diverse as the length of paved roads in the world, species loss, water use, retail outlets, miles traveled, or widgets sold, and we'd see the same sorts of charts with lines that curve sharply up from left to right.

The point here is that you are literally surrounded by examples of exponential growth found in the realms of the economy, energy, and the environment. Far from being a rare exception, they are the norm, and because they dominate your experience and will shape your future, you need to become acquainted with them and recall these two things: (1) they matter a lot if your stadium has a fixed limit and (2) things speed up at the end as you approach those limits.

This helps us to better understand why it is that things seem to be speeding up lately and why we should assume that will be even more true as time goes on. Right up to the end.

The Rule of 70

As I said before, anything growing by some percentage is growing exponentially. The stadium example is one handy way to bring the concept home. Another way is to flip the whole growth concept around and be able to quickly answer the question *"How long will it be before something doubles in size?"*

For example, if you are earning 5% per year on an investment, the question would be, *"How long will it be before a $1,000 investment has doubled in size to $2,000?"* The answer is surprisingly easy to determine using something called the "Rule of 70."*

To calculate how long it will be before something doubles, all we need to do is divide the percentage rate of growth into the number 70. So, if our investment were growing at 5% *per year*, then it would double in 14 years (70 divided by 5 equals 14). Similarly, if something is growing by 5% *per month*, then it will double in 14 months.

Pop quiz: How long before something growing at 10% per year will double?

Answer: 70 divided by 10 is 7, so the answer is 7 years.

Here's a trick question: *Suppose something has been growing at 10% per year for 28 years. How much has it grown?* Intuitively, we might be tempted to say, *"Well, if it doubles in 7 years, and 7 goes into 28 four times, then it must be 2 × 4 = 8 times larger?"*

The answer is, again, nonintuitive. Welcome to exponentials! Did I already mention they aren't wired into our human hardware?

The correct answer is that something growing at 10% per year will be 16 times larger after 28 years, because each doubling builds off the last one (2 → 4 → 8 → 16). One doubles to two after the first seven years, then two doubles to four, then doubles to eight, and finally eight doubles to 16, which is *twice as large* as our intuition might have guessed.

Here's where we might use that knowledge in real life. You might have read about the fact that China's electricity consumption grew at a rate of 10.9% per year between 2004 and 2018, which at first might sound like something we could shrug at and safely ignore. However, using the Rule of 70 we discover that China was fully doubling the amount of electricity

---

*Some use "the Rule of 72," which is more accurate in some circumstances, but less easy to calculate in our heads, so we'll stick to 70 for now, as it is perfectly accurate for our purposes.

it consumed every 6.4 years. After 6.4 years of 10.9% growth, China was not using just a little bit more electricity, it was using 100% more. Twice as much! If China needed 500 coal-fired electricity plants to meet its needs in 2004, then after 14 years of 10.9% growth it would have needed 2,190 such plants. If the pattern holds, by 2024 China will need the equivalent of 4,380 such plants.

Before too many more such doublings, China alone would require the entire world's coal supply, and eventually the entire world's supply of all energy, which, obviously, isn't going to happen. The doublings will cease first, peacefully or otherwise. If this seems rather dramatic and nontrivial to you, we share that in common.

Time for another insight about doublings delivered in the form of a trick question: *Given the 6.4-year doubling time, which do you suppose is a larger amount of electricity, that which China used between 2011 and 2018 (one of its doubling times), or the amount of electricity China used throughout **all** of its history prior to 2011?*

The intuitive answer would be that the total amount of electricity consumed throughout all of China's electrified history is far larger than the amount consumed over a single 6.4-year period, but the correct answer is that the most recent doubling is larger in size than all the prior doublings put together.[4]

This is a general truth about doublings, and it applies to anything and everything that has gone through a doubling cycle.

To make sense of this preposterous claim, let's use the legend of the mathematician who invented the game of chess for a king. So pleased was the king with this invention that he asked the mathematician to name his reward. The mathematician made a request that seemed modest: to be given a single grain of rice for the first square on the board, two grains for the second square, four grains for the third square, and so on. The king agreed to this deal, but had intuitively arrived at a very bad deal as he committed to a sum of rice that was approximately 750 times larger than the entire annual worldwide harvest of rice in 2009.

Here's how that works out. A single grain of rice was placed on the first square; the next square, the first doubling, had two grains placed upon it.

Here on the very first doubling, we can observe that more rice was placed on the board than was already on the board: two grains compared to one grain. Because two is larger than one, this first doubling was larger in size than all of the grains that had come before it. What about the next doubling? Well, here we find that four grains are placed on the third square, which is indeed larger than 2 + 1 (all the prior doublings).

And the next? Here we place eight grains on the board, which is a larger total than the seven (1 + 2 + 4) that are already upon it. And so on to infinity. In every doubling, we'll find that the most recent doubling is larger in size than all of the prior doublings put together. That's one of the less intuitive but more important features of doublings. Each doubling is larger than all the ones that came before *put together.*

Now, perhaps you can begin to better appreciate what it means when it was reported that China's electricity growth had increased by 10% in 2021.[5]

Or, if your town's administrators are targeting, say, 5% growth, what they're *really* saying is that in 14 years' time they want to have more than twice as much of everything in the town than it currently has. More than twice as many people, twice as many sewage treatment plants, twice as many schools, twice the congestion, two times as much electricity and water demand, and everything else that a town needs. Not a few more, but *more than twice as many.* Perhaps 5% doesn't sound quite as harmless to you anymore?

Your Exponential World

The reason we took this departure into discussing exponential growth and doubling times is that you happen to be completely surrounded by examples of exponential growth. And your future, like it or not, will be heavily shaped by their presence.

As you read the rest of this book, it will be helpful to continue to recall these three concepts related to exponential growth and doublings:

1. *Speeding up.* Time really gets compressed toward the end of the exponential phase of growth.
2. *Turning the corner.* This is a very real and extremely important event in systems with limits.
3. *More than double.* Each doubling equals more than all of the prior ones combined.

This information is going to be especially critical when we talk about the idea that our economy, our money system, and all of our associated institutions are fundamentally predicated on exponential growth. As we'll see, it's not just any type of growth that our money system requires, but *exponential* growth.

Up until recently, it was a fine and workable model, but once we introduce the idea of resource limits into our collective story of growth (in other words, once we know just how big the stadium is), we quickly discover some serious flaws in our current narrative.

It turns out the economy does not exist in a vacuum, and it does not have the power to create reality. The economy is really just a reflection of our access to abundant energy and other concentrated resources that we can transform into useful products and services. As long as those resources can continue to be extracted from the earth in ever-increasing quantities, then our economic model is safe and sound. And that is where the trouble in this story begins.

CHAPTER 6

Problems versus Predicaments

John Michael Greer, author and prolific blogger, deep thinker and all-around good guy, made a very important distinction between two common but critical words: "problems" and "predicaments."[1] His distinction is that problems have *solutions* and predicaments have *outcomes*.

A solution to a problem fixes it, returning all to its original (or better) condition. Flat tires get fixed, revenues recover, broken bones mend. Problems can be *solved*.

Predicaments, on the other hand, do not have solutions. They only have *outcomes,* and our only option is to manage predicaments as best we can. Predicaments have to be *managed*.

Given its strict immigration policies, Japan's aging population is a predicament, not a problem. There's nothing short of importing a lot of young people from somewhere that will change that situation.

Forcing a vital species into extinction is a predicament. Creating a lab-enhanced virus that escapes and becomes endemic is a predicament. Once those things happen, they have happened. Only the outcomes can be managed.

Faced with a predicament, people can develop responses, perhaps even elegant and sophisticated responses, but not solutions. There's nothing that can be solved, only outcomes to be managed. The responses may succeed in tempering the losses, they may utterly fail, or they may fall somewhere in between, but no response can correct or erase a predicament.

Greer framed this distinction in terms of the impact wrought by the rise of industrialization and English wars of conquest upon a single prosperous English farming village in 1700. For many villagers, the transformations were wrenching and fatal. What those English villagers faced in the years after 1700 constituted a predicament, not a problem, because change was inevitable and the consequences were unavoidable.

The reason I find this distinction so helpful is this: If we have a problem on our hands, then spending time searching for a solution is a perfectly good use of our time because a solution exists. However, seeking solutions to a predicament is (at best) a complete waste of time and resources because no solutions exist. Today, are we humans chasing solutions to predicaments where none exist? Yes, that's the case, particularly in energy policies. The sooner we recognize that, the better.

Growing older, depleting a finite resource, and developing type 1 diabetes are all predicaments. The historical search for the fountain of youth was a perfect example of an attempt to solve the predicament of aging by finding the solution from a particular body of water. Because no such fountain exists, those efforts were a complete waste of time.

Let us first explore the essence of having a problem. Look at the two gentlemen in Figure 6.1. They have a *problem* on their hands.

I admit that this is an extreme example or a problem, as no prudent climbers would ever put themselves in this particular situation, but it illustrates

FIGURE 6.1   A Problem at the Cliff

Photo: Greg Epperson.

my point. There are a number of *solutions* to this problem that would return both climbers to their original condition of being unharmed and with all their limbs and life intact. Perhaps a big mattress could be placed under them, a rope could be lowered, or the climber hanging by a toe could even reach the rock face and climb down all on his own. Solutions exist that potentially allow both participants to return to their previous, presumably unimpeded state.

The gentleman in Figure 6.2, however, has a predicament on his hands.

No matter how fast or how hard he pinwheels his arms backward, he isn't going to fly back to the top of the cliff. He is going to get wet; that outcome is certain. He needs to carefully manage his current situation to secure the safest outcome that he can, by trying to hit the water feet first instead of belly flopping.

By thinking of clever ways to fly back to the top of the cliff, he will fail.

First, no feasible solution exists that can be deployed in time—people just can't fly. Second, he'll waste time and divert critical mental resources away from the all-important task of *managing* the best landing possible. When faced with a predicament, seeking a solution isn't just a useless thing to do; it is the *wrong* thing to do. Critical time and resources should be devoted to managing the outcome.

FIGURE 6.2 A Predicament at the Cliff
Photo: Brady Jones.

So, where are we facing predicaments today but acting as if we are facing problems? I submit that we are treating predicaments as problems in the economic arena (money printing and debt accumulation are examples), energy (by not seriously addressing Peak Oil), and the environment (by depleting critical resources, ruining ecosystems, causing species loss, and poisoning, well, everything).

In this book, we are going to review reams of data collectively pointing to the fact that we're facing a very large predicament made up of a series of smaller, nested predicaments. The ongoing depletion of energy, the frivolous but deadly serious mountains of debt we have accumulated, the advancing age of baby boomers, and depleting minerals are just some examples of the predicaments we face.

Yet many people and most politicians spend nearly all their time treating these predicaments as if they were problems. Solutions are sought, promised, and counted on where none really exist, possibly because predicaments have been confused with problems.

By failing to appreciate the nature of our collective predicament, we place ourselves at greater risk, because the longer we dither, less time and fewer options remain. We are rapidly running out of time.

As you read this book, be on the lookout for predicaments and problems, and recall the important distinction between the two.

CHAPTER 7

An Inconvenient Lie

The Truth About Growth

All truth passes through three stages. First, it is ridiculed. Second, it is violently opposed. Third, it is accepted as being self-evident.
—Arthur Schopenhauer (1788–1860)

U nless our leadership is careful, they might accidentally pursue growth when what we really want is *prosperity*. The problem is that growth and prosperity used to occur coincidentally, but from now on one will come at the expense of the other. We can't have both because they each result from ample surplus net energy and that is now stagnant and soon to decline. So, if we reflexively fund growth out of habit, we'll see a steady erosion of prosperity. As my website name might indicate, I am a huge fan of prosperity, and I am quite biased toward it over growth.

Growth appears to solve many problems. It creates jobs and adds new money to perpetually hungry government coffers. At the same time, new opportunities often coincidentally arise. Growth is so central to our economic models and thinking that many economists will, and with completely straight faces, refer to recessions as periods of "negative growth." If that doesn't reveal a bias toward growth, I don't know what would.

It's nearly impossible to listen to a presidential press conference on the economy without hearing about growth and how important it is that we create more of it. Economic growth is unquestionably assumed to be desirable, and that's pretty much all there is to the story.

> *Anybody who believes exponential growth can go on forever in a finite world is either a madman or an economist.*
> *—Kenneth Boulding (1910–1993)[1]*

Again, the type of growth upon which our economy is based is *exponential growth*, which is completely unsustainable. So, it's going to end sooner or later; the only question is whether we do it on our terms, or nature's. Because nothing can grow forever, at least nothing that consumes finite resources to fuel its growth, why and how mainstream economics continues to avoid discussing anything other than endless growth is something of a mystery. Maybe elite university educations have room for improvements?

It is my view that this shift to no growth or even negative growth (to use that odd economic term) will happen by 2030, although a ponderous transition is quite likely already underway. Whenever it happens to occur, the recognized end of growth will be destructive to wealth and exceptionally unpleasant for most people and especially their portfolios.

This means that the paradigm of economic growth, along with its presumed necessity and even desirability, needs to be hauled out into the bright light of day and carefully examined lest it bite us in our rear ends.

The necessity of growth is so entrenched that it's something everyone "knows" without being able to say where they came by the opinion or why it's valid. So few people ever question the importance of economic growth that it has become culturally elevated to the same top tier of the winner's podium as other "essentials" such as supermarkets and gasoline stations. Nobody would ever seriously suggest we should up and do away with those, either.

To give you a good example of this assumption, look at how embedded the concept of growth is in this short passage in a 2010 *New York Times* editorial by then–Treasury Secretary Timothy Geithner:

> *The process of repair means economic **growth** will come slower than we would like. But despite these challenges, there is good news to report:*
>
> - *Exports are **booming** because American companies are very competitive and lead the world in many high-tech industries.*
> - *Private job **growth** has returned—not as fast as we would like, but at an earlier stage of this recovery than in the last two recoveries. Manufacturing has generated 136,000 **new jobs** in the past six months.*
> - *Businesses have repaired their balance sheets and are now in a strong financial position to reinvest and **grow**.*
> - *Major banks, forced by the stress tests to raise capital and open their books, are stronger and more competitive. Now, as businesses **expand** again, our banks are better positioned to finance **growth**.*

By taking aggressive action to fix the financial system, reduce **growth** in health care costs and improve education, we have put the American economy on a firmer foundation for future *growth*.[2] The word *growth* appears six times in eight sentences, while the words *expand* and *booming* have starring cameo roles. The message is clear: Growth is what we are after. It is said so often and in so many ways that it no longer jumps out at anybody and goes unquestioned and unchallenged in the press. So, let's challenge the idea. See if it stands up to some commonsense scrutiny.

Businesses constantly seek to grow, local municipalities have growth targets, states and provinces covet high growth, and the federal government constantly seeks to promote economic growth. We'd all like our businesses, as well as our wealth and our stock portfolios, to grow. Meanwhile, the Federal Reserve (a.k.a. "The Fed") has full employment as one of its core mandates: Since the population is constantly growing and new jobs come from an expanding economy, economic growth is a logical mandate for a central bank. More growth = more jobs. The Fed also has a minimum inflation target of roughly 2%, which means that growth of the money supply above and beyond baseline economic growth is a targeted central bank policy. It also means that the money supply needs to constantly grow by some amount above even economic growth (that's what inflation means: more money in circulation for any given set of economic outputs).

Recall, if you will, that anything growing by any percentage over time is exhibiting exponential growth. Since the inflation target is expressed as a percentage over time (per year), exponential monetary growth is an express goal of the Federal Reserve. The implications of this are quite profound and we'll unpack them throughout this book.

How did economic growth come to be so deeply embedded in our language, ideas, and philosophies?

For a long time, longer than anyone reading this has been alive, economic growth has been synonymous with increasing prosperity. By prosperity, I mean a higher standard of living defined by more of everything, easier access to all the conveniences, luxuries, products, and services that define modern life, and plentiful and varied jobs and opportunities.

The Industrial Revolution brought an explosion of both growth and prosperity. When you read today about how many people live below the poverty line, it's helpful to realize that nearly every citizen of any developed country today lives at a level of prosperity and comfort that is equivalent to a level enjoyed only by royalty in the not-too-distant past.

If growth delivered this prosperity, then it is easy to understand why growth would be revered and sought. If growth brings prosperity, then let's have growth! From there, it's just a hop, skip, and a jump to the measurement and pursuit of economic growth as an end all its own, and that is where we find ourselves today.

But is it actually true that growth equals prosperity? What if it doesn't? What if prosperity was entirely coincidental with growth and neither had any role in causing the other? More worryingly, what if growth and prosperity are only related by the fact that they share the same underlying causal factor? If that's the case, we'd better do what we can to understand that thing, whatever it is.

So, let's start with growth. Thought about one way, we might observe that growth is actually a consequence of, and dependent on, the condition of having surplus. For example, our bodies will only grow if they have a surplus of food. With an exact match between calories consumed and calories burned, a body will neither gain nor lose weight. A pond will only grow deeper if more water is flowing in than flowing out. With a deficit of food or water, growth of bodies and ponds will cease and then reverse. Growth in these and countless other examples is a function of surplus.

But exactly what sort of a "surplus" is economic growth dependent on? It's not a surplus of money, or labor, or ideas, although each of those can be an important contributing factor. All economic growth is dependent on what economist Julian Simon called "the master resource"—**_energy_**.[3]

We'll have much more to say about that later on, but for now we'll just make the claim that without energy an economy will simply not exist.

Prosperity too is dependent on surplus. Here is an example: Imagine a family of four with a yearly income of $40,000 that is sufficient to precisely cover life's necessities. For this family, there is a perfect balance between income and outflow. Now suppose that good fortune befalls them, and they receive a 10% boost to their household income. This windfall will allow them to _either_ afford to have one more child (i.e., grow) _or_ to shower a little bit more spending on each person (i.e., economic prosperity), but they can't do both. There's only enough surplus money in this example to do one of those two things, so this family will have to choose between additional growth or more prosperity. When the amount of surplus is sufficient for only one or the other, either growth _or_ prosperity can be increased, but not both at once. "Funding" both growth _and_ prosperity at the same time can only happen during periods when there's enough surplus to fund both.

From this simple example, we can tease out a very basic but profound concept: _Growth does not equal prosperity._ For the past few hundred years, we've been lulled into linking the two concepts, because there was always sufficient surplus energy that we could have both growth _and_ prosperity. And, because both happened at the same time, we began to inappropriately conflate the two (with a lot of help from politicians who wanted more power and a happy populace, and a lazy media that forgot to ask basic questions). The surplus, as we'll see, was really more of an artifact of a fossil fuel bonanza, not because humans' cleverness assures the permanent presence of both growth and prosperity.

If growth in structures and population by itself were responsible for raising prosperity, then Quito, Ecuador, and Calcutta, India, would be among the most prosperous places on earth. But they're not.

If growth in a nation's money supply brought prosperity, then Zimbabwe would have been the wealthiest country on the planet in 2010 when it was producing 100 trillion-dollar bills. But clearly that didn't do the trick.

Growth alone does not bring prosperity, and, worse, under conditions of insufficient surplus, growth can steal from prosperity.

In wealthier countries where an energy and resource bonanza can provide enough surplus for both growth and prosperity, we see both. In poorer countries that can only afford to fund one or the other, we typically only see population growth. For the past 200 years, the developed world has not had to choose between growth and prosperity—it could have both, and it did.

The most important resource of them all is energy. Surplus energy is *the bomb*, and our twin pursuits of growth and prosperity rest entirely on surplus energy.

As long as energy supplies can continue to grow forever, there is no conflict between growth and prosperity, and we'll never have to choose between the two. But someday, total surplus energy dependent on finite resources will decline, and the world will discover that a dogged focus on growth will steal from its prosperity. Unless we're careful, there will come a time when 100% of our surplus money or energy will be used to simply grow, and the result will be a stagnant economy and declining prosperity.

This was the case in Europe in 2022, where the sudden loss of energy supplies from Russia very rapidly morphed into household and business energy bills that spiked as much as 10-fold in a matter of months, stealing from both growth and prosperity at once. If European leaders had bothered to read the first edition of the book back in 2011, they might have avoided the wrenching disruptions they chose for themselves and their citizens by following the first rule of life: Fill your energy tanks to the brim, *then* put sanctions on Russia.

The inconvenient truth about growth is that it only really serves us if there is sufficient surplus to fund both growth *and* prosperity. Once there is not enough surplus for both, which one gets funded becomes a contest.

Our slavish, unexamined devotion to growth is so deeply embedded within our language and cultural ideology that we will seek out more growth by default because we're unaware that it is prosperity we'd actually rather have if given the choice.

The most important decision of our time, and the one by which we will be remembered (fondly or otherwise) by future generations, concerns how and where we utilize our remaining energy and other natural surpluses. Choices must be made. We cannot have *both* any longer. We can either spend our surplus resources toward trying to figure out how to simply grow, or we can spend them toward increasing and enhancing our prosperity.

My strongest preference would be to see continued prosperity along with progress in energy production and efficiency, medical technology, and other significant advancement opportunities modern society can offer. These are but a few of the things we place at risk if we allow ourselves to do what is easy—that is, to take the path of least resistance and simply grow—instead of doing what is right, which would be to put the brakes on growth while we intelligently dedicate our remaining energy surplus to a more prosperous future.

CHAPTER 8

Complex Systems

I'm a generalist. A systems guy. I like to see things from 30,000 feet before I zero in on the details. That's been my superpower these past few years, and I'd like to share this way of thinking with you. It rests on understanding what systems are and a few properties of how they behave.

The dictionary says a system is "a set of things working together as parts of a mechanism or interconnecting network." So, your cell phone is part of a system that routes and stores information. Your body is a system housed within the solar system. Humans in groups, especially nation-sized groups, operate as a system.

What we call the economy and the environment are also each a system, but a special kind of system called a "complex system." There are huge insights that come from understanding complex systems, so we're going to spend a far too brief moment here going over complex systems.

Usually there's plenty to learn and nothing wrong with listening to experts. But sometimes they cannot see the forest for the trees. If you want to know about a particular tree, ask a tree expert. But if you suspect there's a forest fire on the way, you need to understand the whole forest, and quickly!

Systems—Open versus Closed

There are two types of systems: open and closed. An open system is one that can transfer energy between the system and its surroundings. A closed system cannot.

The universe is a closed system. There is no "outside" the universe, no other system beyond its boundaries that it can interact with. Everything that happens within that universe is a function of the energy and matter already contained within it.

A glass of hot water on a kitchen counter is an open system. It will lose its heat to its surroundings, transferring energy across its boundary. The earth is an open system; it sits in the middle of a river of energy streaming from the sun, which it both absorbs and radiates back into space. Your body is an open system, which is constantly involved in taking in food, oxygen, and water while radiating heat and excreting waste back into its surrounding environments.

Now, here's the thing about systems and their relationship to energy. Our universe is governed by certain laws and the laws of thermodynamics govern the transfer of all energy within, among, and between all the systems in the entire universe, no exceptions.

First law of thermodynamics: Energy can neither be created nor destroyed, but it can be changed from one form to another.

The first law tells us that the amount of energy in a system is all it's got, unless it can get more from outside of its system somehow. The earth has only two sources of energy and one large battery. The sun is the obvious main source; while another is nuclear fission, which involves the conversion of matter directly into energy via the process of splitting an atom. Earth's "battery" is the geothermal heat left over from its formation billions of years ago, that even now is percolating to the surface most dramatically in places like Iceland, where volcanos and hot vents make life a bit more interesting for the locals.

What about wind power, you ask? Well, that's a derivative of the sun's heat causing the air to circulate. Hydropower is the sun's heat causing water to evaporate and then fall as rain at higher altitudes, creating potential energy. Fossil fuels are ancient sunlight captured by photosynthesis and then deposited in ancient seabeds and swamp floors over hundreds of millions of years.

So, the earth has an allotment of energy it can tap into and use, and a daily budget of new energy from the sun. Why is all that at all relevant? Because of the second law of thermodynamics.

Second law of thermodynamics: Any system will tend toward maximum disorder (entropy) over time.

"Entropy" is a very useful word that packs a lot into it. Entropy is "the measure of a system's thermal energy per unit temperature that is unavailable for doing useful work." What this means is that, over time, any system will tend to wind itself down, having less and less ability to perform "work," which can mean many things. We'll get to those soon.

The first and second laws of thermodynamics are immutable. They are *laws* in the eyes of physics, elevating them far beyond mere hypotheses and theories. They've never been experimentally violated, ever, and every bit of data we have confirms them. Like gravity, these laws operate at all times and are completely uncaring as to whether anybody believes in them or not.

To unpack that second law, let's consider a diesel locomotive. Outside of the engine is the atmosphere, hanging around at roughly 1 atm at sea level, or 15 psi, and let's say a temperature of 50° F. Inside of a given operating diesel piston at the moment of ignition the pressure will be around 300 psi and the temperature 500° F. It's the extreme difference between the pressure and temperature inside the piston versus outside that allows useful work (moving the piston up and down forcefully, if not violently) to be performed.

Let's imagine we run this diesel engine until it runs out of fuels. By the end it's smoking hot! Lots and lots of heat in that engine block. Touch it and you will be burned, so clearly it still has lots of energy in it. But can it perform useful work? No, that piston will not crank up and down simply because of the waste heat, the entropic heat, it still contains. Yes, the engine system has plenty of energy within it, but not enough to perform any useful work.

It has succumbed to the second *law* of thermodynamics.

It's the reverse of this process where the magic happens. A system that can get more energy from the outside can do something truly wondrous and upon which all of life itself is based: ***create order***.

A system without more energy flowing in will, over time, tend toward maximum entropy, a condition of having all its energy evenly and uselessly and blandly distributed within its "walls," thereafter remaining in that form for all of eternity.

Yawn. Sounds boring (because it is).

But a system with energy flowing in and through it? *Zing!* Now we have something to talk about!

With available energy to exploit, systems can run the other direction and create more order out of less order. Work can be performed and in the case of life that work takes the form of making fantastically complicated and complex forms out of base molecular building blocks. With energy, more order and complexity can arise. Without energy, less order and complexity results.

And that is the great mystery and metronome of the universe—energy pulsing through various systems allowing for the most amazing expression of complexity: life itself. You, in other words. But also, trees and fish and bumblebees. All of it.

The sun's primary energy beams down and is captured by photosynthesis. This allows large, complex, and well-organized molecules to be fashioned out of carbon dioxide and water, the two molecules at the tail end of life's own entropy cascade (as they are "fully oxidized" and have no more chemical energy to give to an oxygen-dependent pathway).

The lesson here is that as long as an open system has energy flowing through it, it will maintain its vital and unpredictable complexity. If it doesn't, then it will immediately begin to become less complicated, less interesting, and possibly terminally boring.

In other words, ***energy is everything***.

Because of this insight, it seems pretty obvious that one of the most vital things you could possibly track for any open system about which you care would be the energy flows. This brings us, sadly and in the wrong way, to the dreary profession of economics.

Economists—Closed Minds

Learn how to see. Realize that everything connects to everything else.

—Leonardo DaVinci

Everything is so intimately interconnected that it's actually foolish to only study things in isolation, and no profession is quite as stubbornly and expertly foolish these days as mainstream economics.

One of the (many) ways classical economists go astray is by assuming that the economy exists in a vacuum, a complete little private universe that can be understood on its own, without considering "externalities" in the form of the resources that cycle in and the waste that must cycle out.

The problem with this view is that the economy is an open system. It is absolutely **not** a complete little universe all its own and it clearly and obviously owes its order and complexity to the flows of energy that run through it and sustain its many moving parts doing useful work.

Most mystifyingly, mainstream economists still use closed-form equations while operating an open-form system. It's as if they had never heard of the second law of thermodynamics and are still using approaches last seen in the late 1700s to try and make sense of the world.

Why are they doing this? Because it gives them tidy answers. Open-form systems equations are notorious for not giving a static answer. There's no "equilibrium state," only a temporary equilibrium dependent on all sorts of things that might themselves be changing in dynamic feedback with the thing you wish to be in equilibrium.

From Wiki:

> *An economic equilibrium is a situation when the economic agent cannot change the situation by adopting any strategy. To fully grasp the concept of economic equilibrium, it must be highlighted that it has been borrowed from the physical sciences. Take a system where physical forces are balanced for instance. This economically interpreted means no further change ensues.*

The above is, quite literally, the current state of the economic profession. They are seeking "equilibrium" within an open system! And a complex system at that, which we'll unpack in a moment.

It is a fool's errand performed by fools, but unfortunately these fools also have their hands on the printing press.

I have read a lot of economic papers put out by central bankers and leading economics schools. Too many. And not one of them—not one!—has ever paid the slightest attention to the relevance and importance of energy flows to their equations or models. It is simple not included, which means it is fully assumed to be there, like a fish might assume the presence of water.

Where economists assume that needed resources will magically arise because the marketplace demands them, a more holistic model would begin with the observation that the economy only exists *because* the resources are available and then weave in some thinking about what happens to their models if/when those energy resources cannot expand.

The way I see it, the natural world isn't a subset of the economy, it is the other way around—the economy is a subset of the natural world. Economists happily invert that and then build elaborate upside-down models while politicians eagerly applaud the status-quo reinforcing conclusions.

Every single one of these economic models is geared around the idea of perpetual growth. And not just any growth, but a certain percentage growth per year—in other words, **exponential growth**.

If an economy is said to be in long-run equilibrium, then Real GDP is at its potential output, the actual unemployment rate will equal the natural rate of unemployment (about 6%), and the actual price level will equal the anticipated price level.[1]

The only world in which conventional economics and its primary goal of being in a state of perpetual growth makes any sense is in a world without limits, one in which no resource constraints exist.

This is clearly and rather easily proven to be an almost childish level of logical thinking. While economists have PhDs and can run circles around me with their math formulae, none have managed to answer this simple question of mine: "How can the economy grow forever, exponentially, on a finite planet?"

Our Complex World

Our economy has also been growing exponentially in complexity by leaps and bounds, as Eric Beinhocker beautifully captured in his amazing book *The Origin of Wealth*:

Retailers have a measure, known as stock keeping units (SKUs), that is used to count the number of types of products sold by their stores. For example, five types of blue jeans would be five SKUs. If one inventories all the types of products and services in the Yanomamo [stone age tribe] economy, that is, the different models of stone axes, the number and types of food, and so on, one would find that the total number of SKUs in the Yanomamo economy can probably be measured in the several hundreds, and at the most thousands. The number of SKUs in the New Yorker's economy is not precisely known, but using a variety of data sources, I very roughly estimate that it is on the order of 10 to the 10th (in other words, tens of billions).

To summarize, 2.5 million years of economic history in brief: for a very, very, very long time not much happened; then all of a sudden, all hell broke loose. It took 99.4% of economic history to reach the wealth levels of the Yanomamo, 0.59% to double that level by 1750, and then just 0.01% for global wealth to leap to the levels of the modern world.[2]

Wealth and development trundled along for thousands and millions of years without doing much and then suddenly—boom!—here we are typing this on a computer that has thousands of components assembled and delivered over tens of thousands of supply chain miles. The economy suddenly became a *lot* more complex. That did not happen because humans are clever—although we are—but happened because (1) clever humans could (2) access massive energy flows to run through the open system of the economy. It was energy that freed humans from the tedium of mainly spending their time surviving, and it was energy that powered the machinery of commerce, allowing a vast increase in order and complexity to erupt.

No energy means no complexity means no complicated economy. That's my thesis. It seems obvious when seen in this light but given my inability to convert any card-carrying mainstream economists to the view, perhaps it's subtle and tricky after all.

Or perhaps writer, muckraker, and political activist Upton Sinclair was onto something when he said, *"It is difficult to get a man to understand something when his salary depends upon his not understanding it."*

The amount of economic complexity required to build, track, ship, and utilize tens of billions of items is enormous. We can only describe our economy as a complex system that, like any other, owes its complexity to the continuous throughput of energy.

A main purpose of this book is to explore the connection between the economy and energy, and then ask what will happen to our economy when (not if, but *when*) ever-increasing energy (oil) flows through the economy stall out. And then, what happens when those ever-increasing flows go in reverse? Because open systems can only increase their complexity and maintain their order through the use of energy, the simple prediction is that our economy's growth in complexity will also stall at first and then go into reverse. In other words, they will simplify. It doesn't take too much of an imagination to hop, skip, and jump from there to various dire scenarios, up to and including Mad Max.

The hard part is predicting what will happen and when, because one consistent feature of complex systems is that they are inherently unpredictable.

Complex . . . sand piles? Complex systems, besides owing their order and complexity to energy flows, have one more massive "feature" that everybody ought to know about.

They are inherently unpredictable.

Predicting when something will happen in a complex system is impossible. Predicting exactly what will happen is also impossible. Complex systems have what are called "emergent behaviors" and you just have to be patient and wait to see what those are when they finally decide to show up.

Even something as seemingly simple as predicting the behavior of a growing sand pile currently eludes our predictive abilities. Imagine dropping grain after grain of sand into a pile. As you drop the grains one by one the pile grows and grows, but as it does it becomes increasingly unstable. At some point the pile will slump a little, or perhaps even collapse. Knowing when it will collapse (*this next grain will do it!*) and how much (*there will be an avalanche on this side, involving 3,714 grains*) seems as though it should be a straightforward task, but it's really not. It's impossible.

In *Ubiquity: Why Catastrophes Happen* by Mark Buchanan, a tale is recounted of three physicists—Per Bak, Chao Tang, and Kurt Weisenfeld—who set about trying to discover if they could predict when, where, and to what degree sand piles would avalanche. Using a computer model to speed things along, they ran an enormous number of simulations and discovered that nothing could be predicted at all. Not the size of the avalanche, which could range from a single grain tumbling down the face to the complete collapse of the whole pile, not the timing between events, and not whether the next grain would trigger either a cataclysm. None of it was predictable.

You would think that such a simple system could be accurately modeled, but that's not the case. Exactly when the pile will finally slump is unpredictable. Exactly how large the resulting slump will be is also unpredictable. The "when" and the "how much" are unknowable (using current modeling techniques).

All that can be calculated for certain is that a higher pile with steeper sides/areas (a.k.a. "fingers of instability") is more likely to slump sooner and more catastrophically. Ah! That's at least helpful. It tells us that complex systems are more likely to break when their internal stresses get closer to some breaking point.

However, like all good scientific inquiry, they discovered some important properties of complex systems, not least of which is the insight that they are inherently unpredictable.

But this doesn't mean they're *entirely* unpredictable. Knowing something of the "system of sand," we can put some boundaries around what might and might not happen and can therefore "predict" the future within a range of boundaries, even though the timing and precise details might elude us.

For example, we know that a growing sand pile will eventually collapse; we know that it cannot grow to be 10 times taller than it is wide; we know that the higher and more complex the pile becomes, the more likely an avalanche becomes; we know that a sand pile is a complex system and will therefore behave in unpredictable ways. These are all things we now know.

While we cannot predict exactly what will happen and when, we can understand the boundaries of the system and therefore know what is both possible and probable.

We know this from our everyday lives. We don't know when, where, or how large the next earthquake in California will be, but we know that one will eventually happen. Because an earthquake in California is both possible and probable, local building codes seek to mitigate the risks by utilizing specific architectural designs and structural reinforcements.

When we sit at the beach on any given day, we cannot possibly predict the form of every crashing wave and the shape of every turbulent eddy in the water's retreat, but we can easily "predict" a range for the size of the waves that will wash in over the next hour. Based on the gentle one-foot waves lapping the shore we might form an expectation that the next hour of waves will be between 0.5 feet and two feet, but most likely one foot in height. Our internal risk meters would be comfortable letting our children play in the surf, confident that an 18-foot wave won't suddenly arrive to ruin the day. While chaotic and unpredictable in their micro form, the macro-outlines can be understood.

Although events within complex systems are unpredictable in their timing and details, we can still (1) understand that they'll happen, (2) know that when stresses are building the events become more likely (and larger), and (3) recognize the rough boundaries of the system.

CHAPTER 9

Our Money System

Before we begin our tour through the economy, energy, and the environment, it's important that we build a common understanding of this thing we call "money."

Money is something we live with so intimately on a daily basis that it has probably escaped our close attention, much like the distinction between growth and prosperity.

Initially what gave money its start were agricultural surpluses that represented real, tangible wealth that could be stored for relatively long periods of time. Over time, people learned it was far easier to convert stores of food into units of money, which could be exchanged for a wide variety of other goods and services, than it was to barter directly using grain.

Money, of course, is an essential feature of our lives. People in practically every culture ever studied, in every region of the world, even those locked down in supermax prisons, have invented and used some form of money, indicating without a doubt that it is a very common attribute of civilization. Religion and money share that in common. Were all of our paper and electronic currency to disappear, a new form of money would rapidly and necessarily arise to take its place. Humans and money are intertwined. If a group of humans stripped of everything were to colonize a deserted island, sooner or later they'd settle on something to be their "money."

By way of example, in U.S. federal correctional facilities, prisoners used to pay each other with "money" in the form of packs of cigarettes. But those were prohibited in 2004, so what were the prisoners to do? They quite soon came to accept plastic-and-foil pouches of mackerel, which they call "macks,"[1] as their new currency. Prisoners used "macks" to pay for haircuts, get their clothes pressed, and settle gambling debts. The "macks" work because they are inexpensive (they cost about $1 each), but few inmates actually want to eat them, so they remain reliably in circulation. And they don't go bad.

In the great Argentinian economic crisis of 1999–2001, circulating U.S. dollars evaporated practically overnight and people were left with rapidly depreciating pesos nobody really wanted. As a consequence, many businesses closed, and imported products became virtually impossible to buy. Within a relatively short period of time, farmers began using soybeans to barter for new vehicles, and individual provinces rapidly issued their own forms of paper money.

Money is essential, especially to complex societies. Without money, the rich tapestry of job specializations enjoyed today could not exist, because barter is too cumbersome and constraining to support a lot of complexity. Our globalized economic system is 100% dependent on money and were money to disappear, life's many necessities and pleasures would very rapidly disappear, too.

For money to be *money* it must possess three characteristics. The first is that it must be a *store of value*. That is, it can't lose its value over time. Just as gold and silver stick around because they don't rust, "macks" stick around because nobody wants to eat them. These forms of currency represent excellent stores of value. On this basis, modern fiat money, which is under a constant regime of inflation, is actually poor-quality money.

A second feature is that money needs to be accepted as a *medium of exchange*, meaning it's widely accepted within and across a population as an intermediary for all economic transactions. Here again, "macks" work as a currency because enough people in the prison system have agreed to accept them. Outside of prison walls, paper currencies and their digital equivalents obtain their value by fiat, or by force of law. This explains why they're termed "fiat currencies."

Governments declare these pieces of paper (and their electronic equivalents) to be legal tender. You *have* to accept them in settlement for debts, and that taxes can *only* be paid with them and nothing else. The "medium of exchange" feature is enforced by government decree for fiat money, whereas the "macks" are legitimized by a form of cultural consent.

But in all cases, money is an agreement between people. The agreement might be direct and voluntary, or indirect and somewhat involuntary if one is born into a system of law where a currency already exists. I suppose you could try to vote in people who might change our currency, but that's not a quick or terribly realistic idea.

When it comes to money, we agree that *these* bits of paper, but not *those* bits of paper, have value. A stack of $100 bills has a lot of value. A stack of old newspapers not so much. Prisoners seem to have agreed that foil pouches of mackerel are valuable, but not gym socks. If you understand that money is simply an agreement between people, then you understand the essence of money.

The third feature of money is that it needs to be a *unit of account*, meaning each unit must be equivalent to any other unit. A dollar in your wallet is the same as a dollar in my wallet. One is not worth more or less than the other. Along with this idea comes the characteristic that money should be divisible, meaning you can make it into smaller parts, which can then be recombined without harming the value. The "unit of account" in the United States is the dollar. Each dollar has exactly the same utility and value as the next, and you can take a dollar and exchange it into four quarters and then back again without losing any value. Ditto for euros, yen, or yuan.

Diamonds have a very high *value*, but they're not good at being money because they are individually varied and are therefore not perfectly equivalent to each other. Diamonds fail at being a unit of account, and dividing them individually causes them to lose value.

So, diamonds may be quite valuable and great at being beautiful, but they are bad at being money. "Macks," on the other hand, are all exactly the same, so they score high in the category of being a unit of account, but presumably they don't divide very well, so they're not as useful for transactions that cost less than one "mack" or might require a partial "mack." So "macks" are reasonably good at being money, but they're not perfect. But, hey, this is federal prison we're talking about, so close enough is good enough.

Okay, those are all the characteristics money has to have to be money, but what is it *really*? I believe the answer is simple: *Money is a claim on real wealth* (but it is not wealth itself).

Money all by itself (with the exception of "macks," which can be eaten, I suppose) has little to no actual value. Get stuck on a deserted island with a fat stack of cash and you'll quickly wish you had something else, some *real* wealth. Like food, or a gun, or a fishing rod, or a tarp. Money is just the way we store our wealth, in an agreed-upon form, offline but ready to convert into the things we really want and need in life. Money by itself isn't really useful. At all.

As we will see in Chapter 10 (*What Is Wealth?*), primary wealth represents the abundance of the earth. If you move some electronic digits from your bank account to another person's account and gain a productive oil well in the process, you have just used your *claim on wealth* to secure some *actual wealth*.

Now, it's up to that recipient of your money to decide where and when they'd like to claim some wealth of their own, too. This idea of money merely representing a claim is important, especially when we consider that these claims have historically been growing exponentially, because too many claims is a recipe for monetary and social disaster.

Full Faith and Credit

Literally anything can fulfill the role of money in a given culture: cows, bread, shells, beads, and tobacco all served as money in the past. Once upon a time in U.S. history, a dollar was backed by a known weight of silver or gold and the dollars themselves came directly from the U.S. Treasury. Of course, those days are long gone. Now dollars are the liability of an entity called the Federal Reserve, a privately held organization entrusted to manage the U.S. money supply and empowered by the Federal Reserve Act of 1913 to perform this function.

If you pull out a current physical U.S. dollar and read it carefully as though it were a contract (which it is), you'll notice that modern dollars no longer have any language on them entitling the bearer to anything. Dollars are no longer backed by any tangible substance sitting in a vault, warehouse, or silo. You can't demand something from the Federal Reserve or the U.S. Treasury in exchange for a dollar, other than a replacement dollar.

Rather, the "value" of the dollar comes from the language on the front, which reads *Legal tender for all debts public and private*, which means that it's illegal to refuse to accept dollars for debt settlements and that you can't pay taxes in anything else—all of which is to say, money is really a form of a contract. It's a social contract, formed by agreement and enforced by the government.

Dollars have perceived value because they're backed by the "full faith and credit" of the U.S. government, but what this really means is becoming increasingly difficult to justify or explain as debts mount and fiscal deficits are simply always part of the budget cycle. Backed how exactly? By what? As we'll continue to reinforce, money has no value at all unless it can be exchanged for something.

It is therefore vitally important that a nation's money supply be well-managed because if it's not carefully regulated and too much is "printed up," as they say, the monetary unit can be rapidly diminished by inflation. Has this happened before? Yes, of course. Thousands of paper currencies have come and gone throughout history and now no longer exist except in museums and other collections. All were completely devalued as useful money by inflation and other forms of gross mismanagement.

A few examples from the United States include Confederate money, colonial scrip, and the infamous greenbacks issued during the Civil War, which still lend their nickname to modern money despite having lost all of their monetary value long ago. The value of some currencies simply erodes slowly over time until they're no longer useful, and then they're replaced. But a smaller yet noteworthy number suddenly lose all of their value in dramatic, hyperinflationary episodes.

How Hyperinflation Happens

"How did you go bankrupt?" Two ways. Gradually, then suddenly.

—Ernest Hemingway, *The Sun Also Rises*

A relatively recent example of hyperinflation comes to us from Yugoslavia between the years 1988 and 1995. Pre-1990, the Yugoslavian dinar had measurable value—you could actually buy something with a single dinar. However, throughout the 1980s, the Yugoslavian government ran persistent budget deficits and printed money to make up for their shortfalls. By the early 1990s, the Yugoslavian government had used up all of its own hard currency reserves (of dollars and other external currencies) and turned next to the private accounts of citizens as a source of funds. As they rapidly burned through those, and printed even more, the dinar slowly and then more rapidly began to lose value to the process of inflation, successively larger and larger bills had to be printed, finally culminating in a rather stunning example of the use of zeros on a piece of paper: a 500-billion dinar note.

At its height, inflation in Yugoslavia was running over 37% *per day*. This means prices doubled roughly every two days (70/37 = 1.89 days), which is hard to even imagine. But we can try.

Suppose that on January 1, 2022, you had a single U.S. penny and could buy something with it. Inflation running at 37% per day means that by April 3, you'd need a billion dollars to purchase the very same item. Using the same example, but in reverse, if you had a billion dollars on January 1, by April 3 you would have only a penny's worth of purchasing power.

Clearly, if you had attempted to store your wealth in the form of Yugoslavian dinars during the early 1990s, you would have lost it all, which is how inflation punishes savers. It literally steals value from their saved wealth while their money sits in storage. Inflationary regimes promote rapid spending by people concerned about using their money while it has the most value and increase the amounts wagered on speculation in order to at least try to keep pace with inflation.

Of course, investing and speculating involve risks, so we can broaden this statement to make the claim that inflationary monetary systems *require* citizens living within them to risk their hard-earned savings. There's really no escape. You either opt out of risks by holding on to your money and lose for sure, or you play the game by speculating on stocks and bonds and risk losing it in the markets.

However, there is a third way to store wealth and that involves converting all your devaluing currency units (be they dollar or euros or yen . . .) into real assets, usually hard assets. Land, gold, oil wells, trees, water or mineral rights, real estate . . . those sorts of things.

Money Creation

What did I mean when I said central banks were "creating money out of thin air," and how exactly is it that money is created?

John Kenneth Galbraith, the famous Harvard University economics professor, was active in politics and served in the administrations of Franklin D. Roosevelt, Harry S. Truman, John F. Kennedy (under whom he served as the United States Ambassador to India), and Lyndon B. Johnson. He was one of only a few two-time recipients of the Presidential Medal of Freedom.

Clearly, Galbraith was a pretty accomplished kind of guy, one whom you would correctly suppose was a rather calm and collected fellow who wasn't given to hyperbole. He once famously remarked about money: "The process by which money is created is so simple that the mind is repelled."[2]

What he meant by this is that the gulf that exists between the effort required to obtain money by spending one's irreplaceable time working for it and the effortless practice of banks creating money in virtually unlimited quantities by typing a few strokes on a keyboard is too ridiculous to accept. But, it's how the system of money currently operates.

A Quick Anecdote on People's Understanding of Money

One such mind that was repelled belonged to a gray-haired gentleman sitting in the back of a lecture hall in which I was giving a presentation on this very topic. It was 2009. I was covering money creation within the banking system, and he simply couldn't take it anymore. He stood up and shouted, "You have all of that entire wrong! It's pure poppycock!" he yelled. When I asked him who he was and why he thought so, he replied that he was a retired professor of economics from UConn. He'd taught this very subject for years, and I was so far off the mark, he didn't know where to even begin. Banks took in deposits, he said, and they lent them out. End of story.

I was calm because I had an ace in my pocket. Once he'd worked off some steam and settled down, I slowly withdrew a comic book and waved it over my head with the authority usually reserved for a bible.

"In here," I informed him, "is confirmation of everything I have said. I haven't made up a single fact or mechanism. This is *The Story of Money*, and it is produced for children by the Federal Reserve. You can order copies for free from the N.Y. Fed itself."

He huffed once more and left the room, obviously angered. To his lasting credit, a full two years later, he tracked me down by email and admitted he was quite chagrined to learn I was in fact correct.

He shouldn't feel too bad, it wasn't until 2014 that the Bank of England finally figured it out and excitedly produced a paper on the subject that caused much amusement and concern among those of us who'd worked it out years before.[3]

Wasn't that their one and only job? If they hadn't even worked out the basic mechanics of money creation within the banking system, what else didn't they know?

Back to Our Story

Let's begin with a look at how money is created by banks.

Suppose a person walks into town with $1,000 and, lo and behold, a brand-new bank with no deposits has just opened up. This is lucky for the town, because prior to this person arriving, there was no money anywhere in the town. Not even in the bank. The new arrival deposits their $1,000 in the bank. From an accounting standpoint, the depositor has a $1,000 asset (the bank account) and the bank has a $1,000 liability (that very same bank account).

There's a federal rule that permits banks to loan out a proportion—a fraction—of the money deposited with them to other people who wish to borrow some money. In theory, that amount is 90%, although, as we'll see later, banks often loan out much closer to 100% of their deposits. There's no longer any particular requirement that banks reserve any money at all. As the thinking goes, it is very unlikely all of the bank's depositors would demand all of their money back at the same time, so most of it can safely be lent out under the assumption that only a fraction will be demanded by depositors at any one time. Because banks retain only a fraction of their deposits in reserve (10%), the term for this institutional practice is "fractional reserve banking."

So, we now have a bank with $1,000 on deposit, which it is itching to loan out. After all, banks don't make money by holding on to money; they make their living by paying a lower rate of interest to depositors while lending to borrowers at a higher rate. Banks live on the "spread" between these two rates.

For now, let's continue with the idea (wrong though it is) that federal rules permit the town bank to loan out up to 90% of all deposits. The bank then goes about finding an individual who wishes to borrow $900, and a loan is made. This borrower then spends that $900, perhaps by giving it to their accountant, who, in turn, deposits it back in this same bank. It doesn't matter that it's the same bank—that's just to keep the story simple; it could be the same bank or a different bank—the mechanism operates precisely the same.

All that matters is that the money goes back into the banking system, which all money eventually does. For now, to keep things simple, suppose the accountant deposits this money at the very same (the only) bank in town.

With this new deposit, the bank now has a fresh $900 deposit, against which it can loan out 90% once again, which works out to $810. Again, the bank gets busy finding somebody who wants to borrow $810 and makes another loan, which then gets spent and (surprise!) redeposited in the same bank. So now *another* fresh deposit of $810 is available to create a loan of $729 (which is 90% of $810), and so on, until we finally discover that the original $1,000 deposit has mushroomed into a total of $10,000 in various bank accounts and $9,000 of loans. This is how fractional reserve banking with a 10% reserve requirement can, and does, turn $1,000 into $10,000 of spendable money.

Is this all real money? You bet it is, especially if it's in *your* bank account. But if you were paying close attention, you would realize there's more than just money in those bank accounts. The bank records the existence of $10,000 in various accounts, but it also has the notes to $9,000 in debts, which must be paid back. The *original* $1,000 is now entirely held in reserve by the bank, but every *new* dollar in the town, all $9,000, was merely loaned into existence and is now "backed" only by an equivalent amount of debt. How is your mind doing? Is it repelled yet?

If the bank had a 3% reserve requirement instead of a 10% one, that initial $1,000 could have been mushroomed into $33,333 of money and loans. With no reserve requirement, well, there no limit at all. Infinity beckons.

You might also notice here that if everybody who had money at the bank, all $10,000 dollars of it, tried to take their money out all at once, the bank would not be able to pay it out because . . . well, they wouldn't have it. The bank would only have $1,000 sitting in reserve. Period. You might also notice that this mechanism of creating new money out of new deposits works great as long as nobody defaults on a loan. If and when that happens, things get tricky and defaulted loans can quicky lead to bank failures. In our example, if the first two borrowers defaulted, the bank would be completely busted and out of money. But that's another story for another time.

For now, I want you to understand that money is *loaned* into existence. When loans are made, money appears as if by magic. Clickety-clack, a few keys are pressed, loan documents are signed, and the money now exists.

Conversely, when loans are paid back, money disappears, as the debts and the money cancel each other out when the loans are paid back. This is how money is created. I invite you to verify this for yourself. As I mentioned, one place you can do that is the Federal Reserve, which has published all of this information in handy comic book form, which you can order from them for free.[4]

You may have noticed that I left out something very important in the course of this story: interest. Where does the money come from to pay the interest on all the loans? If all the loans are paid back without interest, we can undo the entire string of transactions, but when we factor in interest, we suddenly discover that there's not enough money to pay back all the loans.*

So, where does the money come from to pay back the interest? And where did that original $1,000 come from? We can clear up both mysteries by traveling to the headwaters of the money river to the Federal Reserve.

The Fed

Even though you might have gotten a loan from Bank of America, creating money in the process, the dollars you received don't say "Bank of America" on them; they say "Federal Reserve Note." To find out where all money originally comes from, we need to spend a little time understanding how the Federal Reserve creates money.

Chartered by Congress in 1913 to manage the nation's money supply, the Federal Reserve (a.k.a. "The Fed") has complete and unilateral discretion to decide when and how much money is made available to the banking system, and by extension the entire economy.

But the Fed doesn't just print up a bunch of money and send it out in trucks; it *lends* the money into existence. After all, it is a bank, and banks create money by creating an offsetting debt.

The process works like this: Suppose the U.S. government wishes to spend more money than it has. Perhaps it has done something really historically foolish, like cutting taxes while conducting two wars at the same time, and finds itself short of money. Or it's an election year, which always calls for some extra deficit spending. Or any of a hundred other reasons.

---

*Some argue that there is enough money to pay back all of the loans, but this is only true under highly unrealistic conditions, where every loan creates goods or services that are bought by the bank or bank shareholders, who buy them with interest payments that are perfectly recycled to the very same people who took out the loans. I call this the "theory of perfect interest flows." While theoretically possible, it is not at all realistic and is therefore something of an intellectual parlor trick. Under this model, nobody can ever take out a purely consumptive loan, undertake a failed business venture, or save money without spending it. As soon as any of these three things happens (and they happen all the time in real life), there's not enough money to pay off all the loans. Suffice it to say that this vision of "immaculate interest flows" is an interesting thought experiment, but it is not at all useful in understanding how the system operates in practice and is therefore not terribly helpful as a way of understanding the current situation or future risks.

Now, having abdicated its monetary responsibilities to a third party (the Fed), the U.S. government can't create any money itself, so the request for additional spending money by Congress gets routed through the Treasury Department, which, it turns out, also can't make any money itself and rarely has more than a few weeks of operating cash on hand.

In order to raise the needed cash, the Treasury Department will print up a stack of Treasury bonds (or bills or notes, which are essentially all the same things with different maturities), which is government debt. A bond has a "face value," which is the amount that it will be sold for, and it has a stated rate of interest that it will pay the holder. So, anyone who buys a bond with a $1,000 face value that pays a rate of interest of 5% would pay $1,000 for this bond but get $1,050 back in a year, representing your original $1,000 plus $50 in interest.

Treasury bonds, bills, and notes are sold in regularly scheduled auctions and are mainly purchased by banks, other large financial institutions, or the central banks of other countries. So, if a batch of bonds with a face value of $1 billion is sold at auction, then $1 billion of bonds is exchanged for $1 billion of cash, which then lands in the Treasury's coffers, where it immediately becomes available for the U.S. government to spend. Assuming these are Treasury notes with a one-year maturity, after a year the Treasury Department will return all $1 billion to the purchasers of those bonds, *plus* an amount equal to whatever the rate of interest happened to be.

After all that, no new money has yet been created in the system. Treasury bonds are bought with money that already exists. The interest is paid out of money that already exists. The question remains, *Where does **new** money come from?*

New money, a.k.a. "hot money," comes into being when the Federal Reserve buys a Treasury bond from a bank. When the Fed does this, it simply transfers money in the amount of the bond to the other bank and takes possession of the bond. The bond is swapped for money.

But where did *that* money come from? Ah! This money was created out of thin air, as the Fed literally creates money when it "buys" a debt instrument, which used to mean only U.S. Treasuries, but since the Great Financial Crisis it now can mean mortgage-backed securities (MBSs), or even dodgy positions in failed hedge funds.

Don't believe me? Here's a quote from a Federal Reserve publication titled "Putting It Simply":

> *When you or I write a check, there must be sufficient funds in our account to cover the check, but when the Federal Reserve writes a check, there is no bank deposit on which that check is drawn. When the Federal Reserve writes a check, it is creating money.*[5]

Now *that* is an extraordinary power. Whereas you or I need to work (i.e., expend human labor) to obtain money, and then place that money at risk to have it grow, the Federal Reserve simply prints up as much as it deems prudent and then loans it out, with interest, to its most favored clients, the big banks, who former Fed officials tend to go and work at after their term of "public service" is up.

The answer to how money originally comes into existence is very simple: It's loaned out of thin air by the Fed. In whatever quantities it deems fit. And without ever being audited by a public firm in a public way.

Is your mind repelled yet?

Two Kinds of Money—One Exponential System

So, now we know that there are two kinds of money out there. The first is bank credit, which is money that is loaned into existence, as we saw in the first bank example. Bank credit comes with an equal and offsetting amount of debt associated with it, consisting of a principal balance and a rate of interest that must be paid on that balance.

Because this money, which is also created out of thin air, accumulates interest charges, it promotes the growth of the money supply, even though the principal balance must be paid back. The interest represents money that accumulates over time, and as long as everything is working according to plan, it does so exponentially because it accumulates on a percentage basis.

That's the nature of a loan. It is a principal balance that must be paid back at a rate of interest that is expressed on a yearly basis. Again, anything growing by some percentage over time, is growing exponentially. If you borrow $250,000 for a mortgage at 5%, you will end up paying back $483,141 over the life of a 30-year loan.

The second type of money is also printed out of thin air, but it is created by the Fed, and it forms what is known as the "base money supply" of the nation. If you're thinking of "base" as in a solid foundation, as in permanent, then you have the right mental image. This money forms the base of all other loans, which, as we saw earlier, can be multiplied fantastically due to the miracle of fractional reserve banking.

Base money, too, is loaned into existence, and a quick glance at the Federal Reserve's balance sheet reveals nothing but various types and forms of debts that it has swapped for thin air money. Together these two forms of money

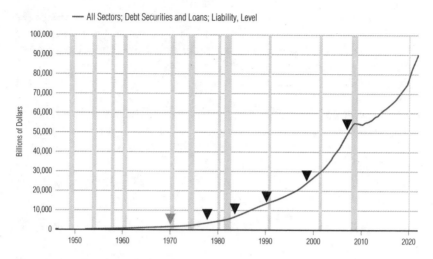

FIGURE 9.1   Total Credit Market Debt

All forms of debt are represented here: federal, state, municipal, corporate, and household.

Source: Federal Reserve.

(base and credit) conspire to create a money system that will expand exponentially. Loaning money into existence, at a rate of interest, virtually assures this outcome.*

The very mechanisms of our money system promote and even demand the exponential growth of money and debt. If the deconstructed workings of the lending and interest cycle are not enough to make the case, then perhaps some empirical data will do the trick.

In Figure 9.1, we see a chart of the total credit market debt in the United States from 1952 to 2022.

What is total credit market debt? It's everything except liabilities such as underfunded pensions, Social Security, Medicare, and the like. It includes student debt, auto loans, household debt, corporate debt and state and municipal and federal debt.

We can calculate its "doubling time" as being every 7.4 years. The gray triangle marks a starting time in 1970 when a grand total of $1.55 trillion of outstanding debt was in the system. The first black triangle represents the first doubling to $3.1 trillion in 1977 (7 years). The next triangles represent

----

*I know that I have skipped over a number of details, some of them quite important for the sake of accuracy, but we've covered enough of the process for the purposes of this book. For more complete explanations, please see *Crash Course* at **www.peakprosperity.com/ crashcourse**.

$6.2 trillion in 1983 (6 years), then $12.4 trillion in 1989 (6 years), then $24.8 trillion in 1998 (9 years), and then finally $49.6 trillion in 2007 (9 years). The most recent doubling is taking a bit longer due to the Great Financial Crisis of 2008/2009, seen on Figure 9.1 as the one and only "hump." As soon as that gets to $99.2 trillion, we can score that one as accomplished.

In other words, debt accumulation in the United States is running at about one and a third doublings *every decade*. This is far faster than GDP growth, which is doubling every 25 years or so, which means debt is piling up more than three times as fast as the nation's income, an unsustainable condition that many other countries replicate.

If the future is going to resemble the past, the next doubling will be to ~$100 trillion of total debt and the one after that takes us to $200 trillion. Then $400 trillion and pretty soon we're talking about real money! Just kidding, the total U.S. debt pile is already larger than the entire world's GDP, which is real money in anybody's book.

In Figure 9.1, once again, we see a nearly perfect hockey stick, but this one is composed of debt. If we perform something called "a curve fit" to test how closely the data conforms to a particular mathematical function, we get the best fit using an exponential curve fit. It's nearly perfect (with an "R-squared" of 0.93 for you math buffs . . . 1.0 is a perfect fit for everybody else, so it's a damned good fit). Armed only with this information, and without knowing any of the details that underlie money creation and policy, we could use this curve fit observation to form a quite strong hypothesis that the system we're studying grows exponentially. Not just "sort of exponentially" but nearly *perfectly* exponentially.

The Trouble with Future Claims on Wealth

The fact that our money/debt system is growing exponentially is an exceptionally important observation, and it has enormous bearing on how claims on wealth will be settled in the future. Or, more bluntly, if they even will be.

Remember, money is simply a claim on wealth. When money is exponentially accumulating (growing), it carries both an implicit and *explicit* assumption that the economy will be exponentially larger in the future. After all, the claims have to match the real goods.

If the economic future turns out to be smaller than expected, but there is exponentially more money and debt floating around, then all of those monetary claims will be chasing a smaller stack of goods, which means all that money will be worth a lot less than its current value. That is, we'll experience a lot of inflation, which is not "things costing more" but instead is best thought of as "money being worth less as compared to things."

Therefore, when we see money and debt growing exponentially, as it is, our very first task should be to assess whether the economy is growing similarly. If it is not, then we might rationally question whether we wish to try and save our wealth in a depreciating fiat currency. Might it make more sense to hold wealth itself, not claims against it? We will go into more detail about wealth in Chapter 10 (*What Is Wealth?*).

What we've just learned about money allows us to formulate two more extremely important concepts. The first is that all dollars are backed by debt. At the level of the local bank, all new money is loaned into existence. At the Federal Reserve level, money is simply manufactured out of thin air and then exchanged for interest-paying government debt. In both cases, the money is backed by debt—debt that pays interest.

Because our debt-based money system is always continually growing by some percentage, it is an exponential system by its very design. A corollary of this is that the amount of debt in the system will always exceed the amount of money.*

I'm not going to cast judgment on this system and say whether it's good or bad. It simply is what it is. But I'll gladly point out that it is a patently unsustainable system. It cannot last in its current form. By understanding its design, though, you'll be better equipped to understand that the potential range of future outcomes for our economy are not limitless; rather, they are bounded by the rules of the system.

All of which leads us to another concept, the idea that perpetual expansion is a *requirement* of modern banking. Without a continuous expansion of the money supply (via credit expansion), all sorts of trouble emerges, including debt defaults, which are the Achilles heel of a leveraged, debt-based money system.

Just to be clear, I'm not saying that this requirement to expand is written down somewhere, neither etched in legal stone in the basement of the world's centers of power nor forever enshrined in Google's search cloud. Instead, I use the word "requirement" in the same way your body requires oxygen. Yes, the system can operate for brief periods without it, but it's a lot happier and more productive with it.

By understanding the requirement for continual expansion, we are in a position to illuminate the future and make informed decisions about what is likely to transpire.

---

*Again, for those who prefer data over theory, consider that in the United States at the end of 2021, there were more than $88 trillion of total credit market debt, but only approximately $21.5 trillion of money (and money equivalents). This means that we now have far more debt than money. It's a "feature" of the system: always more debt than money, 4× to 5×, typically.

CHAPTER 10

What Is Wealth?

(Hint: It's Not Money)

Once, as I drove around southern New Hampshire, Vermont, and western Massachusetts looking for a home to buy and a place to settle, I suddenly noticed something. Beyond the usual list of criteria including a nice neighborhood and proximity to culture and shopping, I had one non-negotiable item on the list: good soil. I wanted to have a big, lush garden and it's much easier to have one if you start with good soil.

My trick was to keep an eye trained on the types of trees and plants in each area, looking for the plant-based clues would let me know if the soil underneath was good quality or not. I knew that an excess of pine trees often indicates weak, sandy, and acidic soils, while maple trees portend rich, sweet soils.

After passing through a succession of small towns, each established 150 or more years ago, a relationship between the types of trees and architecture emerged. In the towns surrounded by pine trees, the historic churches were small, modest affairs, generally without steeples. The churches looked poor. But in the towns with maple trees, the churches were invariably grander, with large, ornate steeples attached. All at once, the saying "dirt poor" took on new meaning to me.

The phrase originally dates from the Great Depression and may well have meant "poor as dirt," but to me, from that trip on, it could only convey that one is as rich as one's soil. If you were poor once upon a time it was because your soil was poor and only offered meager returns for your efforts. This insight, I am sure, was quite obvious to our ancestors, whose lives and livelihoods depended on agriculture, but for me it was a revelation.

There it was, in fine stonework, ornate woodwork, and soaring steeples. For thousands of years nobody had to tell people that wealth came from the land.

If two people work just as hard as each other, but one enjoys fine, rich soil and the other struggles with poor dirt, they will reap very different rewards for similar efforts. One will be wealthy and the other will remain poor; one is dirt poor and the other is dirt rich. My modern and middle-class lifestyle had permitted me to completely escape that basic reality of life.

We probably lost sight of this connection in recent decades because we are bestowed with the most amazing abundance of magical, wealth-producing stuff ever pulled out of the ground: petroleum. It has masked the previous direct relationship between wealth and land-based resources, a central part of true wealth for every generation except the most recent ones. It allows trade to be conducted at such great distances that people are often separated from the source of the food on their plate by many thousands of miles. Is that a temporary or a permanent condition of life?

The Hierarchy of Wealth

Let's begin by describing what we mean by "wealth." We can think of wealth as coming in three layers, like a pyramid of sorts. At the bottom of the pyramid sits primary wealth, then above that is secondary wealth, and finally tertiary wealth.

Rich soils, concentrated ores, thick seams of coal, gushing oil, fresh water, and abundant fisheries are all examples of *primary wealth*. The foundation of the wealth pyramid comprises these concentrated resources. Today, we might call this our "natural resource base," but once upon a time your access to these things (or lack thereof) meant the physical difference between a life of ease and a life of hardship.

Secondary wealth is what we make from primary wealth. Ore becomes steel, abundant fisheries lead to dinner on the table, soil becomes food in the store, and trees turn into lumber. The richer, closer, and more concentrated your primary wealth, the easier the task of creating secondary wealth and the more likely you were, in the past, to be wealthy, or rich.

If your soil was "dirt poor," then you had a weak source of primary wealth, and no matter how devotedly or intelligently you worked, you could never achieve the same level of productivity (or wealth) that would be possible if you were working rich soil.

The landed gentry of antiquity were as wealthy as their lands were productive and their holdings expansive. Before the Industrial Revolution (in other words, not all that long ago), this very basic connection was not only well understood, but it also formed the basis for societal hierarchies. There were wealthy people who owned land, and then there was everybody else. The same is true for weak grades of mineral ores compared to high grades, or an overharvested fishing ground as compared to a healthy one.

Poor primary wealth translates into poor secondary wealth.

We can transform primary wealth into secondary wealth more intelligently, quickly, and cost-effectively with every passing year because of continued improvements in technology and processes. But no matter how good we get at making these transformations, there can be no secondary wealth unless there is primary wealth to begin with. Unless there are trees to send to the mill, there's no lumber; no crude oil in the ground means no gas at the pump; without ore there is no metal; and if soils lack nutrients, plants will not grow. Without primary wealth there cannot be secondary wealth. The second depends on the first; it's a *requirement*.

The final layer, *tertiary wealth*, consists of all the paper abstractions that we pile on the first two sources of wealth—derivatives, stocks, bonds, and every other paper vehicle you can think. Such "wealth" is nothing more and nothing less than a claim on primary and secondary wealth. Tertiary wealth is not really wealth. If you grow wheat, you can always eat it if circumstances require, but good luck obtaining any sustenance from your (paper or electronic) wheat futures contracts. To repeat, third-order wealth is a *claim* on sources of wealth, and not a *source* of wealth itself. The distinction is vital.

Without the prior two forms of wealth, third-order wealth has no value and no meaning at all. For example, imagine that we hold stock in a mining company. One day the stock has lots of value, perhaps billions of dollars' worth. But if the next day the mine collapses into a hole, our stock shares in the mining company—our tertiary claims on that mining wealth—become totally worthless. A billion dollars of perceived value disappeared in the blink of an eye. But what if the reverse happened? What if we had a productive mine with good ore and the stock market tanked and decided that the billion dollars of stock value was now worth $0? Would the mine actually be worth $0? No, of course not. It will contain precisely the same resources regardless of how it is valued in the tertiary markets.

The earth is the source of all primary wealth. The long chain from primary wealth to tertiary wealth begins with the abundance of the earth and ends with some impressively complicated paper-based abstractions even the brightest Wall Street minds sometimes have trouble deciphering.

As you read this book, it will be helpful to recall that what most people call "wealth" isn't actually an independent *source* of wealth, but is instead a dependent *claim* on wealth. Money is a store of value, not wealth itself.

We live at the tail end of a *very* unique and odd moment of human history where it is even necessary to write this chapter. We've been afforded the luxury of forgetting what real wealth actually is and where it comes from. For many of us, tertiary wealth is all we know and have known. Because of this, it seems to be even more real than reality itself, and we often base our future expectations and dreams on how much of it we hold.

It bears repeating, however, that *all* wealth begins with primary wealth; without it, there is nothing. Today, when there is more abundant luxury available to more people than at any point in history, much of it traveling from very far away to arrive in our lives as if by magic, it has been easy to lose sight of this fact, but it remains as true today as ever before.

Money and Wealth

What about currency or what we call "money" (even though it fails the "store of value" test)? How does it factor into the wealth story? Currency or money can and should be a store of wealth, but as I've said it's not wealth itself. It's a way for us to conveniently measure and transfer ownership of true wealth from one person or entity to another, but just like a stock, bond, derivative, or any other financial product, money is simply a *claim* on wealth.

It also happens to be an exceedingly important social contract, one that we vest with extraordinary powers such that it can entirely shape the trajectory of lives, nations, and destinies. Ultimately, though, what we call "money" is either a piece of paper (indistinct from any other except for the ink patterns on it) or it's an ephemeral collection of numbers that exist as a series of magnetically determined ones and zeros on a computer hard drive.

Money has value because, and only because, we collectively agree it can be exchanged for something. If we go far enough backward or forward in any line of transactions, that "something" is *always* some form of primary or secondary wealth. Perhaps we exchange money for a college education; this might seem to be quite different and less tangible than the examples of primary or secondary wealth I've already described. But if we keep following the path of money in that exchange, we'll eventually find the money in the pocket of a college professor who will ultimately use it to buy food, or clothing, or a house, or some other form of primary or secondary wealth. If we buy a service like a back massage, we still will eventually find that the spa paid a masseuse who then bought food or filled a gas tank or otherwise spent it on some form of primary or secondary wealth.

The point of money is to help us store our surplus effort so we can secure the things we need when we need them. The most vital are found at the very bottom of Maslow's hierarchy of needs.* There we find the physiological needs

---

*Maslow was a psychologist who proposed that humans have many needs existing in a hierarchical structure in which the higher levels will not be sought and met until the lower ones are met. At the bottom of his pyramid are the physiological needs of breathing, being fed, obtaining water, sleeping, and excreting. The next layer up covers our safety and security, and self-actualization resides at the very top of the pyramid.

of food, shelter, and warmth. Once those are met, we are free to progress one layer higher and see to our safety and security. In other words, we're investing a huge amount of faith in money and we are trusting that it will reliably be there for us so we can see to our own survival and that of those we love.

It's vitally important, then, that money be stable and trustworthy, because if it's not, and people begin to suspect money might fail to enable them to meet their basic needs, the entire social contract money fulfills will begin to fray. Trust breaks down rapidly within a society when money breaks down. Gangs form, safety is lost, commerce grinds to a halt.

As long as money exists in a balance with actual primary and secondary *sources* of wealth, then it will retain its perceived value and perform the important function of being a *store* of wealth. However, when the supply of money gets out of balance with resources, money's value can begin to gyrate wildly. We call this process *inflation* or *deflation*, depending on whether the gyration goes up or down.

The Nature of Wealth

The idea that monetary wealth originates with the wealth of the earth is hardly new, but abundant primary wealth, as described here, has been such an assured feature of the landscape of the past few centuries that it seems to be almost entirely taken for granted. Over 200 years ago, the great economic thinker and observer Adam Smith took great pains to describe how wealth came about, but given that he lived during a time of natural abundance of primary wealth (that it could be safely ignored) and poorly formed tertiary paper-based wealth abstractions, he focused mainly on the role of labor in creating wealth.

Adam Smith turned his attention to secondary wealth and did a most credible job of isolating the essential features by which better-organized labor led to greater wealth. Here he essentially discounts the importance of "soil, climate, and territory" compared to the number of people laboring productively:

> [T]his proportion [between production and consumption] must in every nation be regulated by two different circumstances; first by the skill, dexterity, and judgment with which its labour is generally applied; and, secondly, by the proportion between the number of those who are employed in useful labour, and that of those who are not so employed. Whatever be the soil, climate, or extent of territory of any particular nation, the abundance or scantiness of its annual supply must, in that particular situation, depend upon those two circumstances.[1]

Given the limitless natural abundance of the time, he's saying that those who could transform primary into secondary wealth faster and more productively created wealth the quickest. While he's not wrong, he also lived at a time when you could safely assume resources were so abundant you could more or less set them aside. Now we know differently.

People in the late eighteenth century had a firm grasp on wealth creation and it is my intention to return that view to the front of the conversation. It's not that we've moved beyond an archaic view never to return, we've simply forgotten something both obvious and profound.

We live under very different circumstances than Adam Smith, but the question of how we create wealth and where it really comes from remains as relevant now as it was then. There are thousands of books to help you navigate tertiary wealth, virtually all of them assuming the future will resemble the present, only bigger. But what if that assumption is dead wrong? What if the primary resources essential to all of wealth creation are not only limited in supply, but actually becoming harder and harder to extract? Then what?

All of our money, debts, stocks, and bonds owe much of their current value to the expectation of not just future economic growth, but exponential economic growth.

What causes that growth? What are the primary resources most responsible for enabling economic growth? How much longer can we count on their inputs to the story?

Most importantly, what's a fair price for high-flying stocks and bonds in a world without growth?—because that is surely a future condition of life on this fixed planet.

Someday the people and "the markets" will awaken to that reality. The question is, when?

PART III

Economy

CHAPTER 11

Debt

If something cannot go on forever, it will stop.

—Herbert Stein, economist (1916–1999)[1]

The United States and much of the developed world suffer from a condition I call "too much debt." It's not exactly profound to most people, but our leaders don't seem to understand or care about the impact it has on the rest of us.

We could spend an entire book just on the subject of debt, because (a) it's that important, (b) it's a very complex subject packed with data and a long and rich history, and (c) the trajectory of our debt is completely unsustainable.

But we're only going to spend just enough time on debt to support my main claim: Debt markets are making an enormous collective bet that the future economy will be exponentially larger than the present. It is a dangerous wager, and one which, if it doesn't pan out, places the collective wealth of entire nations and everyone's future prosperity at risk.

When debt markets were disappointed in the past, standards of living suffered, governments were tossed, currencies destroyed, and countries collapsed. We therefore care very deeply about whether our debt markets are at risk of being disappointed, and, if so, what the source of their disappointment might be.

What Is Debt?

In Chapter 7 (*Our Money System*), we learned that all money is loaned into existence. When money is created in our current system of banking, the other side of the ledger carries the loan that was made. In other words, we have a debt-based money system. By itself, that is neither good nor bad. Unfortunately, history proves humans are very bad at avoiding the destructive temptations of debt-based money systems and unerringly make a mess of things.

We now need to spend some time looking at the nature and quantity of those "loans," which are also sometimes referred to as "credit" or "debt." All three terms are interchangeable, and sometimes we'll switch back and forth between them to follow established conventions. For example, government debt and some consumer loans trade on and are part of the credit markets. To really mix it all together, we'll examine a data series called "total credit market debt" or "TCMDO," in Fed speak. If at any time you find the use of a term confusing, feel free to mentally insert whichever word you prefer—loan, credit, or debt. They're essentially the same thing, and their minor differences aren't relevant to our discussion. So, what exactly is a "debt" (or "loan")? A debt is simply a legally binding, contractual financial obligation to repay a specific amount of borrowed money, at some point in the future, at a defined rate of interest—in other words, an IOU.

An auto loan is a debt, a credit card balance is a debt, and mortgages, Treasury bonds, home equity lines of credit, corporate bonds, and municipal bonds are all examples of debts. In every case, there is a piece of paper (or its electronic equivalent) that identifies a borrower, an amount borrowed, a maturity or due date, and a rate of interest.

Auto loans and mortgage debt are known as "secured" debt because in most jurisdictions there is a recoverable asset (like a car or house) attached to those debts. Credit card debt is known as "unsecured" because no specific asset can be directly seized in the event of a default, although other remedies exist.

Because a debt is a legal obligation, if repayment fails to happen on schedule, all sorts of prescribed legal remedies exist for the lender to pursue, ranging from asset seizure, to liens, and to legal judgments.

Debts are distinct from *liabilities*, and it's important to remain acutely aware of the difference between them.

A liability is a form of financial obligation, but it's not the same as a debt. Someone with a young child may think of the potential future college expenditure as a liability, but it's not a legally binding obligation, and therefore it's not a debt. Debts represent known quantities and fixed amounts, whereas liabilities are imprecise and prone to fluctuations.

Many things can change between today's perceived liability and the actual future payout. The child in question may decide not to go to college after all, allowing the parent to evade the entire amount, or the child may decide to go to the most expensive college in the country, drastically boosting the final cost of the liability. However, if the parent decides not to pay for college, no legal remedy exists for the child, because the obligation wasn't a debt.

At the national level, the entitlement programs in the United States (e.g., Social Security, Medicare/Medicaid, and so on) are *liabilities* of the U.S. government. Although they may be vast, huge, enormous liabilities, they aren't debts. At any point along the way, the government could, by way of an act of Congress, completely change the terms of the obligation, perhaps by raising the retirement age to 100 or slashing benefits by 80%, and no legal remedy for any of the affected recipients would be available. So, they aren't debts, they're just vague promises.

With regard to the nation's debts, however, Congress could not pass an act that would reduce the principal repayment of Treasury bonds without triggering a legal default. Once a default is declared, all sorts of legal machinery kicks into high gear. That's the difference between a debt and a liability: Debts are legal obligations, while liabilities are, at best, moral or social obligations.

Realistically, and without getting into Biden's student loan position, there are only two ways to settle a debt: repayment and default. Until one of those two things happen, the debt remains "on the books" as someone's liability (the debtor) and someone's asset (the holder of the debt or note or loan).

Sometimes you'll hear of debts being "restructured," as with Greece in 2010, but that's just a fancy way of saying the debt has either been delayed (i.e., had its payment schedule extended) or reduced in some way, which constitutes a partial default, but a default nonetheless. In this regard, debts are simple beasts—they can either be paid off or they can be defaulted upon.

However, if you happen to have a printing press, as many governments do, there's an alternative way to "pay off" a debt—simply print up the money to pay it off! Because such printing seems to work for a while and offers the least amount of immediate political pain, printing has been a repetitive, if not predictable, feature of economic history. A long time ago this involved physically debasing hard coinage, either by shrinking the precious metal content of each coin or by doing what was known as "clipping," which involved making each coin slightly smaller in size so that a greater quantity could be minted from the same amount of precious metal. Later on, printing money involved actual printing presses churning out paper currency by the wagonload.

These days we have the means to create money electronically without involving paper or coins at all. A few keystrokes on a computer are all that's required. Debasing and/or clipping coins was difficult (as you had to recall them first); paper printing was easier, but you still had to physically print and then distribute the money. Electronic printing is virtually instant and practically free, representing the easiest, fastest, and surest method of them all.

Such printing efforts have never worked for very long because the inevitable result has nearly always been ruinous inflation. In this sense, printing up money to pay off sovereign debts is nothing more than a poorly disguised form of taxation, since it forcefully removes value from all existing money and transfers that value to the debt holders, who otherwise might never have been paid at all. Some might even consider this a form of partial default, because the bondholders, too, are being paid with money that is worth less.

Of all the things I track in my research, the variable I follow most closely is the use of the official printing press to pay for government expenditures, past and present, that cannot otherwise be funded through legitimate means (such as current taxes).

Levels of Debt

The U.S. experience with debt is significant, but most other developed countries are in almost precisely similar straits. Feel free to mentally replace "United States" with the name of some other country, perhaps the United Kingdom or Japan, in the following discussion; the differences are few and have little impact on the final analysis.

The chart of total credit market debt seen in Chapter 9 (*Our Money System*, Figure 9.1) was a beautiful example of exponential growth, and there's quite an interesting story embedded in its data. If we start with the very beginning of the debt data series, in 1951, and then put into table form every doubling since then—encompassing more than 60 years of data—we arrive at Figure 11.1.

The data shows that debt doubles on average every 8.8 years—sometimes a little faster, sometimes a little slower, but it just keeps doubling and then doubling again. As we learned in the chapter on dangerous exponentials, each new doubling has more debt than in all the prior doublings combined!

Everything everybody alive and in power knows about "how the economy works" was learned during a period of time when credit was doubling every 8.8 years.

Date	Trillions	Doubling Time in Years
7/1/1951	0.5	–
7/1/1962	0.9	11.0
10/1/1971	1.8	9.3
4/1/1978	3.7	6.5
4/1/1984	7.4	6.0
4/1/1991	14.7	7.0
1/1/2001	29.4	9.8
4/1/2013	58.5	12.3
		Average 8.8
Next doubling		
??	117.0	?

FIGURE 11.1 Debt Doublings

Time between complete doublings of debt in quarters.

Source: Federal Reserve data.

In order for future decades to economically resemble any of the past seven decades, we might reasonably conclude that credit market debt would have to double once more, from $59 trillion to $118 trillion, and then again to $236 trillion and then again, and again, and again.

This is gut check time. Do you believe it is possible for debts to constantly exponentially increase, with an astonishingly brief doubling time of only 8.8 years, from now until forever? Or, like me, do you intuit that debt accumulation has some sort of math limit imposed, ultimately, by this thing we might dare to call "reality"?

To put the next doubling in perspective, we might note that the next doubling of $58.5 trillion (bottom row of Figure 11.1) represents nearly 3 times 2020 GDP or nearly 6 times the value of all outstanding residential mortgages

What kind of an economy would be required to support $236 trillion of debt? What about the next doubling at $474 trillion? Without getting too fancy and detailed here, such figures ought to cause somebody somewhere to sit up and ask the most basic question of all: Do the resources even exist to support that level of debt? After all, debt is merely a tertiary claim, not wealth itself. How much real wealth actually exists in the world or could exist based on what we know about resources such as oil, copper, lithium, fresh water, productive farmland, and a thousand other forms of primary and secondary wealth?

Short answer: Those resources don't exist.

Snippy add-on: And it's really not very smart to assume they do.

The story of economic growth that has shaped the past seven decades, including many of our expectations about "how the economy works," was heavily dependent on and financed with debt. Without the explosive growth in debt seen over the past seven decades, economic growth would have been a lot smaller than we experienced (and enjoyed). Our experience of "normal" economic conditions was actually an unsustainable illusion, albeit a very pleasant one.

Debt Distorts GDP

To understand how debt grossly distorts the picture of economic growth and health, let's reduce the entire global economy to two small islands, each occupied by a single family earning $50,000 per year ("Family A" and "Family B").

At our first yearly "GDP snapshot" of these two families, we find the GDP of each island is $50,000: they're exactly equal. But in the second year, using a combination of auto loans, credit card balances, student loans, and a home equity line of credit (HELOC), Family B goes out and borrows an additional $50,000, which it uses to purchase various enjoyable goods and services for itself.

Family B lives it up. But Family A, representing the first island nation, prudently plunks their $50,000 in earnings into savings and lives a frugal life, eating homegrown food and making do with last year's clothing, toys, and motor vehicles.

At our second "GDP snapshot" the next year, we see that Family A, still having a GDP of only $50,000, has not increased its earnings and is suffering through a very painful year of flat growth. Therefore, despite their diligent savings, our conventional economic standards indicate this family has suffered through a horrible year of zero percent economic growth (ugh, *no growth!*).

In contrast, Family B—the family that now effectively sports a painful debt-to-income ratio of 1.0—has seemingly undergone an exciting and dramatic 100% growth in their economy (yay, *growth!*) and their island is now sporting a GDP of $100,000. Investors, bankers, politicians, and the media will all cheer the fast growth of Island B and preferentially purchase the currency and debt of Family B's more exciting island nation, eschewing the "anemic growth" of Family A.

But let's be absolutely clear here: Each family still has exactly the same $50,000 of national income. They're economically identical, except that one nation, Family B, is now saddled with debt equal to 100% of its income, while the other, Family A, isn't, and is therefore in far better financial shape. And ironically enough, Family B will be lauded, while Family A will be chided.

As it happens, the conventional way of measuring GDP (which is how all developed nations happen to measure it) doesn't take into account the impact of debt—it completely ignores the accumulation of most forms of debt as if they do not matter. However, as I hope our island nation example has made clear, debt is an absolutely critical component of the story, and excluding it paints a misleading picture.

That debt accumulation is left out of the picture surely cannot be an accident. The impact of debt on distorting the GDP landscape is too easy to understand.

Debt-to-GDP for the high-borrowing family assures they'll be living under the strain of paying down those loans for years to come, which will weigh down their disposable income and future standard of living. This is equally true for a company, a county or a country. Or, as we'll see, an entire world.

To state the debt as an iron law: Time spent living beyond one's means necessitates a future period of living below one's means.

This truism has been borne out and repeated so many times in history that the only surprise left is that some people will be surprised by its reappearance.

Because the conventional GDP measure neglects to factor out the use of credit/debt when measuring "growth," it isn't telling us everything we need to know. This oversight goes a long way toward explaining why the United States, along with every other debt-saturated country, is now in for a very painful adjustment process. Past growth was partially (and unsustainably) bolstered by debt, and future growth will be hindered by debt.

Good Debt and Bad Debt

It's time to distinguish between two major types of debt. Not all debt is bad or unproductive. Many real estate investors use debt wisely to compound their returns.

Debt that can best be described as "investment debt" contains within itself the means to pay itself back. An example would be a loan to expand the seating at a successful restaurant. In the parlance of bankers, these are examples of "self-liquidating debt."

Because these kinds of loans will boost future revenues by enhancing productivity or increasing output, they self-generate the cash flows that will be used to pay them off in the future.

The other type of loan, however, is purely consumptive in nature, such as debt incurred for a fancier car, a vacation, new granite countertops, or perhaps a war that results in a large quantity of destroyed equipment.

These loans don't come self-equipped with the means to pay themselves back. They are called "non-self-liquidating debts" (a mouthful of a term) because they don't lead to additional future revenue, productivity, or profits. In our earlier island nation example, if we postulate that Family B had instead borrowed $50,000 for productive (and not consumptive) purposes, perhaps to build a factory that would then triple its income for the next 20 years, the entire story of which nation is in better financial shape would shift.

The key here is not to just look at the total pile of debt relative to income, but to look at how much of the debt has been spent on non-self-liquidating consumption, as opposed to investments boosting productivity and income. This is easily detected; all you have to do is measure total debt against income.

The Crisis Explained in One Table

Long before the economic crises of 2008 began, I knew such an event was coming. While I admit to wallowing around in massive quantities of base data—I'm a scientist at heart, so data is a kind of like catnip for me—I found my certainty about the trouble ahead in a single piece of evidence. Figure 11.2, all on its own, led me to conclude that the next 20 years are going to be completely unlike the past 20 years, and not in a good way.

This table paints a lousy picture. It says we are borrowing more and more to achieve less and less. It says, without digging more deeply, all on its own, that the United States is using more and more consumptive debt (i.e., "non-self-liquidating"). It takes 4.5 units of debt to create a new dollar of GDP where it used to take 1.6 units. We're borrowing more and more while achieving less and less. If this were a company, you'd sell the stock. If it were your neighbor, you wouldn't lend them any more money.

Billions of Dollars		
Debt Growth	**GDP Growth**	**Debt/GDP**
1960 to 1970	$787	$509	1.55
1970 to 1980	$2,953	$1,752	1.69
1980 to 1990	$9,054	$3,083	2.94
1990 to 2000	$13,697	$4,129	3.32
2000 to 2010	$27,179	$4,762	5.71
2010 to 2020	$22,819	$6,717	3.40

FIGURE 11.2   Debt Growth to GDP

Table of three different eras of debt use in the United States. Era 1 (white box) spans from 1960 to 1980 and saw an average of 1.6 dollars of new debt taken on for every $1 of new GDP added. The second era (light gray shading), from 1980 to 2000, saw an average of 3.1 dollars of debt taken on for every $1 of new GDP added. The third era, 2000 to 2020, saw an average of 4.2 dollars of new debt for each new dollar of GDP added. A lousy trend.

When viewed historically and compared to GDP, the current levels of U.S. debt are unprecedented. There are no maps to guide us in these unknown waters. There's no history, no institutional memory to draw upon, and no experienced leadership prepared to confidently guide us through such a crisis. That's my major point here: Anybody counting on the past to extend seamlessly into the future is headed for almost certain disappointment, both because there's a very low chance of doubling debts over and over again, and because there's nobody in charge with their hands on the wheel. This is all new territory for all of us.

Of course, with more than a single table, I can make a far better case that the future will be quite different from the past, and not in a good way.

The History of Debt

The first part of this story, historically speaking, always begins with the accumulation of debt. Perhaps there are important wars to fund or an exciting new technology in which to invest (e.g., railroads, internet, and so on). Perhaps there's nothing more to show for the debt accumulation than a period of reckless consumption.

The second part of this story involves the psychology of the players who are fully invested in perpetuating the status quo. There are careers to consider, and small matters of legacy to maintain, but mostly there's an overwhelming desire by the leaders of each generation to conform and not rock the boat. Centrism for the (personal career) win!

The circumstance of "too much debt" has been revisited dozens of times throughout history, and the same exact, perfectly understandable and perfectly imperfect human response has been applied nearly every time: Print more money!

This Time Is Different

In their landmark work titled *This Time Is Different*, Kenneth Rogoff and Carmen Reinhart assembled a comprehensive database spanning 800 years of economic data including international debt and banking crises, inflation, currency crashes, and debasements.[2] The one constant throughout history is that many governments, for a myriad of reasons, have gotten themselves wedged into a situation best described as "too much debt."

Throughout history, nearly all governments so stricken by *too much debt* have tried to find salvation by wriggling out through the mechanism of creating inflation. In every case, the same rationale has been used as internal justification for official actions: *This time is different.*

Here are a few of the important conclusions from Rogoff and Reinhart's work:

> *A recent example of the "this time is different" syndrome is the false belief that domestic debt is a novel feature of the modern financial landscape. We also confirm that crises frequently emanate from the financial centers with transmission through interest rate shocks and commodity price collapses. Thus, the recent U.S. sub-prime financial crisis is hardly unique. Our data also documents other crises that often accompany default: including inflation, exchange rate crashes, banking crises, and currency debasements.[3]*

Their work reveals that throughout history, various countries have attempted to live beyond their means and inevitably crashed upon the remorseless math of debt. The response has nearly always been to try and squeeze past the difficulties by printing more money in the hopes that somehow things would eventually work themselves out.

But it has never quite worked out as hoped; "printing" has only served to deepen the severity of the economic and political pain. Yet it has been tried again and again, as if there's some biologically irrelevant human gene that stimulates the desire to print money while suppressing the ability to learn from history.

The work of Rogoff and Reinhardt demonstrates that historically, some form of default always follows the condition of "too much debt," and currency debasement (known as "money printing" in modern times) is the most common form this default takes. Along with these defaults, banking crises, exchange-rate volatility, crashes, inflation, and political and social unrest often arise.

The most important finding from the Rogoff and Reinhart study is that periods of relative global financial tranquility have always been followed by waves of defaults and restructurings. Ebb and flow are a normal part of economic history. In this light, we might then view the past seven decades of debt accumulation as the calm before the storm, rather than the last few steps of a long march toward a final and lasting equilibrium.

The important points to take away here are these: Country-level debt defaults are historically common and economically painful events that typically arise from the condition of too much debt, and the four most dangerous words in economic history are *this time it's different.*

Too Much Debt

Now that we understand the differences between debts and liabilities, can tell good debt from bad debt, and know that debt has been growing far faster than national income (i.e., GDP), we're ready to dive one layer deeper into the debt data as the final step toward assessing the severity and magnitude of the economic predicament.

The pure debt obligations of the U.S. government at the end of July 2022 stood at $30,595,108,567,190.06 (that's $30.5 trillion).[4]

But this is only the debt. Once we add in the liabilities of the U.S. government, chiefly Medicare and Social Security, we get a number somewhere between $100 trillion and $239 trillion, nobody's quite sure. The answer depends on whether you use the Federal Reserve's own estimates or those of people like Boston University economics professor Laurence J. Kotlikoff,[5] respectively.

As mentioned before, these liabilities can be changed at any time with the stroke of a congressional pen, but one thing to remember is that entitlements are a zero-sum game. In other words, if the government decides to save money for itself by slashing benefits, the result will be a lower standard of living for the recipients of those monies. Where the government "saves," the people lose by an equal and offsetting amount. The government will see budget savings, to be sure, but retirees will experience a reduction in cash flows and living standards. Savings in one place translate into losses elsewhere. That's the meaning of "zero sum."

But it's not just the federal government that has underfunded liabilities totaling in the trillions of dollars. States and municipalities are *also* deeply underwater on their pension promises. So too are corporate pensions, at least the few that still exist. Once we add up all the debts and liabilities of the United States, we discover they are more than 10 times larger than GDP and perhaps as much as 20 times larger. How many historical examples can we look upon where a country managed to gracefully grow its way out from under such an enormous pile of unfunded paper promises? None. There are zero historical examples to guide us.

The world-record holder in this category is England, which managed to pull itself out of a debt-to-GDP ratio of 2.6 during the period from 1820 to 1900. It had a little help from this thing called "the Industrial Revolution" and from having entirely dismantled is war machinery after defeating Napoleon once and for all at Waterloo.

Debt's Massive Assumption

The critical assumption inherent in ever-growing piles of debt is this: The economic future will be—*must be*—exponentially larger than the present.

Logically, if debt represents a claim on the future, then ever-larger amounts of debt represent ever-larger claims on the future. Okay, that's easy enough to understand.

But let's recall that debt carries with it the expectation of repayment of *both* the principal *and* the interest components. If the debt has a principal balance of "X," we must not forget that the interest component is a percentage based on "X," a percentage that is paid per units of time, typically a year.

Now is the time to recall that anything growing by some percentage over time is growing exponentially. Because debt comes with time-based interest tacked on, it will behave as an exponential system and it will grow exponentially if left unchecked as we've already seen in the chart of total credit market debt (Chapter 6).

Without knowing any of the underlying details or the myriad of ways in which debt has been deployed, productively or otherwise, we can state unequivocally that an ever-growing pile of debt is an implicit and an explicit bet that the future will be larger than the present. And not just larger, but exponentially larger.

Given that U.S. debts now represent more than 340% of GDP and total liabilities over 1,000% (and maybe 2,000%?) of GDP, there's a whole lot of explicit assuming going on out there. The future GDP of the United States must be larger than today's GDP to pay off today's debt. A *lot* larger.

More cars must be sold, more resources consumed, more money earned, more houses built—*every* facet of economic growth and complexity must increase simply to pay back the loans that already exist. Any continuation of debt expansion will only compound these claims on the future so no more incremental new borrowing can take place during the payback period either.

Banks, pension funds, and governments (whose solvency depends on expanding economic activity) are intimately wedded to the continued exponential expansion of debt, as they all have an enormous stake in its perpetual growth. None of these entities want debt to do anything but *expand*. They have strong incentives to see more borrowing, not less.

This defines the tension in the system and explains why our fiscal and monetary authorities seem to talk of nothing but economic growth. Without economic growth, further debt expansion simply does not make any sense. Without continued debt expansion, large-scale debt defaults emerge, and the financial system will break down.

The internal conflict stalking the financial and economic markets results from (a) preserving the status quo *requires* (there's that word again) the continuous and uninterrupted growth in debt and (b) nothing can continue to grow forever.

Each of us already knows deep down which side of that conflict will win the battle.

How It Unfolds

What do you suppose will happen when the big-time holders of all that debt finally figure out the future cannot grow to infinity?

Well, broadly speaking, when that day comes to pass, the losses will be massive and sudden. Where everybody held the delusion we could simply grow our debts faster than our income forever, they will suddenly come around to the painful conclusion that a protracted period of belt-tightening lies before us.

However, one little wrinkle is that the destruction of wealth can come about in one of two very opposite ways. The first is by *deflation*, manifested as a process of debt defaults, and the second is by *inflation*.

Defaults are easy to explain—the debts don't get repaid and the holders of that debt don't get their money back. Simple as that. The debts vanish in a cloud of smoke. Thus, if the future isn't large enough to pay back the claims, then defaults are simply a way of squaring up past claims with current reality. This path is easy to understand. Perhaps a pension fund that believes in the future of electric pickup trucks holds a billion dollars of the e-car maker Rivian debt, Rivian goes out of business, Rivian debt goes into default and becomes worthless, and pensioners in the future have a billion fewer dollars distributed to them. Defaults destroy wealth like a sniper destroys targets.

Inflation is always the "preferred" route because it does its damage like a hailstorm: widespread and everybody gets a little bit dinged up.

Think of it this way: Imagine that you sold your house to someone, and, to keep it simple, you provided them with a mortgage for $500,000. The terms call for the mortgage to be repaid all at once in 10 years as a single payment of

$650,000, providing you with a nice kicker of $150,000. So far, so good. Well, 10 years pass, and, as stipulated, you are paid your $650,000 right on time. But now, due to inflation, that $650,000 will only buy a house half as nice as the one you sold. Yes, you got paid, but your claim on the future was cut in half by inflation.

In this example, a future $650,000 buys half as much as $500,000 today. In the default scenario, your money is still worth something, but you don't get it back, which also diminishes your claim on the future. In the inflation scenario, you do get your money back, but it hardly buys anything, which also diminishes your claim on the future. In both cases you have less wealth in the future, so the impacts are very nearly the same, but the mechanisms by which you lose out are remarkably different.

The real reason I personally expect an inflationary outcome over a deflationary cataclysm is because deflationary events harm rich people's portfolios and the banks (as they are the holders of the debts, typically) while inflation harms everyone, albeit regressively putting far more hurt on poor people than rich.

Since the rich people hold the keys to power, inflation is where I've placed my bets.

CHAPTER 12

The Great Credit Bubble

In order to understand what the future may hold, we need to see the excessive accumulation of debt between the early 1900s and 2020 for what it really was—an enormous and protracted credit bubble. Debt levels doubled, redoubled, and doubled again with uncanny mathematical precision. Within that larger credit bubble, we had several minibubbles—one in stocks, another in housing, and yet another in debt—and while these were all financially destructive, they were sideshows on the way to the main act.

Because our hopes and dreams for the future rest upon a well-functioning economy, we need to understand what bubbles are and the financial risks they pose. If my analysis is correct, when the current debt bubble bursts we'll be lucky to avoid reverting to 13th century lifestyles and living conditions.

Like all credit bubbles, the current credit bubble is founded on the most enduring of human weaknesses: the desire to get something for nothing.

Before we dive into the Great Credit Bubble, let's spend a bit of time defining an asset bubble and examining some of its more common characteristics.

What Is a Bubble?

Along the continuum of irrational financial behavior, it can be tricky to tell the difference between a bubble, a mania, and a touch of overexuberance. The designation "bubble" is reserved for the height of folly, but unfortunately, history is rich with folly. Throughout the long sweep of history, as I'll demonstrate shortly, the bursting of an asset bubble has always been a financially traumatic event and has often precipitated social and political upheavals. Because they are so culturally and financially painful, bubbles used to be separated by one or usually several generations because it took time to forget the experience.

Bucking this convention, less than 10 years passed between the bursting of the dot-com bubble in 2000 and the housing bubble in 2006—a thoroughly unprecedented event—which calls into question the mindfulness of its participants. And then with another huge round of printing post Covid in spring of 2020, another huge set of bubbles were unleashed this time in stocks, bonds, *and* real estate. I remember all of them!

However, it is my contention that instead of these being separate and distinct bubbles, they were merely sub-bubbles housed within a much larger and more profound credit bubble, which partially (but not entirely) excuses the all-too-close nature of their occurrences.

The Federal Reserve famously likes to claim that you can't spot an asset bubble until it bursts. How they can cling to this view is something of a mystery, because the definition of a bubble is pretty simple.

A bubble exists when asset prices rise beyond what incomes can sustain. There is nothing subjective about the definition, and it provides an easy test that can be founded on solid data.

For example, in 2006, when houses in Orange County, California,[1] rose to the point that the median house cost more than nine times the median income,[2] housing there was clearly in the grip of a bubble. A more normal ratio for housing would be in the range of roughly three times income, while anything over four times income really begins to stretch things a bit.[3] When you get to eight times income, you've been in a bubble for quite a while, it's completely obvious even to casual observers, and it's going to burst with predictable, economically painful results.

China put those numbers to complete shame by advancing their internal housing bubble to the point that every one of their largest cities sported house-to-income ratios of at least 20, with Beijing advancing to an unbelievable ratio of nearly 57. In Figure 12.1, which shows housing price-to-income ratios for the top 18 cities of the world, we see evidence of both massive housing bubbles and the global nature of the phenomenon.

Bubble History

To better understand what bubbles are, how they form, and why they are economically painful, let's take a look at a few historical examples, beginning with the tulip bulb craze in Holland of the 1630s.

In that period, a virus swept through the tulip farms and had the effect of creating beautiful and unique variants in tulip coloration that were transmissible to succeeding generations. Tulips were already an economically important crop for the country, so while it may seem strange to us now that a bubble could develop around flowers, tulips represented an important element of commerce to the people of Holland. Before long, incredible variants with brilliant streaks and accents were developed, and the more spectacular examples

	City	Price-to-Income Ratio
1	Damascus, Syria	147
2	Accra, Ghana	66
3	Beijing, China	57
4	Shanghai, China	51
5	Colombo, Sri Lanka	44
6	Hong Kong, Hong Kong	43
7	Shenzhen, China	41
8	Guangzhou, China	38
9	Isfahan (Esfahan), Iran	37
10	Manila, Philippines	36
11	Taipei, Taiwan	35
12	Ho Chi Minh City, Vietnam	33
13	Tehran, Iran	33
14	Phnom Penh, Cambodia	32
15	Bangkok, Thailand	32
16	Seoul, South Korea	31
17	Beirut, Lebanon	30
18	Buenos Aires, Argentina	29

FIGURE 12.1 Price to Income, Housing Top 18 Cities, 2022

Table of the top 18 most expensive, bubbly cities in the world. In Buenos Aires, Argentina, in mid-2022, the average household would have to spend **100%** of their disposable income for 147 years to afford the average home. And they're the "best" on this list. Bubbles are no longer a rare feature, but a matter of serial policy by all the world's central banks, led by the Federal Reserve, and it's a dangerous and ultimately destructive path.

Source: https://www.numbeo.com/property-investment/rankings.jsp.

began trading at higher and higher amounts, building a speculative frenzy. Complicated trading routines built up around the products, and before long nearly all trades were conducted using credit.

At the height of the bubble, a single bulb of the most highly sought-after example, the Semper Augustus, which sported red petals and racy white streaks, commanded the same selling price as the finest house on the finest canal. A tulip bulb!

The tulip bubble could not have occurred were it not for the presence of ample credit. Credit is a necessary fuel for all bubbles; without it, no bubble can develop. After all, if the very definition of an asset bubble is that it grows "larger than incomes can sustain." It means that funds to support the bubble's growth have to come from *somewhere* besides current cash flows (i.e., current income). It's why credit is necessary. People can't pay for bubbles; they have to borrow to create bubbles. True to form, tulip-bulb trading soon outstripped the local money supply, and people began trading on credit.

Records indicate that the tulip craze ended even more suddenly than it began, crashing nearly to the bottom in a single day at the start of the new selling season in February of 1637. When bidding opened on that day, no buyers would bid, and prices rapidly cratered, never to recover. The people holding the last batches of purchased bulbs recorded major losses, creditors went bust, and an enormous amount of wealth evaporated, never to be seen again. Lives were ruined, fortunes were lost, and people promised themselves, *Never again.*

A second example of an early recorded bubble comes from the 1720s and is known as the South Sea Bubble.

The South Sea Company was an English company that had been granted a monopoly by the government to trade with South America under a treaty with Spain. The fact that the company was rather ordinary in its profits prior to the granting of the monopoly did not deter people from speculating wildly about its financial potential.

Even more startlingly, people were undeterred in snapping up shares of its stock, despite the fact that the company rather accurately billed itself as "A company for carrying out an undertaking of great advantage, but nobody to know what it is." That's about as clear a scam warning as an investor will ever receive, but bubbles have a way of shutting down critical thinking in the masses.

Sir Isaac Newton, when asked about the continually rising stock price of the South Sea Company, said he "could not calculate the madness of people." But then he, too, apparently went mad for company stock. He may have invented calculus and described universal gravitation, but he also ended up losing over 20,000 pounds,[4] a massive fortune in those days, to the burst South Sea Bubble. Even a truly rare intelligence can be outwitted by a bubble.

For some reason, bubbles are extremely hard for most people to spot in advance. A bubble begins when people start relying on hope instead of reason, but a bubble really hits its stride when prudence is replaced by greed.

Bubble Characteristics

History is littered with the wreckage of financial bubbles involving a surprising diversity of assets, with more recent examples involving railroads, swamp land, internet stocks, housing, and even government bonds, if you can believe it. The asset itself, whether land or tulips or pieces of paper, is irrelevant. What matters is having the right story—usually involving massive riches soon to come, a credulous mob, short-sighted (or greedy) lenders, and an ample supply of credit. If any one of these things is missing, no bubble for you!

What's interesting is that nearly every bubble shares the same common, and therefore predictable, features. Despite these, we seem to be unable to prevent them from forming, so we have to assume that's not really the goal.

Bubbles are self-reinforcing, meaning that on the way up, higher prices become the justification for higher prices. Once the illusion is lifted, the game is permanently over, but not instantly, as it takes a little bit of time for reality to set in.

Figure 12.2 demonstrates two important traits about bubbles. Note that the amount of time it took the Dow Jones to run up to its price peak in 1929 is roughly the same amount of time that it took for prices to fall back to their starting levels. The first characteristic of bubbles is their rough symmetry. They first rise, and then they fall, but not all at once, revealing that bubbles take time to develop and then to unwind.

First, the psychology has to be built into a frenzy, a mob has to be formed, fear of missing out has to set in, and then all that energy has to be slowly dissipated, one disillusioned person at a time. With all that said, bubbles typically deflate just a little bit faster than they develop perhaps showing the fear acts more quickly than the greed.

The second characteristic of bubbles that we see reflected in Figure 12.2 is that asset prices will usually fully retrace to their starting point, if not just a little bit further. Whatever the starting point was for the asset prices in question is a reasonable place to suspect they'll eventually end up at some point in the future.

To reinforce this point, Figure 12.3 shows the stock price of General Motors (the black line) between the years 1912 and 1922 and Intel (the shaded line)

FIGURE 12.2 Dow Jones Industrial Average, 1922–1935
Source: Yahoo! Finance.

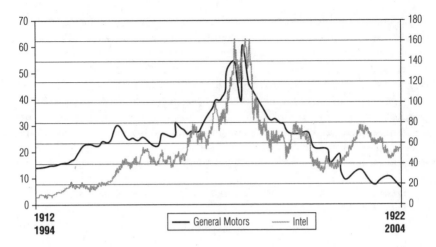

FIGURE 12.3 Stock Prices: GM and Intel

Source: Yahoo! Finance.

between 1992 and 2002, periods during which both stocks were swept up in bubbles. Here we might also note that the price data looks very similar for both stocks, despite the fact that one was a car company in the 1920s and the other was a high-tech chip manufacturer trading some 80 years later. Again, we might note that they share the two characteristics of bubbles we've already discussed: a rough symmetry in both time and price. They crescendo, then crash, and end up right where they began.

The fact that bubbles display the same price behaviors over the centuries and decades tells us they're not artifacts of particular financial arrangements, cultures, or legal systems. Instead, the constant factor is people. Bubbles do not develop as a condition of poor financial engineering or specific financial laws and regulations that happen to be present, nor because of particular cultural practices, but as the by-product of greed, hope, and excessive credit. Wherever these circumstances exist, bubbles will eventually develop, which is why investors should hold onto their wallets whenever they spot such conditions.

Asset bubbles, therefore, aren't so much financial phenomena upon which we can conduct meaningful financial postmortems as they are sociological events best understood through the study of human psychology and mob behavior. Perhaps we can even speculate that bubble behavior is wired into our biological software, an evolutionary remnant once useful in our deep past but is now a profound liability when it comes to making investment choices.

That bubbles happen isn't the surprising part of this story; rather, it's well-educated people responsible for knowing about such things have apparently never learned that bubbles aren't rare and random events but are very common and predictable features of the economic landscape. In their defense, perhaps these people have learned about bubbles, but then mistakenly overestimate their ability to manage their destructive effects (yes, I am talking about Alan Greenspan, Ben Bernanke, Janet Yellen, and Jay Powell here).

By way of illustration, the Federal Reserve entirely missed the opportunity to nip both the 1990s stock and 2000s housing bubbles in the bud, and even devoted considerable internal resources to the task of proving to itself that no housing bubble existed. Even as a number of analysts and commentators (including me) were warning of a housing bubble back in 2004, the Fed released a study titled "Are Home Prices the Next Bubble?," which concluded that the answer was no:

> *Home prices have been rising strongly since the mid-1990s, prompting concerns that a bubble exists in this asset class and that home prices are vulnerable to a collapse that could harm the U.S. economy. A close analysis of the U.S. housing market in recent years, however, finds little basis for such concerns. The marked upturn in home prices is largely attributable to strong market fundamentals: Home prices have essentially moved in line with increases in family income and declines in nominal mortgage interest rates.[5]*

All of that sounds perfectly logical, and the paper is stuffed with comforting and supportive data, but it is also completely and hopelessly wrong. Although they should arguably have known better, the Fed's researchers were simply doing what millions of people did; namely, falling prey to the belief that somehow "this time is different." That's just how bubbles are.

People take leave of their senses, using all manner of rationales to justify their positions, but then suddenly one day the illusion lifts, and what was once unassailably true no longer makes any sense at all. Once that tipping point occurs, there's really nothing left to do but track the speed of the bubble's collapse and the damage it will cause.

A Bubble 50 Years in the Making

> *There is no means of avoiding the final collapse of a boom brought about by credit expansion. The alternative is only whether the crisis should come sooner as the result of voluntary abandonment of further credit expansion, or later as a final and total catastrophe of the currency system involved.[6]*
>
> —*Ludwig Von Mises*

All of this review of bubbles was meant to get us to the point where we could talk about the biggest, and what will almost certainly be the most destructive, bubble in history: The Great Credit Bubble.

So far (as of 2022), this bubble, like every serious bubble worthy of mention, has largely escaped attention. Most economic experts are convinced a credit bubble doesn't exist, and few people think twice about using credit in their daily lives or dwell on the past four decades of debt accumulation. Bubbles that have not yet collapsed are incredibly hard for most people to detect; that's pretty much what allows them to exist in the first place.

As mentioned in Chapter 10 (*Debt*), total credit in the United States doubled five times over the five decades between 1970 and 2020. At the end of 2000, when the stock bubble was bursting, total credit market debt stood at $26 trillion, but by the end of 2008 it stood at an astounding $52 trillion. By January of 2022 it had hit $90 trillion. This $64 trillion increase in borrowing was 4.4 times larger than the increase in U.S. gross domestic product (GDP) over the same period of time.

If debt is meant to be paid back, and that is the whole idea, then over the long term, debt cannot rise faster than income. That's just how the math works out. At the household level it would be like having a credit card you never paid off that had a rate of interest on it of two times your yearly salary increases. Sooner or later that's a straight-up cash flow problem but it was a math problem the entire time. We have a huge math problem and hardly anyone is talking about it.

Now, let's look at the increase in the size of the United States' debt compared to its GDP, representing the national income, over the past 30 years.

Where debts have increased by just over 1,900% since 1980, GDP has advanced by just under 770%. It is a thoroughly unsustainable proposition.

Now, here's the question. If your debts are constantly expanding faster than your income, what's the one thing that could buy you some time? That's right, negotiating a lower rate of interest!

The U.S. Federal Reserve, in order to facilitate and allow this ill-advised exponential expansion of debt, has engineered constantly falling interest rates since 1982 (see Figure 12.4).

But this trick of lowering interest rates can only go so far. The European Central Bank experimented with taking the rate below zero, giving the world the spectacle of negative yielding bonds, but it's far from clear the experiment was a success.

The more adult and obvious thing to do would be to let free markets set the rate of interest and keep the amount of money in circulation nice and tight. That way bad ideas wouldn't get funded, non-self-liquidating debt would be too expensive to really get out of hand, and the system would have a chance at self-regulating.

But, instead, we have the Fed and its foreign brethren consisting of very small groups of unelected people (many of whom have never held a real job) setting the price of money lower and lower and lower to keep the whole charade alive for a little longer.

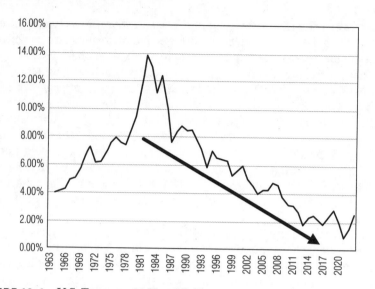

FIGURE 12.4 U.S. Treasury 10-Year Yield

The 10-Year Treasury Bond Interest Rate has continuously declined since 1984.

Withering Heights

How was it possible to keep such a bubble going for so long? One essential factor was that interest rates constantly fell even as the total amount of credit market debt rose.

Here's why falling interest rates matter.

Imagine you had a credit card with a most unusual feature, whereby the rate of interest declined as the balance grew. The more you charged, the lower the interest rate became, which had the effect of stabilizing or even reducing the minimum payment due. Clearly, such an arrangement would allow more borrowing than if the interest rates had not fallen (let alone risen). It is highly doubtful the credit bubble would have developed without U.S. interest rates steadily falling over the 30 years between 1980 and 2010 (see Figure 12.4, earlier). This was really a perverse development when you think about it; interest rates should *rise* with a rising balance of debt, not *decline*. But there's no law saying these things have to make sense.

This practice of lowering interest rates to keep the game alive for a while longer has a natural limit: Rates cannot go below zero. In 2010, we saw the Federal Reserve set interest rates for overnight money to between zero percent and 0.25%, and we saw the interest rates on two-year Treasury notes go below 0.50%. In short, interest rates hit bottom in 2010 and were held there for 11 long years in an effort to keep the credit bubble expanding. It worked.

Unfortunately, all good things come to an end, and doubly unfortunately, we're going to have to deal with the aftereffects of *too much debt* at the same time a dozen other critical projects are going to be competing for attention and funds.

As for the timing? It could hardly be worse. Dealing with a bursting credit bubble is hardly the sort of challenge we need at this particular moment in history, where energy and environmental issues loom large. But here we are. The stewardship and vision displayed by the Federal Reserve and Washington, DC, in shepherding us to this position has been reckless and, to the degree they chose winners and losers (the wealthy over the poor, the older over the younger, and the reckless over the prudent), immoral.

So, what can we expect from a collapsing credit bubble? Simply put, everything that fed upon and grew as a consequence of too much easy credit will collapse back to its baseline position. Where we lived beyond our means for too long, we will have to live below our means until the excesses are worked off. Living standards will fall, debts will default, and times will be hard. Those, at least, are the lessons history provides.

But there's more to this story than the simple accumulation of debt, even as serious as that is all by itself. We'll explore more of the story later when we discuss the role of energy in supporting economic growth. For now, let's just hold onto the idea that in order for the next 20 years to resemble the past 20 years, total debt will have to double and then double again. How likely does that seem to you?

Hold that thought . . .

CHAPTER 13

Like a Moth to Flame

Our Destructive Tendency to Print

When the Great Credit Bubble first began to lurch about unsteadily in 2008 as the consumer withdrew, most governments of developed nations predictably turned to Keynesian stimulus to try and keep the bubble going. Meaning, they racked up enormous and unprecedented levels of debt trying to stabilize the situation, and this debt will someday need to be paid back.

History is quite clear on the subject: Whenever governments or countries have found themselves saturated with too much debt totaling more than could possibly be paid back out of their productive economy, they've nearly always resorted to printing more money. In times past this meant physically debasing the coinage of the realm by reducing the purity of the silver or gold in the coins, or by making the coins smaller, or both.

The Moths

In the fourth century BC, Dionysius of Syracuse became the first recorded ruler to debase his currency in order to pay down his accumulated debt. The trick he used was to recall the circulating money, melt it down, and make all the coins a bit smaller. Presto! More money! But this was relatively hard work because they had to perform the tasks of actually getting the physical coinage back, melting it down, and then refashioning it into coinage.

Far easier was the task of running paper printing presses and churning out truckloads of paper currency, as Germany did in the 1920s and Zimbabwe did in the 2000s.

Today, "money printing" means using computers to generate electronic entries on computer hard disks that represent money. It's as simple as typing a few keys on a keyboard and—presto!—a billion or even a trillion dollars are instantly created.

The difference between antiquity and today is that when money is conjured up out of thin air the resulting debasement is virtually instantaneous and far less readily observed by the common person. Where it took several decades for the Roman Empire to debase its coinage (contributing to its downfall), it only took Germany about five years to accomplish the same task in the 1920s using paper printing presses.

Today, it's possible to create unlimited quantities of money almost instantly with just a few strokes on a keyboard. All that's needed to unleash the money is some sort of an emergency to justify it all. In 2020, Covid provided that emergency. In truth, the Federal Reserve had already begun to print in earnest beginning in September of 2019 due to a "repo emergency" and so they were looking for an excuse, any excuse, to print even more.

While an arcane bit of financial plumbing, what happened in the "repo" market was extraordinarily important. On September 17, 2019, interest rates on overnight repurchase agreements, or "repos," suddenly doubled and then doubled again, shooting over 10% when they had been ~2.5% just a day earlier. This was an enormous emergency for the Fed and they had to tamp it down with massive injections of "liquidity," by which I mean freshly created currency.

To the Federal Reserve, Covid was a welcome justification that came at just the right time.

And print they did. Not just a little bit, either; they effectively engineered more new money creation within the U.S. system in just nine months—an astonishing $3.8 trillion!—than had entirely existed within the system in 1980. From the start of Covid through July 2022, more than 6.2 trillion new dollars had been created within the U.S. banking system (see Figure 13.1).

This is truly astonishing! Perhaps even more astonishing is how confused the Federal Reserve officials acted when inflation spiked to 40-year highs in 2022. Not one question was asked of Federal Reserve Chairman Jerome Powell about the Fed's role in creating inflation by any "journalist" in any press conference I watched. To be somewhat fair to these journalists, they know they'd never be invited back if they did actually ask any tough questions, as very publicly happened to *Wall Street Journal* reporter Pedro De Costa in 2015 after he asked a Janet Yellen a "toughie."[1]

Despite all of our technological "advances" in the arena of electronic money creation, the core of the matter has not changed one bit over the centuries. In all instances, additional money was created without the benefit of anything else being produced. The very definition of inflation is the creation of money divorced from the process of creating additional produce or value.

Once we understand that money is a *claim* on wealth, but not wealth itself, it becomes obvious why simply printing more of it does not create wealth but instead robs a tiny bit of stored purchasing power from every outstanding unit of money. It's the same as when you were a teenager and you added water to your parent's vodka to cover up the fact that you pinched some. Yes, there's more volume in the bottle, but the vodka is now diluted.

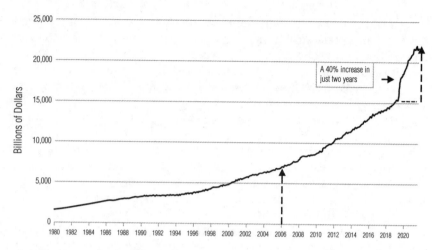

FIGURE 13.1   The U.S. Money Supply (M2)

"M2" is a measure of money in the system. It includes all physical cash, checking and savings accounts, CDs, and money market funds. From the beginning of Covid in March of 2020 through July of 2022, 6.2 trillion new dollars were created within the banking system.

Source: Data from US Federal Reserve; chart created by author (C Martenson).

The purpose of this chapter isn't to present an exhaustive recounting of economic history, although there are many fascinating tales to be told, but to help us assess what the future might hold.

In order to mitigate our economic risks, we have to have a clear bead on what they actually are. *Which path or outcome is most likely? Will we head down a path of inflation or deflation? Should I hold cash, gold, land, stocks, bonds, or something else? What chance is there that the entire system will blow up so I'd better have a garden, some chickens, and a dozen really close friends?*

The Flame

Recall from Chapter 11 (*Debt*) that there are only three ways for a government to get rid of its debt:

1. Pay it off.
2. Default on it.
3. Print money (which is a less honest form of default).

If we put ourselves in the shoes of politicians, there really isn't any other choice besides option 3. Option 1, paying it off, is a nonstarter because that involves telling voters that they are the ones who are going to have to live below their means to pay back the excesses of prior generations. That's just super unpopular, is called austerity, and is *never* willingly chosen. Greek politicians had it forced on them by external forces in the aftermath of the Great Financial Crisis but, as I said, it was forced on them.

Option 2, default on the debts, is an exceptionally rare outcome mainly because it shafts powerful institutions like major financial companies and big banks as well as endowments and billionaires who hold all the debt. Since these people and institutions have vastly more power than politicians, this option is also never selected.

In 2009, things got away from the keepers of the system and despite their significant efforts, defaults rippled through the system threatening big companies like AIG and Goldman Sachs. The political response was as swift as it was predictable: bail out the big companies, guarantee their bad bets, make them and their stock- and bondholders whole, and saddle the U.S. taxpayers with the bills. That those bailouts eventually cost a lot less than feared due to the markets stabilizing and recovering was anything but an assured outcome when the bailouts were crafted. The initial response was to slap the taxpayers with the bill, so the wealthy did not experience any losses. It is an easy prediction to make that we'll see many more bailouts in the future until something external forces this behavior to stop. It won't be anything internal like integrity, ethics, or a sense of social responsibility.

Covid represented another massive bailout of the system courtesy of the most aggressive printing spree in all of history, bar none.

Further, because debt is a claim on the productive output of a country, the first option, paying off the debt, is deeply painful, as each payment redirects the nation's productive output into the hands of creditors. In practical terms, "paying off debt" means the government has to tax its citizens so it can hand that money over to the debt holders. That translates into lower economic growth, higher unemployment, fewer goods and services, and unhappy voters.

Throughout all of history, raising taxes has *always* been a deeply unpopular move, but even more so if the collected taxes are siphoned away and don't result in any additional benefit to the citizens in any form. *Hey, our debts are lower!* is not a compelling political argument.

This leaves us with the third option, money printing. This is the most politically viable of the three options and explains why it's almost always the preferred avenue. The irony here is that it's also the most dangerous path to take, but because its destructive effects are inevitably lodged in the future somewhere, it pushes the day of reckoning to a later time (when it could very well be somebody else's problem anyway). It offers a convenient sliver of rationalized hope, too. *Hey, it just might work this time! This time might be different!* It never is.

Alan Greenspan made a number of crucial errors during his tenure as chairman of the Federal Reserve, but before he held that position, he wrote this remarkably lucid and correct assessment of gold and its role in helping to shield people from the effects of governmental money printing (written in 1966, when he was managing the consulting firm Townsend-Greenspan & Co. in New York).

In the absence of the gold standard, there is no way to protect savings from confiscation through inflation. There is no safe store of value. If there were, the government would have to make its holding illegal, as was done in the case of gold. If everyone decided, for example, to convert all his bank deposits to silver or copper or any other good, and thereafter declined to accept checks as payment for goods, bank deposits would lose their purchasing power and government-created bank credit would be worthless as a claim on goods. The financial policy of the welfare state requires that there be no way for the owners of wealth to protect themselves. This is the shabby secret of the welfare statists' tirades against gold. Deficit spending is simply a scheme for the confiscation of wealth. Gold stands in the way of this insidious process. It stands as a protector of property rights. If one grasps this, one has no difficulty in understanding the statists' antagonism toward the gold standard.[2]

Although Alan Greenspan "got it," his actions as Federal Reserve chairman ran dead against his earlier insights. His policies set the stage for decades of increasingly bad Federal Reserve policies. Ben Bernanke, then Janet Yellen, and currently Jerome "Jay" Powell have carried Greenspan's monetary excesses to higher and higher extremes.

Inflation's political benefit has the effect of reducing the real value of public debts; it makes them smaller by making the money in which they're denominated worth less. Inflating debt away represents a stealthy form of default; it is a multitude of micro-defaults on the concept of money being a store of value.

To draw once again from Rogoff and Reinhart's remarkable 800-year romp through history[3], we observe that monetary history consists of periodic episodes of sovereign defaults scattered across a constant backdrop of inflation. What is stunning is that every country in both Asia and Europe experienced an extended period of inflation over 20% between the years 1500 and 1800, and most experienced a significant number of years with inflation over 40%. But they also experienced pronounced deflations that tended to follow each inflationary episode, so after all the ups and downs were eventually netted out, prices tended to remain constant over the centuries.

In the period from 1800 to 2006, Rogoff and Reinhart note that inflationary eras became ever more frequent and attained higher levels, thanks to the ease offered by modern printing presses. Prior to 1900, the world cycled between inflation and deflation on very short cycles of around 10 years, again keeping price levels roughly in check around a median value. But since the last deflationary episode in the 1930s, the world has spent the next 80 years in one long, sustained inflationary episode, with virtually no deflationary downdrafts.

It is also very much not a coincidence that oil has yielded nearly all of its energy bonanza to humanity over the same span of time. As we'll see in the upcoming chapter on energy economics, a vast surplus of oil energy can cover up a host of monetary errors and accidents.

One more point—fiat money only lost its final tether to the firmament of earth when President Nixon cut the dollar's tie to gold on August 15, 1971.*

The uninterrupted march of inflation is intimately tied to these events. The particular style of debt-based money on which we operate requires the very sort of continuous expansion that petroleum offers, while spending massively beyond one's means requires that no physical, tangible anchor exist to limit the spree.

This means that *this time it really is different*, because the story now involves so much more monetary excess and fiscal imprudence as seen throughout history. This time, the entire globe is involved and there are critical resource issues involved. This time, the entire world is operating on a debt-based monetary system that requires perpetual exponential growth to avoid collapse.

Quantitative Easing

The prediction I made in the video version of the Crash Course in 2008 was that we'd enter a period of profound money printing by the Fed in order to try and "fix" things. I based that on history and knowing human behavior is what it is.

Given the fact that the Federal Reserve and other central banks in Europe and Japan began an aggressive monetary printing program in 2008, continuing through the time of this writing (2022), this "prediction" is now an observation. The printing had already started in earnest. These money-printing programs go by the fancy name of quantitative easing (QE), which simply refers to creating money out of thin air and then using it to buy various forms of debt, both governmental and nongovernmental.

----

*On August 15, 1971, President Richard Nixon "slammed the gold window," ending the Bretton Woods I agreement, which allowed foreign countries to convert their paper dollar holdings into U.S.-held gold at the fixed price of $35 per ounce. From that moment on, foreign exchange rates lost their anchor to gold and "floated" freely on the international market.

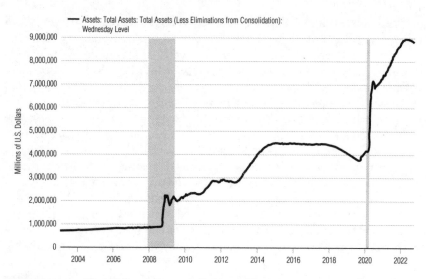

FIGURE 13.2 The Federal Reserve Balance Sheet

The slow and careful accumulation of assets (debts) spiked sharply upward at the start of the credit crisis in 2008 and then climbed until mid-2014 where they more or less stalled for four years. Then assets turned up again during the repo panic of 2019, before exploding higher in response to Covid.

Source: Chart copied from Cleveland Federal Reserve.

Between 2008 and 2022, the Fed's balance sheet expanded from $800 billion to just over $8,900 billion (or $8.9 trillion), all of which represents money created out of thin air for the purpose of monetizing existing debt (see Figure 13.2).

Keep a journal, folks! This level of excess has never been tried, never been seen before. This is/was history being made. It was a truly desperate move and anybody who claims it was made carefully and with plenty of supporting evidence is either ignorant or lying.

The Central Bank's Reign of Error

The U.S. Federal Reserve, which is a privately held banking cartel (yes, that's true) deserves very little of the credit and credibility granted to it by the public. It manages to cause larger and larger crises as it flails about seeking remedies for the problems caused by its prior sets of "solutions."

In 1987, the stock market crashed by 25% in a single day. At the time it was quite traumatic, and Alan Greenspan swept into action—*just this one time*—to get stocks moving again the correct direction: up. Crisis averted! Like a drunk driver avoiding a ditch, Alan Greenspan cranked the monetary wheel to the left and got us back on the road. But he oversteered a bit.

Then in 1994, all that hot money he'd introduced to stave off further stock declines crept over into the corporate bond markets, where trouble was suddenly brewing. The solution was bold: get more money into banks' hands so they could lend more and stave off the bursting corporate bond bubble.

Greenspan accomplished this by fully removing the last vestiges of banks needing to hold anything in reserve by introducing something called "sweep accounts." This was a sleight-of-hand move that allowed banks to reclassify your demand account money as something else.

From the Federal Reserve itself we get this description of sweep accounts:

> *Since January 1994, hundreds of banks and other depository financial institutions have implemented automated computer programs that reduce their required reserves by analyzing customers' use of checkable deposits (demand deposits, ATS, NOW, and other checkable deposits) and "sweeping" such deposits into savings deposits (specifically, MMDA, or money market deposit accounts). Under the Federal Reserve's Regulation D, MMDA accounts are personal saving deposits and, hence, have a zero statutory reserve requirement.*[4]

Crisis averted! Now, completely untethered from having to hold any money in reserve at all, the banks could create as much as they want any time they wanted! Greenspan once again cranked the monetary steering wheel, this time to the right, with even greater force than before.

The effect of this program was to effectively remove reserve requirements altogether, allowing a flood of new lending to proceed. Sure, that fixed the corporate bond market tightness, but it also gave us the massive stock bubble of the late 1990s. Oops.

Along the way, the Long-Term Capital Management (LTCM) disaster blew up in 1998 and again Greenspan grabbed this wheel and cranked it hard to the other side, this time creating a massive moral hazard as Wall Street's biggest players learned something very important: If you're going to fail, fail so big that you are a "risk to the system." That way, you get bailed out and made whole. Heads, you keep your profits and winnings. Tails, the Fed will make you whole.

But then the 2000 stock market crash required more Fed activism (crank! steer!), and then the 2008 Great Financial Crisis (bigger crank, larger steer!!), and then various other crises in 2011, 2013, 2015, 2019, and finally 2020, where Jerome Powell spun the wheel so hard it's no longer connected to the steering column.

Problem, reaction, overreaction, overreaction to the overreaction, wildly swinging this way and that, with the amplitude of each swerve violently increasing.

Finally, you are reading this wondering how all this could happen without a single person able to cast a single vote for any of the people causing such a mega-disaster. Undoing any of this will not be easy mechanistically and all but impossible politically.

In reality, putting money *into* the system is far easier than taking it back *out*. When the Fed puts the money into the system, an institution delivers a debt instrument to the Fed and receives a large pile of cash in return. Reversing this process requires an institution to have a large and ready pile of cash on hand to give to the Fed in exchange for the debt instrument that, by definition, will be falling in value (as they flood the market).

Cash is rarely left piled up at financial institutions; it is generally put to work quite rapidly when it's received, so raising cash usually requires selling other things elsewhere. For this reason, putting cash out into the marketplace is a lot easier for the Fed than reeling it back in.

As the first edition of this book claimed in 2011, "if they don't (or can't) reverse these monetary injections, then there's an incredibly high chance of destructive inflation emerging at some point in the future." Boy, did that ever turn out to be accurate.

CHAPTER 14

Fuzzy Numbers

What if it's true, as author Kevin Phillips states, that "[e]ver since the 1960s, Washington has gulled its citizens and creditors by debasing official statistics, the vital instruments with which the vigor and muscle of the American economy are measured"?[1] What if it turns out that our individual, corporate, and government decision making was based on deeply misleading, if not provably false, data?

That's what we're going to examine here, uncovering the ways that inflation and gross domestic product, or GDP, are measured, or, as we might say, *mis*measured. The instrumentation of the United States is rigged to make things look better than they actually are and this is preventing us from having the sort of honest conversation we ought to be having. After all, if you've convinced yourself you are 25 but you are actually 55, you are going to make a few errors out in the field of life.

Inflation is an active policy goal of the Federal Reserve,[2] and for good reason: Too little inflation, and our current banking system risks failure; too much and the majority of people noticeably lose their savings, which makes them angry and politically restive. So, keeping inflation at a "Goldilocks" temperature—not too hot and not too cold—is the name of the game.

On January 25, 2012, the Fed made a historic shift when Ben Bernanke announced that the Fed would adopt an explicit inflation target of 2%. Before then it had been known that the Fed favored inflation, but it wasn't an explicit target with a set of supporting policies.

Recalling our Rule of 72, if the Fed had its way, your savings would lose one-half of their value every 35 years (70/2 = 35). It should be noted that the Fed has badly miscalculated, as predicted in the first edition of this book, and, at the time of this rewriting of the book, inflation is running closer to 9% at which rate money will lose one-half of its value in only 7.7 years. Over time, this adds up. It's reverse compounding, where our money loses some percentage value over time. The Fed's track record makes it look like it hates the dollar or something (see Figure 14.1).

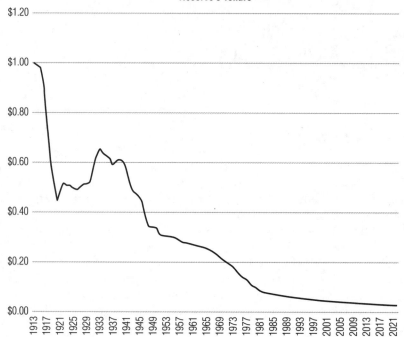

FIGURE 14.1   The Fed's Dismal Track Record

The dollar's value during the Fed's tenure. To develop this chart the CPI (Consumer Price Index) was deducted from the value of the prior year's result.

By the time you are reading this, especially if you are in Europe, the rate of inflation will probably be far higher. The reason? Again, nobody in power has the stature to weather a round of punishing austerity, so they will concoct another reason to print, and then print even more.

It's important that we understand what inflation is and what it isn't. The definitions have been so muddied over time that people rarely share much about what it is, what causes it, and what it isn't.

Let's begin with what it isn't. Inflation is not rising prices. Those are a symptom. Instead, inflation is the value of your currency falling.

Inflation results from a combination of two components. The first is simple pressure on prices of goods and services due to too much money floating around. If goods and services remain constant but circulating money rises, inflation will result. (More money) + (the same number of things) = higher prices.

The second component lies with people's expectations of future inflation. If people *expect* prices to rise, they tend to spend their money today, while the getting is still good, and this serves to fuel further inflation in a self-reinforcing manner. The faster people spend, the more they expect inflation to rise, and the more inflation does rise.

Zimbabwe was a textbook-perfect example of this dynamic in play during the years 2001 to 2008, when inflation nudged over 100% on its way to a peak of more than 230,000,000%.[3]

Post-Covid there was a third dynamic pressing on the "spend it now" philosophy due to disrupted supply chains and people's worry that they'd better buy things now while they were still available, at any price. That too contributes to rising prices, but because of the perception if not the reality of scarcity. There, the equation is (the same amount of money) + (fewer things) = rising prices. If, God forbid, you have the worst of all possible equations then you're really screwed: (more money) + (fewer things) = explosive inflation.

Accordingly, official inflation policy seeks to goose the money supply just enough to achieve the desired amount of inflation, while it seeks to anchor inflation expectations to help keep them in check.

How exactly is "anchoring" accomplished? You might be surprised at the answer. Over time, the management of your inflation expectations has evolved into little more than telling people that inflation is lower than it actually is.

The details of how this is done are somewhat complicated, but they're worthy of your attention because it helps to know when you are being lied to. Trusting bad data can be hazardous to your wealth.

Before we begin, I'd like to be clear on one point: The tricks and subversions that we'll examine did not arise with any particular administration or political party. Rather, they arose incrementally during each administration from the 1960s onward. If I point fingers, I'll be pointing at actions, not ideologies or parties. There are plenty of examples implemented by both of the major U.S. political parties, and there's absolutely no partisan slant to this game. Every politician and statistical bureaucrat is in on it.

Administrative Bias

Under President Kennedy, who disliked high unemployment numbers, a new classification was developed that scrubbed so-called "discouraged workers" from the statistics. Doing so made them disappear from the rolls, and so there were fewer unemployed to count, which caused the reported unemployment figures to drop.

Discouraged workers, defined as people who desire to work but aren't currently looking due to poor employment prospects, just weren't counted anymore. Problem solved! The reported unemployment numbers went down, and Kennedy was said to be pleased with the outcome. Of course, the exact same number of people were unemployed both before and after this statistical revision, but the *reported* number went down, so things looked better. No president since has seen fit to reverse this practice, so "discouraged workers" are still dropped from the rolls and not counted as unemployed. They are, instead, discouraged.

President Johnson created the "unified budget" accounting fiction we currently enjoy, which rolls Social Security surpluses into the general budget, where they are spent just like ordinary revenue. Even though the surplus Social Security funds have been spent and represent a debt of the U.S. government, budget deficits are reported after taking into account the positive impact of the "donated" Social Security money (which reduces the cash deficit) but not the future negative impact of this borrowing. In this sense, the federal budget deficits you read about are fiction.

President Nixon bequeathed us the so-called core inflation measure, which strips out food and fuel, to create a measure of inflation "ex food and fuel," which financial commentator Barry Ritholtz says is "like reporting inflation ex-inflation." For the rest of us, it's very strange to think about inflation as consisting of the prices of our essential daily needs minus the eating, driving, and heating parts.

By adopting the Boskin Commission recommendation on inflation, President Clinton bestowed upon us the labyrinthine statistical morass that's now our official method of inflation measurement, the monthly reported Consumer Price Index or CPI, which we discuss in detail shortly.

Those are just a few of the examples of a pathological instinct to buff the numbers into a rosier hue since the Kennedy administration. With every new administration the permanent bureaucracy of Washington, DC thinks of new and more creative ways to statistically torture the national economic figures, always in the direction of overstating how good things are.

I know of no examples of a new economic measure being adopted that served to make things seem a bit drearier or worse off. The process of debasing our official statistics has always been strongly biased to the upside.

Economic activity was always adjusted higher, inflation was statistically tormented downward, and jobs were made to seem more plentiful than they actually were. Untangling any one of the messes would require a deep-dive forensic exploration of footnotes to monthly reports stretching back decades.

Unfortunately, the cumulative impact of all this data manipulation is that our measurements no longer match reality. In effect, we're telling ourselves lies, and these untruths serve to distort our decisions and jeopardize our economic future. A few economic fibs during the good years seemed harmless enough, and they probably were during times of amply surplus fossil fuel energy. However, with the current and emerging economic difficulties, we will find them to be as severe a liability as a defective cockpit altimeter would be to a pilot navigating a gap through the Rockies at night.

Next let's discuss in detail the way the most important indicators we rely on for understanding our economic picture are adjusted, measure by measure.

Inflation

We begin with inflation, which is reported to us by the Bureau of Labor Statistics (BLS) in the form of the Consumer Price Index (CPI). If you were to measure inflation, you'd probably track the cost of a basket of goods from one year to the next, subtract the two, and measure the difference. If you did, your method would, in fact, mirror the way inflation was officially measured right on up through the early 1980s. It's a perfectly logical, defensible, and sensible method.

But in 1996, Clinton implemented the Boskin Commission findings, which championed the use of three new statistical tools—substitution, weighting, and hedonics—that are applied to measured prices after they're collected but before they're reported.

The costs of goods and services are no longer simply measured and reported from one year to the next, now that we have adopted the use of the "substitution effect." Thanks to the Boskin Commission, our measurements now assume that when the price of something rises, people will switch to something cheaper. So, any time the price of something goes up too rapidly, it's removed from the basket of goods and a cheaper item is substituted. For example, if rib-eye steaks go up too much in price, they'll be removed from the basket and replaced ("substituted") with, say, sirloin steak (or whatever form of steak is cheaper).

To illustrate the impacts of these statistical tricks, let's imagine that our goal is to accurately assess whether a group of 20 of our former high school classmates have gained weight or had lost weight since high school. Following current government statistical conventions in our experiment, we'd first weigh all 20 subjects and choose the 10 showing the least weight gain, assume those reflect the actual status of the group, throw out the 10 heaviest, and report our findings.

To the BLS, "substitution" means that if steaks become too expensive, people will buy chicken. They will substitute a lower-cost item for a higher-cost item. By this method the BLS is free to wander around our consumer lives assuming we're always buying the cheaper item, even if we're not and even if they aren't even the same category, as with chicken versus steak. The main complaint of using substitution is that it's not measuring the price increases, it's measuring the cost of survival.

Using this methodology, the BLS reported that food costs rose 4.9% in 2007.[4] However, according to the Farm Bureau, which doesn't employ these tricks and simply tracks the same shopping basket of the exact same 30 goods from one year to the next, food prices rose 9.2% in 2007.[5] That spread of 5.1% makes a huge difference. Recall from the Rule of 70 in Chapter 5 (*Dangerous Exponentials*) that a 5% rate of growth will result in a complete doubling in just 14 years. What this means is that after 14 years of the BLS telling us that "food costs X" it will instead be true that food costs 2X. Every year I've tracked the BLS, food inflation is said to be lower than a simple Farm Bureau–style method.

Even smallish-seeming underreporting of inflation will result in big differences over time. One critique of using substitution as a method is that our measure of inflation no longer measures the cost of *living*, but rather the cost of *survival*.

The next statistical method, *weighting*, has the effect of reducing the amount of those goods and services that are rising most rapidly in price by mysteriously making them a smaller portion of consumer basket than they actually are.

This is the least defensible of all the statistical tricks, because over time it has deviated widely from reality. For example, the Bureau of Economic Analysis (BEA—a different agency from the BLS) reports that health care represents about 17% of our total economy, but the BLS only weights it as 6% of the CPI.

Because health care costs have been rising extremely rapidly, including less of it in our basket has the effect of making inflation seem lower than it is. It's a thoroughly ridiculous practice and infuriating to anyone who pays health insurance premiums or has had to listen to a story about someone with a broken leg refusing an ambulance ride because they were terrified by the expected bill.

Next comes the most outlandish statistical adjustment of them all, *hedonics*, a word whose Greek roots translate to "for the pleasure of." This adjustment is supposed to account for quality improvements, especially those that lead to greater enjoyment or utility of a product, which makes sense in a world of increasing product quality, but which has been badly overused.

Here's an example: Tim LaFleur is a commodity specialist for televisions at the Bureau of Labor Statistics (BLS) where the CPI is calculated. In 2004, he noted that a 27-inch television priced at $329.99 was selling for the same amount as the previous year but was now equipped with a digital tuner.[6] After taking this subjective improvement into account, he adjusted the price of the TV downward by $135, concluding that the benefit derived from the tuner improvement was the same as if the price of the TV had fallen by 29%. The price reflected in the CPI was not the actual retail store cost of $329.99, which is what it would actually cost you to buy the TV, but the hedonically adjusted price of $195. Bingo! Deflation!

Based on that adjustment, the BLS concluded that televisions cost a lot less than they used to, and in response, inflation was reported to have gone down. However, at the store, you'd discover these same televisions were still selling for $329.99, not $195.

Another complaint about hedonics is that they're a one-way trip. If I get a new phone this year and it has some new buttons, the BLS will declare that the price has dropped because of all the additional enjoyment I will receive from using the new features attached to those buttons. But if my new phone lasts only eight months before ceasing to work, instead of lasting 30 years like an old rotary phone, no adjustment will be made for that loss of service life (or the hassle of having to drop everything to go and get a new phone, transfer everything over, etc.). In short, hedonics rests on the improbable assumption that new features are always beneficial and these features can be thought of as synonymous with falling prices. I'm not entirely against the practice—I really like the many ways my 2016 Nissan Pathfinder is not like a 1978 Ford Pinto—but the use of hedonics can easily be overdone, and it usually is.

Over the years, the BLS has expanded the use of hedonic adjustments and now applies these adjustments to everything: DVDs, automobiles, washers, dryers, refrigerators, health care, and even college textbooks.

What would happen if you were to strip out all the fuzzy statistical manipulations and calculate inflation the way it used to be? Luckily, John Williams of shadowstats.com has done exactly that, painstakingly following these statistical modifications over time and reversing their effects.[7] If inflation were calculated today the exact same way it was in the early 1980s, Mr. Williams has determined it would be roughly eight percentage points higher than currently reported, which is an *enormous* difference.

The social cost to this self-deception is enormous. For starters, if inflation were calculated the way it used to be, Social Security payments, whose cost-of-living adjustment (COLA) increases are based on the CPI, would be close to 100% higher than they currently are.[8] That would make a huge difference in the lives of millions of elderly households.

Because Medicare increases are also tied to the woefully understated CPI, hospitals are receiving lower Medicare reimbursements than they otherwise would and are increasingly unable to balance their budgets, forcing many communities to choose between closing their hospitals and cutting off service to Medicare recipients. A little harmless fibbing and self-deception is one thing; losing your only community hospital is quite another. These are a few of the grave impacts in our daily lives that result from living with a statistically tortured CPI.

But aside from paying out less in entitlement checks, politicians gain in another very important way by understating inflation.

Gross Domestic Product (GDP)

Gross domestic product (GDP) is the story we tell ourselves about how well our economy is doing. In theory, the GDP is the sum total of all value-added transactions within a country in any given year. Just like the CPI (inflation measure), the GDP measure has been so twisted and tweaked by government statisticians that it no longer tells a recognizable version of the truth. As before, there was no sudden, secret adjustment where GDP slipped off the rails; it has

been stealthily and systematically debased under every presidential administration since the 1960s, like an old house with a thriving termite colony.

Here is an example of just how far from reality GDP has strayed: The
reported GDP amount for 2003 was $11 trillion, implying that $11 trillion
of money-based, value-added economic transactions occurred. But that did
not actually happen. To begin with, the $11 trillion included $1.6 trillion
of so-called imputation adjustments, where economic value was assumed
("imputed") to have been created, but no cash transactions had actually
taken place. Despite the fact that there was no trade and nothing changed
hands, a value was still assigned to these assumptions and reported as part
of the GDP.

The largest imputation represents something called "owner's equivalent
rent," which assigns a value to the benefit homeowners receive by not having
to pay themselves rent. If you own your house free and clear, the government calculates "the amount of money owner occupants would have spent
had they been renting"[9] . . . from themselves (Figure 14.2).

It's not a trivial amount; it totaled $2.3 trillion in 2019.[10]

Another is the benefit you receive from the "free checking" provided by
your bank, which is imputed to have a value because if it wasn't free, then,
as the logic goes, you'd have to pay for it. So, a value is assigned to all the
free checking in the land, and that, too, is added to the tally. Together, all of
the imputations added up to $3.375 trillion in 2020, out of a total reported
national GDP of $20.8 trillion, or 16% of the total.[11]

Finally, like the CPI, the GDP also has many elements that are hedoni-
cally adjusted. For instance, computers are adjusted to account for the prospect that faster and more feature-rich computers must be worth more to our
economic output than prior models.

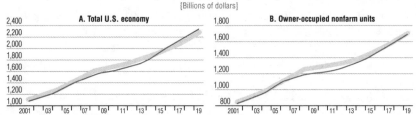

**Annual Current-Dollar National Levels of Personal
Consumption Expenditures Housing Services, 2001–2019**
[Billions of dollars]

FIGURE 14.2 Owner's Equivalent Rent

Amount the BEA calculates for the value of owners of houses not having to pay
themselves rent.

Source: BEA, **https://apps.bea.gov/scb/2021/05-may/0521-housing-services.htm**.

So, if a computer costing $1,000 was sold, it would be recorded as contributing more than a thousand dollars to the GDP to account for the fact that it's faster and more technologically advanced than the thousand-dollar model sold the previous year. Of course, the extra money is fictitious; it never traded hands and doesn't actually exist. This is similar to a toilet paper manufacturer reporting higher revenues because its product was softer and fluffier this year, even though the same number of units was sold last year at the same price.

Add it all up and GDP is an imperfect measure with enough statistical quirks and oddities that we should really view it aspirational bureaucratic folk art.

And All the Rest

Statistical wizardry similar to that which we've explored here for GDP and the CPI is also performed on income, unemployment figures, house prices, budget deficits, and virtually every other government-supplied economic statistic that you can think of. Each is saddled with a long list of lopsided imperfections that inevitably paint a rosier picture than is warranted. Taken all together, I call the economic stories we're handed by government statisticians "fuzzy numbers." To quote Kevin Phillips again: " . . . our nation may truly regret losing sight of history, risk and common sense."[12]

Add it all up and we're flying blind—telling ourselves stories that aren't actually true, which overstates our vigor and strength.

CHAPTER 15

Crumbling Before Our Eyes

The Story of Concrete

The first time I was confronted with the idea that perhaps, maybe, the United States was no longer number 1 in the world was in the spring of 2001, while returning from a trip to Europe. I was in the back of a taxi heading home from JFK airport outside of New York City trying to complete an important phone call with a new client.

"What?" I asked, "I couldn't make that out . . . " as my phone connection went fuzzy. Just then, the taxi hit an enormous pothole, its third in as many minutes, and I lost the phone connection. Physics tells me these were unrelated events, but they felt connected. Redialing, embarrassed, and apologizing for the lost connection, I was struck by the thought that I had not had a single dropped call while I was in Europe, not even when traveling on a train through the 26-mile-long Chunnel connecting the UK to France beneath hundreds of feet of rock and water. Not even in elevators. Nowhere.

While stewing over the lost phone call and the rough ride from the airport, it struck me all at once just how shabby and decrepit much of the U.S. physical infrastructure had become. As I recall, the business deal turned out okay, but instances such as these surrounded some of my first budding doubts about the health of our country.

Every few years, the American Society of Civil Engineers performs a comprehensive assessment of the condition of 12 categories of U.S. infrastructure, including bridges, roadways, drinking water systems, and wastewater treatment plants. The 2017 report gave the United States an overall grade of "D+" and calculated that $2 trillion of new investment would be needed over the next five years to bring the United States back up to First World standards.[1]

It obviously costs a lot in terms of money and resources to build new infrastructure, but it also costs a certain amount just to keep what you've already built. Maintenance and eventual replacement are part of the game.

Choices matter, and the United States has repetitively chosen to defer maintenance and upgrades on essential economic infrastructure until some future date. There's a long story there, but for now, we can simply note that one of the many demands on the United States' limited pool of future funds will be the required investment in, and repair of, its physical infrastructure.

The point I wish to make here is that simply keeping what we've got may prove to be a challenge, let alone growing and building out new infrastructure. What we need to assess here for ourselves is just what the challenges of the next few years and decades really are, and can we meet them all without hardship?

Sometimes it's a little story, one element that can bring the whole into light. It's time to talk about concrete.

The Story of . . . Concrete?

It's time to talk about reinforced concrete specifically. That's the stuff you see in buildings, bridges, dams, foundations, piers, roadways and runways, and perhaps, it's the floor of your basement or garage. It's plain old concrete that has been poured around a metal lattice.

The problem? This article in *The Conversation* lays it out rather well:

> By itself, concrete is a very durable construction material. The magnificent Pantheon in Rome, the world's largest unreinforced concrete dome, is in excellent condition after nearly 1,900 years.
>
> **And yet many concrete structures from last century—bridges, highways and buildings—are crumbling. Many concrete structures built this century will be obsolete before its end.**
>
> Given the survival of ancient structures, this may seem curious. **The critical difference is the modern use of steel reinforcement, known as rebar, concealed within the concrete.** Steel is made mainly of iron, and one of iron's unalterable properties is that it rusts. This ruins the durability of concrete structures in ways that are difficult to detect and costly to repair.
>
> The writer Robert Courland, in his book Concrete Planet, estimates **that repair and rebuilding costs of concrete infrastructure, just in the United States, will be in the trillions of dollars—to be paid by future generations.**[2]

Concrete itself can last thousands of years, as the 2,000-year-old Parthenon attests. But concrete alone is only good for what are called compression loads, meaning you can place a lot of weight on them as long as the forces are all aligned properly (inward and down), as they are in the Parthenon.

To get concrete to perform under what is called tension requires steel reinforcement. Done properly, concrete slabs can be poured thinner, saving construction costs, and long beams can be created such as those you might see spanning a highway.

But it's now clear that this comes with a catch—a big one. The steel inside slowly rusts away and when it does, it expands and leads to something you've seen but perhaps not recognized: concrete cancer. In every single reinforced concrete structure, behind the smooth exterior the concrete is silently breaking itself apart due to the steel inside that is rusting and expanding. The process can begin in as few as 10 years after the concrete is poured. The estimated lifespan is somewhere between 50 and 100 years. Max.

What all this means is that literally everything made of concrete will need to be replaced within a hundred years of its installation. Every bridge, every building, every roadway . . . all of them.

They're just rotting away from the inside, silently and relentlessly. When this rotting goes far enough, it leads to something called "spalling," which is when the surface of the concrete crumbles away to reveal the rusted steel beneath.

Once you notice this, you'll see it everywhere.

Now, of course, it's true that *anything* you build will erode over time and require maintenance and care to provide longevity. The problem with reinforced concrete is that it's extremely difficult to remedy once it's poured because the affected parts are inside and hard to reach. Yes, it was a lot more convenient and cheaper to build with steel-reinforced concrete but it was also a disposable mindset. The thinking, if there was any, seems to have been, "Well, we can always just replace that when the time comes."

But what if we can't because the energy for that job is simply not available to get the whole job done?

If we project forward just a few years into the future, we find hundreds of trillions of dollars of global debt, hundreds more trillions of unfunded liabilities, depleting fossil fuels becoming ever more expensive, all competing with a crumbling concrete-built environment that will have to be torn down and more or less entirely replaced. All of these issues will be clamoring for time, energy, and money at the same time. Can we service them all? If not, which do we jettison?

And, we don't get much for replacing a crumbling piece of infrastructure. When you tear down a bridge and replace it, you still have one bridge performing the services of one bridge. Yes, you occupy a number of people in the construction and manufacturing trades while the bridge is being rebuilt, but you don't get any additional economic activity above and beyond that. It's not the same as putting in a new bridge to a new location and opening up a new area for greater economic activity. That's a different story.

You just get your bridge replaced. One for one; an economically neutral trade except one that happened to cost a lot of money.

My larger point here is to ask if all the competing future demands will even allow all of the current concrete infrastructure to even be replaced, let alone expanded.

What if there's not enough energy for that task plus the demands of feeding and sheltering and defending ourselves?

I believe we'll regret this short-term mentality that led us to trade durability for lower cost. Further, I contend that the future competing demands will prevent us from replacing all the crumbling infrastructure with similar copies.

Either they won't be replaced at all because we cannot afford to do so (see Detroit) or we will have to bite the bullet and begin installing truly durable structures that won't simply tear themselves apart from the inside in a few short decades.

Summing It Up

Putting it all together, we find that some short-sighted decisions have left us with a rather massive load of liabilities at the federal level, a profound failure to invest in infrastructure, and have deployed building practices so far from durable they might better be described as disposable.

All of these deficits will exert demands on our national wealth in the relatively near future, and this leads me to conclude that the next 20 years are going to be completely unlike the past 20 years, and not in a good way.

How did we get here? How did this happen? As a former consultant to Fortune 500 companies, I observed that if the leadership of a company was financially reckless or had a moral disregard for its workers, this same behavior could be reflected throughout all the remaining layers of the company. The U.S. government became fiscally reckless beginning in the mid-1980s, failed to live within its means, borrowed more and more, and not only failed to properly fund the entitlement programs but raided the funds and then excluded themselves from having to properly report this fact.

The Federal Reserve aided and abetted these fiscally unsound practices by constantly engineering the interest rate lower (so the government could borrow more) while simultaneously flooding the markets with more and more currency. Congress failed to appreciate the predicament and did not appropriate sufficient money for necessary upkeep and improvements.

Coincident with this loss of fiscal prudence and monetary recklessness, corporations, municipalities, states, and individuals all took their cues from above and went along with the party vibe of the times.

All on their own, these financial and monetary practices were unsustainable, but they take on a far more worrisome aspect when we wrap in the story of resources along with concrete.

PART IV

Energy

CHAPTER 16

Energy and the Economy

Now that we have seen how our economy is based on perpetual exponential growth, and we've explored how all systems owe their increasing order and complexity to the energy available to them, we are ready to get to the heart of the matter: linking energy to our economic system. This chapter is *essential* to appreciating why our economy cannot continue on as it has.

The Master Resource

When oil first began to be used for industrial purposes in the early 1900s, the world's population stood at 1.7 billion people, the most common profession was farming, and sailing ships still plied the waters alongside coal steamers. During its first century on the world stage, oil helped propel the expansion of world population by 4 times, energy use by more than 16 times, and the global economy by 18.5 times.[1] The twentieth century was thus the first era dominated by fossil fuels, and the 16-fold rise of their use since 1900 created the first high-energy global civilization in human history.[2]

The resulting exponential chart of global GDP (see Figure 16.1) perfectly illustrates the immense power of unleashing vast quantities of surplus energy into a system that feasts upon energy to grow in complexity.

The fact that it takes energy to run an economy should be intuitively obvious too. All you have to do is sit and view any city, airport, or highway for a few minutes through the right lens and it all becomes staggeringly obvious. Everything that is moving represents "economic activity." Every car is someone going somewhere, using up gasoline (part of GDP), wearing down their

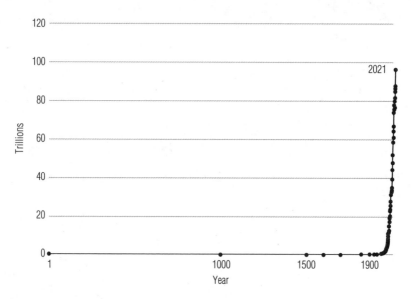

FIGURE 16.1 Global GDP

Global GDP since the year 1. A perfectly exponential chart that "turned the corner" right when fossil fuel use exploded onto the scene.

Source: **OurWorldInData.org**.

car (GDP), carrying insurance (GDP), and on their way to some building or other (GDP). Every truck is "GDP on the hoof" doing something important, ferrying about hundreds if not thousands of those stock keeping units (SKUs).

More subtly, every person you see is a walking expression of fossil fuels as the calories they ingested were heavily subsidized by fossil fuels to grow, store, transport, and cook.

Every single thing in our economy can be tied back to a primary source of energy if we just dig a layer or three. Once you slip on these energy goggles, it all begins to take on new meanings. Literally nothing in our economic system happens without energy being involved. That's one of the iron laws of life and it applies to every organism equally. If you want to live, you need to be taking in more energy than you are expending. If you want your population to grow in size, the same law applies. If you want your babies to grow, again, the same condition applies.

We're all familiar with the massive benefits bestowed by this explosive liberation of human potential in the forms of technological and intellectual advances. In order to appreciate the delicacy of the continuation of this abundance, we need to understand the actual role of energy in forming our society. If we recall back to Chapter 7 (*An Inconvenient Lie*), I made the point that both growth *and* prosperity are dependent on surplus. In the case of economic growth and prosperity, nothing is more important than surplus energy.

Imagine two separate societies: One has barely enough food energy to survive, and the other is blessed with a vast surplus of food energy. Assuming they possessed the same cultural proclivities toward inventiveness, we would find the society with the subsistence level of food supply to be very rudimentary and not terribly complex compared to the society with more ample food supplies. It would be clear that the surplus energy in the food supply had been "funding" complexity, specialization, and what we call economic growth for the more well-bestowed society.

Which is why we say that among all energy sources, food most commands our attention when it's in short supply. Spoiler alert: The amount of food we'll be able to grow in the future is also very closely tied to the energy we have to throw at the project.

By way of example, we could compare the state of societies' complexity before and after the Agricultural Revolution some 10,000 years ago. Before the Agricultural Revolution, humans lived in small nomadic tribes that subsisted by hunting and gathering. There were few job roles, and only small, hand-held artifacts from this period have been found and studied today. After the revolution, complex societies with multiple producing and nonproducing job specializations arose, building enduring works of architecture, art, music, law, and all the other trappings of societal complexity familiar to us today. All this only became possible once there was a surplus of food to "fund" specialized roles and activities.

Before agriculture, human society was limited in its complexity by the amount of food it could gather and crudely store, which represented a very limited energy budget with a skimpy and uncertain yearly surplus. After the agricultural revolution, enormous leaps in complexity were powered by the ability of farmers to create an excess of food calories that effectively freed up other people for other pursuits. But what unleashed the "third epoch"— the exponential explosion in complexity—that began some 150 years ago and continues today? It was energy, of course, but it wasn't food energy. It was 300 million years' worth of ancient sunlight stored in the form of fossil fuels.[3]

Instead of waiting for the rather diffuse and comparatively parsimonious energy from the sun to fall upon the earth and slowly grow their planted crops, humans learned how to utilize the unbelievably dense and usable forms of coal, oil, and natural gas.

Nature will occasionally build up a massive store of potential energy, which will be unleashed in a furious burst. Thunderheads will build up enormous electrical potential energy and then discharge it all at once with a bolt of lightning. A steep slope will accumulate an enormous weight of snow before its potential energy avalanches destructively into the valley below.

Ancient sunlight was stored as immense concentrations of potential energy, waiting in store for some spark to release it. That spark was us humans, and we've consequently liberated close to half of all those tens and hundreds of millions of years of stored energy in a span of a little over 150 years—faster than lightning, in geological terms.

Just as food energy is vital to the effective functioning of our bodies, which are very complex machines, energy that can perform useful work is the lifeblood of complex economies. The key word here is "work." Without energy, no work could ever be performed, but not all forms of energy are useful for doing work. The tiny amount of potential energy stored up in the spring of a wristwatch can perform the useful work of moving the watch's hands and mechanisms, but the enormous heat energy contained in one of the Great Lakes can do almost no work, because it isn't concentrated enough to be of any practical use. Dense energy is where it's at. That's the good stuff. The denser the better.

The more energy density something contains, the more useful it is. This is why the fossil fuels—oil, natural gas, and coal—are so desirable. They represent concentrated forms of energy capable of doing a lot of work. Without them, our economy would be a pale shadow of its current bright self. Probably medieval, if you catch my drift. Given the importance of energy to the continued smooth functioning of our economy, we owe it to ourselves to understand the ideas and the data that underlie the sources and amounts of energy that course through our economic arteries.

Energy Budgeting

To help us on this journey, let's take a quick tour through the concept of energy budgeting. If you have a household budget or have ever run the numbers for a business, this will be an easy topic.

Imagine that at any given time there is a defined amount of energy available for us to use as we wish. This will be our budget to spend as we see fit, but instead of dollars, this budget consists of units of energy. Let's put every source of currently existing energy into this budget: solar, wind, hydro, nuclear, coal, petroleum, natural gas, biomass, and so on.

This list represents our total energy to use any way we please; it's our "energy budget." It's like an interest-free savings account. We can draw upon it as needed, but in the case of fossil fuels, we only get to use it, or burn it, once.

Our first mandatory expenditure from this budget will be the energy we need to use in order to ensure that we'll have more energy next year.

Consider it an unavoidable energy tax. It takes energy to find and produce energy. Oil and natural gas wells have to be drilled and maintained, and coal has to be mined from the earth.

Also included here would be the energy required to maintain our existing energy infrastructure—all the dams, electrical pylons, power plants, refineries, and innumerable other installations must be maintained. Eventually, they have to be replaced, also at an energy cost.

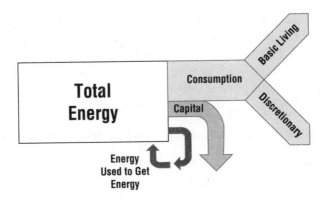

FIGURE 16.2 Energy Budgeting

In a proper energy budget, a certain amount of primary energy must be reinvested (darkest arrows) back into the project of obtaining more energy, with the remainder divided between maintaining existing capital stock, and end-consumer consumption.

Along with all of this, we must also reinvest some energy in building and maintaining the capital structure (labeled "capital" in Figure 16.2) that allows us to collect and distribute energy and to maintain a complex society. Things like roads, bridges, and all of our commercial and residential buildings fall into this category. Together, all of this can be considered our mandatory energy expenditures, meaning they are unavoidable.

Finally, whatever is left over, we ordinary people get to consume. Some of that has to be dedicated to nonnegotiable basic living activities such as eating, not freezing in the winter, and keeping ourselves cool in the summer. The last bucket of use would be discretionary. Ah! That's where life gets fun. That would include trips to Cancun, a nice drive in the fall in New England to see the colorful leaves, and driving massive SUVs to go get a bag of chips.

Energy budgeting is simply reminding ourselves that it takes energy to make energy and a good portion of it is entirely spoken for, unavailable for economic growth and adding to overall complexity. As we'll see, the day rapidly approaches when fossil fuels will be unable to deliver any additional units of energy. Coming at us even faster than that is the next major energy concept of *net energy*.

Net Energy

This is the most important concept of this chapter and one of the most important concepts of the book. I want you to ignore how much energy costs in money terms, because the cost is an irrelevant abstraction (especially when your money is printed out of thin air).

Instead, we're going to focus on *how much energy it takes to get energy,* because, as I'm going to show you, this is even more important to our current and future well-being than the raw amount of energy that we can produce each year. The concept is straightforward, and it's called "net energy."

Because it takes energy to both find and produce energy, we're going to look at the returns delivered from energy exploration and production activities in terms of the ratio between what is invested and what is returned. Imagine that the total energy it took to find and drill an oil well were one barrel of oil, and that 100 barrels came to market as a result. We'd say that our net energy return was "one hundred barrels to one," or 100:1. In this example, our mandatory expenditure was 1 out of 100, or 1%. Another phrase for this that you're likely to encounter in the literature is energy returned on energy invested, which goes by the acronym EROEI.

I find this easier to visualize in graphical form, shown in Figure 16.3.

In Figure 16.3, we're comparing the relationship between energy out and energy in. The darker part (above) is the amount of energy we put in ("invest"), and the gray part (below) is how much energy was returned representing the *net* energy that's available for society to use for whatever purposes it desires.

All the way on the left side of the *x*-axis of the chart, the energy out divided by energy in yields a value of 50, meaning that one unit of energy was used to find and produce 50 units of energy. In other words, 2% was used to find and produce energy, leaving us a net 98% in the gray part to use however we see fit (1/50 = 2%).

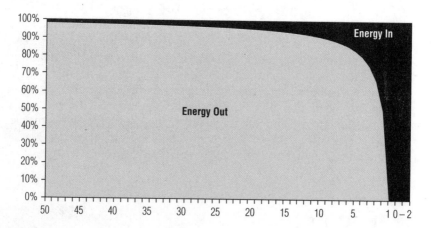

FIGURE 16.3   The Energy Cliff: Energy Returned on Energy Invested

This figure expresses the relationship between energy invested and energy returned. Note that together the invested and returned energy always sum to 100% and the lines hit zero percent at a reading of 1, where it takes one unit to find one unit for a zero percent return.

This represents the surplus energy available to society; it's the stuff used to create 100% of the economic order and complexity we see all around us. As we scan across the chart, we can observe that the surplus energy available to society remains quite high all the way down to a net energy ratio of about 10, where it suddenly falls off a cliff. We might also note this is yet another non-linear chart of great importance to our future.

Now, I want to draw your attention to what happens on part of the chart between the readings of 10 and 5. The net energy available to society begins to drop off quite steeply and nonlinearly. Below a reading of 5, the chart really heads down in earnest, hitting zero when it gets to a reading of 1, which is where it takes one unit of energy to get a unit of energy. At that boundary, there's zero surplus energy available and there's really no point in going through the trouble of getting it.

Given that energy is *the* master resource, and no economic activity is possible without energy, how much net energy is available should be a matter of great concern to everyone, but especially policymakers. What Figure 16.3 allows us to begin to appreciate is that it's not "energy" we really care about, but *net* energy, the light gray part below, because it's the area that literally makes possible almost everything we care about. It allows the lights to come on, food to appear on our plates, warmth to fill our homes, and the big brown truck of mail-order happiness to pull into our driveways.

To further explore why this is an enormously important chart, let's take a look at our experience with net energy with respect to oil (Figure 16.4).

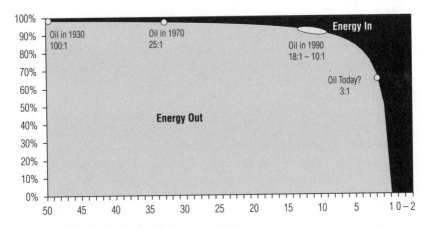

FIGURE 16.4 The Energy Cliff (2) and Oil

The energy returns of oil production over time have been declining.

Source: C. J. Cleveland, "Net Energy from Oil and Gas Extraction in the United States, 1954–1997," *Energy* 30 (2005): 769–782.

In 1930, for every barrel of oil used to find oil, it's estimated that 100 were produced, giving us a reading of 100:1, which would be way off to the left in Figure 16.4. By 1970, fields were a lot smaller and the oil was often deeper or otherwise trickier to extract, so, unsurprisingly, the net energy gain fell to a value of around 25:1—still a very good return with lots of light gray beneath it. By the 1990s, this trend continued, with oil finds returning somewhere between 18:1 and 10:1.[4]

It's estimated that new oil resources found after the year 2010 will return a much lower net energy, perhaps as low as 3:1, although nobody really knows for sure because careful analyses have not yet been performed. Still, we might observe that gigantic rigs drilling through thousands and thousands of feet of water and rock as they chase after smaller and smaller fields will intuitively have less favorable energy returns than prior efforts located in shallower zones on dry land.

Why is the net yield dropping? In the past, a relatively tiny amount of embodied energy was contained within the smallish rigs that were used to exploit finds that were massive, plentiful, and relatively shallow. Two of the larger finds in the world's history, Spindletop in Texas and the Ghawar field in Saudi Arabia, are both only a little over 1,000 feet below the surface.

The Macondo field in the Gulf of Mexico, which was the site of the *Deepwater Horizon* incident in 2010, was beneath 5,000 feet of water and a further 13,000 feet of rock and sediment, and held perhaps 1/1,000th of the oil in Ghawar. All that drilling, miles of piping, and a massive oil rig were required to find a relatively minor amount of oil, illustrating why the net energy of oil discoveries of today are so much lower than the past. And the Macondo field was neither particularly deep nor disappointingly small by current standards.

Today, much more energy is required to find energy. Exploration ships and rigs are massive, requiring significantly more steel to create than the humble drilling rigs of the 1930s. And today, more wells are being drilled to greater depths in order to find and produce smaller and smaller fields, all of which weigh upon our final net energy return.

And what about the massive amounts of oil allegedly contained within the tar sands and oil shales (not "shale oil" but, confusingly, oil shale)? These are often wrongly described as equivalent to "several Saudi Arabias." The net energy values for these are especially poor and are in no way comparable to the 100:1 (or higher) returns actually found in Saudi Arabia. Tar sands have a net energy return of around 5:1,[5] and tar shales are thought to be even worse, in the vicinity of 2:1 or less.[6] So, while there may be the same *volume* of oil locked in those formations as there is in Saudi Arabia's magnificent treasures, there isn't the same amount of useful, desirable, delicious net energy in them. Nowhere near as much.

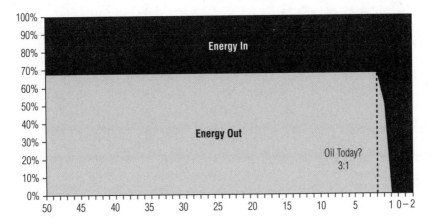

FIGURE 16.5   The Energy Cliff (3)

Trying to live on 3:1 net energy.

If we were to try and subsist entirely on the energy offered by a new source that was sporting a 3:1 net energy return, Figure 16.5 shows the world in which we'd live.

Look at how much less gray area and how much less surplus energy there is in this chart after we've begun to slide down the energy cliff, compared to the ones where there were 10:1 or 20:1 returns. The gray area represents how we "fund" our growth and our prosperity. The gray area is the net energy that feeds and supports our economic complexity. If we can appreciate how two societies, one abundantly supplied with food and the other nearly starving, can differ on the basis of their available net food energy, then we can also appreciate how a high-net-energy economy will be fundamentally more robust, complex, and interesting than a lower-net-energy economy.

And what about renewable energy sources (Figure 16.6)? Methanol, which can be made from biomass, sports a net energy of about 2.6:1,[7] while biodiesel offers a net energy return of somewhere between 1:1 and 4:1, depending on whether we count just the biodiesel itself or include the energy left in the crushed meal, which can be burned.[8] Corn-based ethanol, if we're generous, might produce a net energy return of just slightly over 1:1,[9] but could also be negative, according to some sources.[10] Ethanol produced from sugar cane in Brazil has an EROEI of closer to 8:1[11] (largely because the sugarcane itself can be burned to fire the process), making it a viable proposition there, and some exciting work is being done on cellulosic and other forms of ethanol that might have much higher EROEIs than any other biofuels, but those are

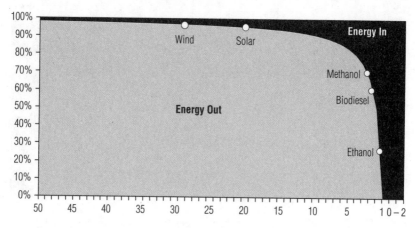

FIGURE 16.6   The Energy Cliff (4): Net Energy from Renewables

Not all energy forms are fully comparable on the basis of net energy returned. Solar and wind do not produce liquid fuels.

not yet out of the demonstration phase. We should work with all due haste on these prospects, but not count on them to arrive at the appropriate time and at the appropriate scale to save the day.*

If we add in all the other new usable liquid fuel sources we've just talked about, we see that they're all somewhere "on the face of the energy cliff." Solar and wind[12] are both capable of producing pretty high net returns, but it's important to note that these produce electricity, not liquid fuels, which

---

*While there are a number of potentially exciting new technologies and energy sources in the labs and even in pilot demonstrations—including cellulosic ethanol, methanol, and algal biofuels—I set a high bar; in order to be included in this book, they actually had to be in commercial production at a level that cracked the 1 percent-of-total-fuel barrier.

Why? Simply because if Peak Oil is only 5 or even 10 years from the writing of this book, any technology that has less than a 1% market share already, no matter how promising, is exceedingly unlikely to allow our economy to continue along uninterrupted.

And that's the main point of this book: to illustrate why the next 20 years are going to be completely unlike the past 20 years.

Yes, I will be quite excited by and will closely follow the developments of new energy technologies. But no, I will not stake a significant portion of my future strategy on the mere hope that these will arrive in time. Hope alone is a terrible strategy.

This book is meant to inject a dose of numerical reality back into the discussion, and that's what I am driving at here. In order to be considered as a potential solution, the technologies and/or processes in question have to have a solid chance of affecting the outcome.

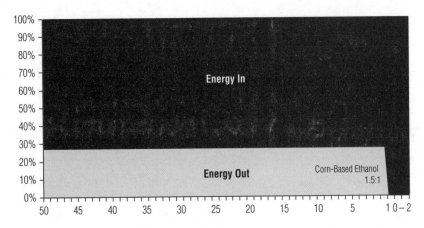

FIGURE 16.7   The Energy Cliff (5): Trying to Live on Alcohol Alone

means that they are not at all comparable. Peak Oil represents "peak liquid fuels," and that's the primary issue here for petroleum. Once we get to Peak Coal (and we someday will), or begin to operate our transportation infrastructure on electricity, then electricity from the sun is more directly applicable to meeting our needs and solving our challenges. If we were to try and make a go of it on corn-based ethanol alone, Figure 16.7 shows the world in which we'd (be trying to) live.

There's no gray zone to speak of left in that chart, and practically no surplus at all to fund even the basics of life, let alone a rich, complex economy full of prosperity and opportunities.

Unless we very rapidly find ways of boosting the net energy of the remaining energy options, we'll simply find that we have far less surplus energy to dedicate to our basic needs and discretionary wants than we came to expect and enjoy from fossil fuels. We'll be using far too much energy in the essential, mandatory practice of finding and producing more energy, and we'll find ourselves with far too little left over to use as we wish. Our energy investment costs will skyrocket even as the returns dwindle. That's just the basic reality of the situation; it's not possible to fool nature with fraudulent accounting.

Oh, and where's the so-called "hydrogen economy" in Figure 16.7? It's below the x-axis in negative territory because it has to be produced from other forms of energy—perhaps electricity (via hydrolysis) or from natural gas. There are no hydrogen reservoirs anywhere on earth; every single bit of it has to be created from some other source of energy—and, here's the kicker, *always at an energy loss*. In other words, hydrogen is an energy *sink*, not a *source*; its tiny bubble would have to be placed below the zero percent mark in Figure 16.7. In creating hydrogen, we *lose* energy. That's not pessimism; that's the law—the second law of thermodynamics, to be exact. We'll talk more alternative energy in Chapter 19.

The Economy and Energy

A massive abundance of surplus energy, liberated by the lightning bolt of humanity, has enabled historically unparalleled levels of prosperity to be enjoyed by billions of people. But respect for the role of energy in providing this abundance has largely gone missing from the economics profession, which will prove to be a rather tragic mistake. Heck, it's more or less missing from every major field of study. It's quite odd that the primal importance of energy to the quality of our lives and improvements in living standards has been thus ignored, because the evidence for the connection between growth in energy utilization and economic growth (and prosperity) is extremely well documented and also intuitively obvious.

To counter this, presented here are the most important charts in all of economics. Or, at least they should be. The first is seen in Figure 16.8, which plots global GDP against global energy use. After some adjusting in the 1960s, which saw energy use climbing faster than GDP for a while (boxed area),

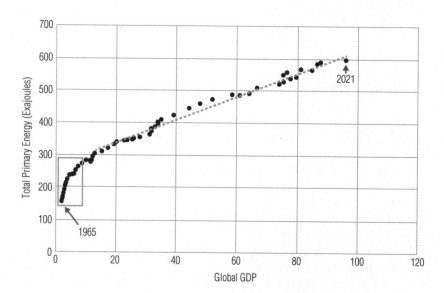

FIGURE 16.8 Global GDP plotted Against Total Global Energy Use

Ever since 1975, the relationship between total global GDP and total global energy use has been perfectly linear. Well, almost perfectly.

things have settled down into the system we have today, producing a very linear relationship ever since.

This is the most robust and important chart I have in my entire economic arsenal. It tells the whole tale. For the past 50+ years, every increment of GDP growth has been accompanied by a steady increment of additional energy consumption. The conclusion is easy to draw: Any future economic growth will require new increased energy consumption. The data is remarkably and inescapably clear on that point.

Perhaps you've heard of the idea of energy decoupling, which posits that advanced economies like those in Europe or the United States have been able to "decouple" from energy use. A chart might even show that for an individual country or area. But what happened was the United States and Europe outsourced its energy-intensive activities like steel and heavy manufacturing to China, among other places. So that energy use doesn't show up in their respective GDP-to-energy charts.

This is why we have to view this data for the whole world at once. That way, any tricks of outsourcing are avoided, and we get the complete picture. If the world economy were decoupling from energy, it would look like Figure 16.9.

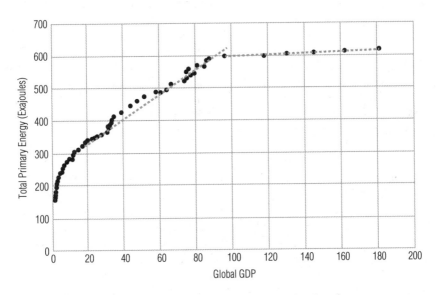

FIGURE 16.9 What Energy Decoupling Would Look Like If It Were Happening

With energy decoupling we'd see more and more GDP for the same amount (or even less) energy use. The line would bend down and we'd see a kink it in as has been mocked up here.

Since there are no visible kinks in the global GDP to energy data in the past 50+ years, it's not yet happening. More economy means more energy. Period. We know the global debt markets are assuming that energy will be there, but will it? And what if it's not?

Even less well appreciated is the degree to which economic *complexity* owes its existence not just to the total amount of energy being utilized, but to the net free energy that flows through society. Of all the sources of energy, petroleum stands out as the most important of them all, due largely to its presence in nearly every consumer product that is made, transported, and sold. Oil is richly woven into our economic tapestry, and there are no substitutes waiting in the wings. Where we once transitioned from wood to coal, and later from coal to oil, there is currently no established candidate waiting to replace oil.

We Live Like Gods

In order to understand why oil, in particular, is so important to our economy and our daily lives, we have to understand something about what it does for us. We value any source of energy because we can harness it to do work for us. For example, every time you turn on a 100-watt light bulb, it's the same as if you had a fit human being in the basement pedaling as hard as they can to keep that bulb lit. That's how much energy a single light bulb uses. While you run water, take hot showers, and vacuum the floor, it's as if your house is employing the services of 50 such extremely fit bike-riding slaves in the basement, ready to pedal their fastest, 24 hours a day, at the flick of a switch. When you jump in a car, depending on your engine, it's the same as a king harnessing up a carriage to 300 horses. This "slave count," if you will, exceeds that of kings in times past. Given the fact that even kings of times past could not whip out a credit card on a whim and find themselves halfway around the world in less than a day, it should be said that we enjoy the power of gods.

And how much "work" is embodied in a gallon of gasoline, our favorite substance of them all? Well, if you put a single gallon in a car, drove it away from your home until the gas ran out, and then got out and pushed the car home, you'd find out exactly how much work a gallon of gasoline can do. It turns out a gallon of gas has the equivalent energy of somewhere between 350 and 500 hours of human labor.[13] Given that a gallon of gas can perform that much human work, how much value would you assign it? How much would 350 to 500 hours of your hard physical labor be worth to you? $4? $10? Assuming you decided not to push your car home and paid someone $15 an hour to do this for you, you'd find that a gallon of gasoline is "worth" $5,250 to $7,500 in human labor.

Here's another example: It has been calculated that the amount of food an average North American citizen consumes in a year requires the equivalent of 400 gallons of petroleum to produce and ship.[14] At $3/gallon, it works out to $1,200 of your yearly food bill spent on fuel, which doesn't sound too extreme. However, when we consider that those 400 gallons represent the energy equivalent of close to 100 humans working year-round at 40 hours a week, then it takes on an entirely different meaning. This puts your diet well out of the reach of most kings of times past. Just to put this in context, as it's currently configured, food production and distribution uses fully two-thirds of the U.S. domestic oil production. This is one reason why a cessation of oil exports to the United States would be highly disruptive; most of our domestic production would have to go toward feeding ourselves.

If we add up all the fossil fuel use in 2019 and covert it to a fit human adult working eight hours a day and 365 days a year, we discover that it was as if 7.8 billion people had 468 billion energy slaves quietly and uncomplainingly working in the background (see Figure 16.10).

According to **worldhistory.org**, a large castle estate in pre-fossil fuel eras might have had a staff of 50.[15] In today's world, on average each person has a staff of 60 working for them. A standard house of four individuals then has 240 energy slaves. But, unlike actual staff or slaves, the energy slaves do what is asked without complaint, no drama, and no food or medical care needs to distract their lords and ladies with.

Aside from the way oil, in particular, works tirelessly in the background to make our lives easy beyond historical measure, oil is a miracle in other ways.

In the industrial processes, oil is the primary input feedstock to innumerable necessities of life, such as fertilizer, as many became acutely aware during the energy crisis of 2022 when the natural gas feedstock for that process

Fossil Fuel Provided Human Equivalents in 2019	
Coal	150,167,808,219
Natural Gas	134,561,643,836
Oil	183,630,136,986
Total	**468,359,589,041**

FIGURE 16.10 Energy Slaves

The energy services provided to humanity in 2019 was equivalent to more than 468 billion fit and health humans working eight hours a day, without any breaks, all year.

Source: Author's calculations (C Martenson).

suddenly became unavailable and/or very costly. Then there are plastics, paints, synthetic fibers, countless chemicals, and fuels for every sort of engine in planes, trains, trucks, and automobiles.

It could be said we all live like kings, but truthfully, even the wealthiest king of times past couldn't click on a link, order an item made halfway around the world, and have it in his hands the next day.

That ability is something the ancient Greeks would have recognized as the power of a god, and that's exactly the power we wield today compared to times past.

CHAPTER 17

Peak Oil

If you were to glance up from this book and scan your surroundings, you'd be unable to point to a single human-made object that did not somehow, in some way, get there because of oil.

Petroleum fuels and products are involved in every part of our economy. If you enjoy a modern lifestyle, you enjoy a ridiculously high standard of living, and oil is responsible for every bit of it. Your clothes, your car, your food, your home—everything.

Everything that is manufactured and transported either or indirectly.

That DoorDash vegetarian combo meal with cold-brewed iced tea delivered by a bicycle-riding vegan named Trevor? Yes, oil was intimately involved. The bicycle tires directly, the frame of bike mined by massive diesel-fed machines, the components all shipped to final assembly by truck, Trevor himself eating foods grown hundreds, if not thousands, of miles away using gobs of oil-based products ranging from fertilizer to tractors to plastic row covers and, you guessed it, trucked to his belly. Your food too.

It's impossible to overstate just how central and irreplaceable oil is to our entire economic system and way of life. But it's certainly possible to overlook it, and most people do. It is simply an assumed part of the landscape, a permanent feature that can safely be ignored. It will always be there for us, right? If you haven't yet heard of Peak Oil, this chapter is going to be a real eye-opener. My purpose here is not to recreate a complete treatise on Peak Oil—that would take an entire set of books, and they've already been written by others[1]—but to establish just enough logical facts we can use to tie the three Es together and arrive at the conclusion prudent adults should seriously consider: the possibility that the future is far less certain than advertised and it's time for you to begin preparing and becoming more resilient.

As we discussed in Chapter 16 (*Energy and the Economy*), energy is the lifeblood of any economy (or any complex system, for that matter). Our economy is a complex system, society is a complex system, and even energy production is a complex system. All of them are interwoven with and interdependent on each other.

Those relationships are far too complicated to unravel and, besides, these are complex systems so we cannot possibly predict what's going to happen and when. But we can apply the golden rule about the role of energy in enabling complex systems to become more orderly and more complicated, and understand that less energy will mean less order, and less complexity.

Without energy constantly flowing through complex systems, order and complexity shrink as the system inexorably winds down and tends toward disorder (a process called "entropy," as we've learned).

When an economic system has been built around exponentially driven debt-based money, the energy that fuels the exponential expansion of both debt and the economy deserves your very highest attention. Why? Because of "bubble symmetry," it's a virtual certainty that any system that expands exponentially will also contract exponentially. As the old saying goes, what goes up must come down. The worry is that once its energy supports are knocked out, the economy will collapse at the same speed it expanded—*fast*.

Falling out of a window at the top of a tall building is never fatal, but hitting the sidewalk is. It's not the destination, it's the pace of change that gets you there—the speed at which you hit the concrete. Right now, at this moment in history, here in the first half of the 2020s, we risk the largest and fastest pace of change in all of human history outside of Noah's flood.

Nothing is more important to the continuation of our current way of life than our ability to extract and deploy ever-larger amounts of energy. Where exactly that energy will come from has really not been competently addressed. How such an oversight could have happened is outside of the realm of logic and reason, and we must turn to psychology for insights.

Our entire economic system is predicated on the implicit assumption that the future will not only be larger than the past, but *exponentially* larger.

Tomorrow's economic growth is always the collateral for today's debts. But we have to ask, if that growth does not occur, then what exactly is today's mountain of debt actually worth? How certain are we that the energy to fuel all that extra growth will be there?

Petro-Realities

In order to understand what "Peak Oil" means, we need to share a basic understanding about how oil fields work and how oil is extracted. A common misperception is that an oil rig is plunked down over an oil field, a hole is drilled, a pipe is inserted, and then oil gushes from a big underground lake or pool that eventually loses pressure and gets sucked dry. Let's call this the "straw in a firmly gripped juice box" model.

The reality is that what you find deep underground is pretty much the same thing you find when you dig a hole near the surface of the ground: solid material. No caverns, lakes, or pools; just solid earth.

FIGURE 17.1   Juice Box vs. Frozen Margarita Model

One of these more accurately represents an oil field. (Hint: It's the one on the right.)

Sources: Margarita image copyright Wacpan; juice box image copyright Neiromobile. *Image:* Molly McLeod.

So, how do we find water and oil under the surface? Extractable liquids are only found in porous rocks, like sandstone, or fractured rocks that permit the oil or water to flow through extremely tiny crevices, fissures, and pores in between and around the granular structure of the stone.

If you were to hold a chunk of rock from an oil-bearing formation, you'd perceive it to be a greasy but quite solid piece that you could use to pound a stake into the ground. Therefore, it's more accurate to think of an oil field like a frozen margarita than an underground juice box, where the oil is the tasty stuff and the rock is the crushed ice. We'll call this the "frozen margarita" model (see Figure 17.1).

When an oil field is tapped, we find that the amount of oil that comes out of it over time follows a tightly prescribed pattern that typically ends up resembling a bell curve. At first, when the frozen margarita is discovered upon the insertion of just one straw (the exploratory straw), the rate at which the beverage can be extracted is limited by having only one thin tube through which the drink can flow. As more and more straws are stuck into the delicious slush, more and more drink flows out of the reservoir at a higher and higher rate.

Eventually the dreaded slurping sound begins, and then, no matter how many new straws are inserted and no matter how hard those straws are sucked on, the amount of margarita coming out of the glass declines until it's all gone and we're left with only ice. That's more or less how an oil field works.

So far, every single mature oil field has exhibited the same basic extraction profile as the one caricatured in Figure 17.2. The amount of oil extracted over time grows higher and higher until it hits a peak, and then it progressively shrinks. Just like with a frozen margarita, once the oil is gone, it's gone, and no amount of late-night wishing or desperate attempts at more careful slurping will cause that circumstance to change. And what is true for one

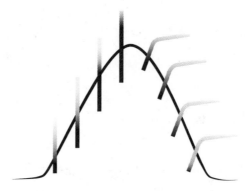

FIGURE 17.2 Basic Extraction Profile

With each new straw, up to the first four, the rate of liquid extraction increases. After a time, the flow rate begins to decline and the insertion of straws 5 through 8 does not increase the flow rate. *Image*: Molly McLeod.

oilfield is equally true across the sum of many oil fields. Because individual fields peak, so do collections of fields.

Peak Oil, then, isn't a theory, as some have tried to portray it; it's an observation—one witnessed on every single oil well ever drilled, which now number in the millions. Peak Oil is an extremely well-characterized physical phenomenon. We have many decades of data and experience to draw upon when making that claim. This isn't some idle theory we're waiting to confirm through additional observation.

Some of the most carefully recorded items in the world are the barrels coming from an oil well. That's money, lots of money, and most often with multiple interested partners involved, so there's a huge incentive to track and track them accurately.

As have individual wells over time, entire oil fields comprised of many smaller finds have depleted in front of our watchful eyes. Dozens of nations have undergone this process of peaking. We *can* theorize about how much oil remains to be discovered and produced, but we cannot debate whether this is true or not. Like aging, Peak Oil is not a theory; it's an observed fact of life.

Bombshell! Saudi Arabia Fesses Up to Peak Oil

July 20, 2022, will be a day I always remember. It was the day I heard that Saudi Arabia announced it had hit Peak Oil. I will remember it both for the importance of the announcement and for how little attention it drew from the media and the public.

It was, given Saudi Arabia's vital role as an oil exporter, quite literally the most vital piece of news one could imagine. It settled the long mystery of exactly where Saudi Arabia was in its oil story, the truth of which Saudi officials had been hiding and kept shrouded in mystery for decades.

On that fateful day, Mohammed Bin Salman, crown prince of Saudi Arabia said to the world (during President Biden's trip there to ask for more oil), "The kingdom will do its part in this regard, as it announced an increase in its production capacity to 13 million barrels per day, **after which the kingdom will not have any additional capacity to increase production.**"

That part in bold is a fancy, gentle way of saying "we'll be at Peak Oil." The potential impact to a world economy still completely and totally dependent on oil could not have been more profound and serious. Now that you understand the exponential nature of our money and economic systems, and the intimate role of energy in sustaining our complex systems, I hope the impact of this lands solidly.

As profound as this was, Saudi Arabia was hardly the first to announce that it was at Peak Oil. In April 2021, Russia's Energy Ministry announced that it was "most likely" that Russia oil production would never again hit the levels of output seen in 2019.

This means that the number-two and number-three producers of oil in the world had said out loud the unthinkable: Peak Oil is real and it is upon us (Figure 17.3).

The good news is that the Energy Information Agency (EIA) predicts that the United States will produce roughly the same amount of oil it did in 2021 for the next 30 years. The bad news is that the executives of U.S. oil-producing companies don't believe it to be true and are on record as saying that the United States will hold steady for perhaps five years and then also slip into terminal decline.

> *The real energy crisis isn't even here yet. The U.S. Energy Information Administration forecasts U.S. oil production to average 12.5 million barrels per day for the next 30 years. **This is all but impossible. Shale will likely tip into terminal decline in about five years as the main shale plays run out of locations.** Unfortunately, by then, most of the individuals with incumbent knowledge about offshore and international development will have retired. The brain drain in the industry will create a real and much larger crisis in the mid-to-late 2020s.*
>
> *Comment from an oil executive to the Dallas Regional Fed*

Whoops. That's a huge difference, and I have to say I side with the oil executives on this one. As was true of the CDC and FDA during Covid, the EIA has mostly become a political agency saying whatever is most politically

The 10 Largest Oil Producers and Share of Total World Oil Production in 2021

Country	Million Barrels per Day	Share of World Total
United States	18.88	20%
Saudi Arabia	10.84	11%
Russia	10.78	11%
Canada	5.54	6%
China	4.99	5%
Iraq	4.15	4%
United Arab Emirates	3.79	4%
Brazil	3.69	4%
Iran	3.46	4%
Kuwait	2.72	3%
Total top 10	68.82	72%
World total	95.57	

FIGURE 17.3 Table of Oil Producers

The top three oil producers completely dominate this table, comprising 43% of total world output, with the top 10 comprising 72%. The other 100 or so oil-producing countries make up the rest, but more than 60 of them are already past their own peak of production.

Source: EIA.

expedient rather than what is most accurate and data informed. Yes, it matters when your main institutions lose the plot line and consistently fail at their missions.

It's Not "Running Out"

Far too often, Peak Oil is inaccurately described as "running out of oil," as if we'll produce more and more, and then, suddenly, we'll just run out. This is misleading and inaccurate. As described earlier, Peak Oil involves producing slightly more and more until the peak, and then producing slightly less and less. In fact, given the difficulty in extracting the second half (which has to be carefully pumped out) in contrast to the first half, there's usually a longer span of time to be found *after* the peak than *before* the peak. A quicker rise up, and then a longer slower tail. Roughly speaking, at the moment of the peak, roughly half of the oil has been extracted and the second half remains to be extracted.

But something interesting happens at the halfway mark. Where oil gushed out under pressure at first, the oil represented by the back half of the curve (the downslope) usually has to be laboriously pumped or squeezed out of the ground at a higher cost, in terms of both energy and money, than when it gushed from the ground under pressure. Where every barrel of oil was cheaper to extract on the way up, the reverse is true on the way down: Each barrel becomes *more* costly to extract in terms of time, money, and energy. Eventually, it costs more to extract a barrel of oil than it's worth, and that's when an oil well, or field, is economically abandoned. There's still oil down there, sometimes a lot, but it's just not worth the effort to get it.

Figure 17.4 shows crude oil production in the United States from 1900 to 2019. Starting with the first well drilled in 1859 in Titusville, Pennsylvania, more and more oil was progressively pumped from the ground until 1970

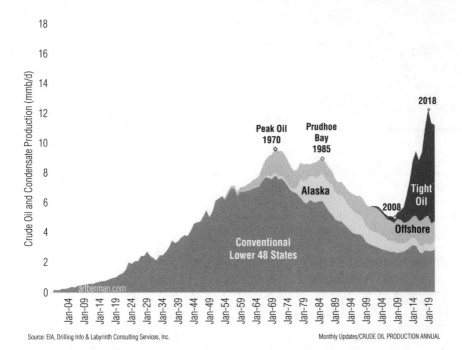

FIGURE 17.4 U.S. Crude Oil Production, 1900 to 2019

Oil production displayed by major region and also source (for tight oil which comes from many regions).

Source: Courtesy of Art Berman, Labyrinth Energy Consultants.

Country or Region and Most Recent Year of Peak Oil	
Venezuela	1970
Libya	1970
Kuwait	1972
Iran	1974
Romania	1976
Indonesia	1976
Trinidad and Tobago	1978
Brunei	1978
Tunisia	1980
Peru	1982
Other Europe	1986
Egypt	1993
Gabon	1996
United Kingdom	1999
Total Europe	1999
Uzbekistan	1999
Australia	2000
Argentina	2001
Norway	2001
Syria	2002
Yemen	2002
European Union	2002
Mexico	2004
Denmark	2004
Malaysia	2004
Vietnam	2004
Italy	2005
Chad	2005
Equatorial Guinea	2005
Algeria	2007
Sudan	2007
Angola	2008

Country or Region and Most Recent Year of Peak Oil	
Total Africa	2008
Other Asia Pacific	2008
Azerbaijan	2010
Nigeria	2010
Total Asia Pacific	2010
India	2011
Colombia	2013
Qatar	2013
Ecuador	2014
Total South and Central America	2015
Turkmenistan	2015
China	2015
Oman	2016
Saudi Arabia	2016
United Arab Emirates	2016
Other Middle East	2016
Total Middle East	2016
Thailand	2016
Canada	2018
United States	2019
Total North America	2019
Kazakhstan	2019
Iraq	2019
Republic of Congo	2019
South Sudan	2019
Other Africa	2019

FIGURE 17.5   List of All Oil-Producing Countries or Regions and Year of Maximum Production

While a few countries are likely to exceed their peak of production (notably Argentina, Saudi Arabia, briefly, and Canada), the vast majority of countries are not only permanently past their peak, but in steady decline.

Source: BP 2021 Statistical Review.

("the peak"), and after that point, less and less came out of the ground until shale oil came along.

The massive finds in Alaska and the Gulf of Mexico could not overcome the rate of depletion in the lower 48 states to achieve a new high-water mark of oil production. The United States' peak of oil production in 1970 was just under 10 million barrels a day, and 40 years later it produced just a little over five million barrels a day.

Shale (or "tight" because of the extremely stingy rock it hails from) oil is such a monumental event it gets its own chapter (*Shale Oil*, Chapter 18).

Before shale oil, the United States was using what is called "conventional oil," which is synonymous with "cheap and easy" oil. Cheap is another way of saying high-net-energy oil, while "shale oil" is another way of saying expensive, low-net-energy oil.

Because they are so different in every possible way—in terms of costs, net energy, decline rate, and quality—we're going to examine conventional and shale oil separately.

For conventional oil, what we saw within the United States' history (mirrored in every other conventional oil procuring nation so far) is a nearly textbook-perfect example of Peak Oil: a steady rise in oil production to a peak, followed by a bumpy plateau (1970–1985) and then a steady decline in oil production.

According to the incredible and valuable *BP Statistical Review*, which they put out every year, of 55 oil-producing countries or regions in the world, 46 are more than five years past their peak of oil production and in decline, leaving only nine to try to both cover the declines occurring in other areas and add more oil to fuel the story of growth. Again, these aren't theories, but facts (see Figure 17.5).

Despite headlines to the contrary, the United States consumed more oil than it produced in 2021, a condition that I expect will become permanent with the decline of shale oil fields. Japan, lacking any domestic oil source, imports nearly 100% of the petroleum it needs. The United Kingdom, having gone past peak in the incredibly productive North Sea fields in 1998 (which now produce less than half as much as their peak amount), became a net importer of both natural gas and petroleum in 2004 and 2005, respectively.[2] Australia's oil hit peak in 2000, and by 2009 Australia was importing close to 40% of its petroleum needs.[3] By 2022 Australia was importing more than 90% of its petroleum.[4]

However, China is the biggest part of this story. It announced to the world, again to too little fanfare, that it had hit its own peak of oil production in 2018. But well before then, China's own appetite for oil was greatly exceeding its own domestic production. China became a net importer in 1993 (see Figure 17.6).

The issue for an oil-importing country isn't how much oil it produces, but whether or not it can import what it needs. If we scoot back up to a very high

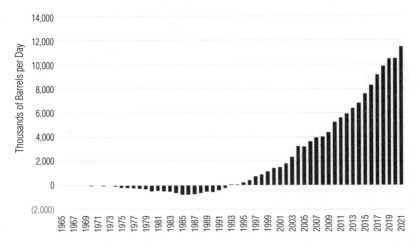

FIGURE 17.6   China's Oil Imports

In 1993 China became a net oil importer. In 2014, it surpassed the United States as the number-one importer of oil in the world. In 2021, China imported five times as much oil as the United States. This sets the state for future conflicts.

Source: BP 2021 Statistical Review.

level, we can see it's a tale of a few regions producing the surplus that other regions consume (Figure 17.7).

Seen this way, it's a bit more obvious just how important the Middle East and Russia are to Europe and Asia. Given that oil production is already being slightly exceeded by demand, it will be a miracle if the next decade passes without a major kinetic war. Virtually all wars in history have been resource wars: food raids by the Vikings, plundering by expanding and hungry empires, and soon *the oil wars*.

Find First, *Then* Pump

It's impossible to pump oil out of the ground if you haven't found it, so another unavoidable fact about oil is that in order to extract it, you have to find it first. Even after a major oil field is discovered, a fairly significant gap exists between the time of its initial discovery and its date of maximum production.

There are two main reasons for this: The first is that it takes time to drill the wells and develop the necessary infrastructure to get the oil away from the fields and to market (pipelines, storage facilities, and separating units all have to be sited and built). The second is that a careful approach to maximizing production has to be developed to avoid accidentally damaging the field and possibly stranding some oil in place by pumping it too quickly.

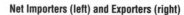

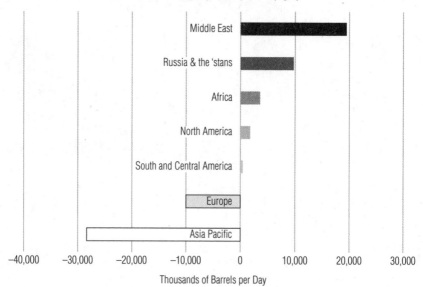

FIGURE 17.7   Net Importers and Exporters, 2021

Europe and Asia import; the rest of the world exports to varying degrees. In 2021, the importers exceeded the production capacity of the exporters by more than four million barrels per day, which led to a large drawdown in global oil stocks. This continued throughout 2022.

Source: BP 2021 Statistical Review.

To understand this second point, imagine you have been given an inflatable mattress glued to the floor filled with creamy peanut butter, and you have the task of getting as much of the peanut butter out of the fill nozzle as possible. You'll be paid $100 for every tablespoon you get out. But if you ever accidentally create a small pocket of left-behind peanut butter, it's lost and cannot be claimed.

You'd probably begin by carefully massaging the mattress from the edges working your way around slowly. This would be no small challenge, and from time to time, you'd stand back and assess your progress, maybe making a few measuring pats here and there just to be sure all is going well. If you decided to get some out as fast as you could, you'd just jump on the middle of the mattress and, sure, you'd get plenty out quickly, but you'd also ultimately get out a fraction of what you could if you did so more carefully.

Similar to this peanut butter mattress analogy, it's no small challenge for oil producers to maximize the ultimate production from their oil fields, which are often enormously complicated in their underground topography (imagine you had to work around random baffles and blind cavities in the inflatable

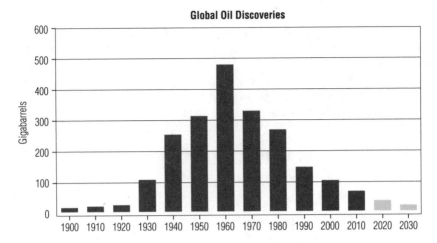

FIGURE 17.8   Global Oil Discoveries Peaked in 1964

Because discoveries necessarily precede production, a time lag exists between discovery and maximum production.

Source: Association for the Discovery of Peak Oil and Gas (ASPO).

mattress while being blindfolded and wearing mittens). They must work carefully and diligently to get as much out of the ground as they can. Given these realities, it can take anywhere from a few years to several decades for any given field to finally achieve maximum production.

In the United States, conventional oil discoveries peaked in 1930 and conventional oil production peaked in 1970, which yields a gap between a peak in *discovery* and a peak in *production* of almost exactly 40 years. Perhaps that 40-year gap was unique to the United States' particular geology and the oil demand of the times, but the United States is a very large country, and we might reasonably consider this experience to be a plausible proxy for the entire world.

This is where the story gets interesting. Figure 17.8 shows that worldwide oil discoveries increased in every decade up to the 1960s, but have decreased in every decade since then, with future projections (2010 through 2030) looking even grimmer.

If you've got to find it before you can pump it, and it takes time to develop fields to achieve maximum production, and the global peak in discoveries was in 1964, then we know there's a peak in production coming at some point. The United States' experience of a 40-year gap between its discovery and production peaks suggest that perhaps 40 years is as good a starting point as any to begin looking for a world production peak (1964 plus 40 equals 2004.)

The main problem is that because of hostile environment/governance/ social (ESG) rhetoric and oil prices that dipped crushingly below investment thresholds in 2015 through 2020, global capital investment by oil companies simply failed to happen. The oil business slashed investment by a staggering 50% in 2015, and then failed to invest an estimated $1.5 trillion over the next five years.

Because you have to find it before you can pump it, these investment shortfalls represent oil that will not be coming out of the ground over the next few years. Remember, it takes years to bring a new oil field online and so the shortfalls today reflect a failure to invest anywhere from five to seven years ago. There's no quick or easy way to make up for that lost time, even if the funds were immediately available and dedicated to the cause.

A Global Peak?

Now, let's turn our attention to global oil production. In 2018 and 2019, the world hit a peak of production that was clobbered in 2020 due to Covid, and then failed to regain to that peak in 2021 despite very strong demand that was,

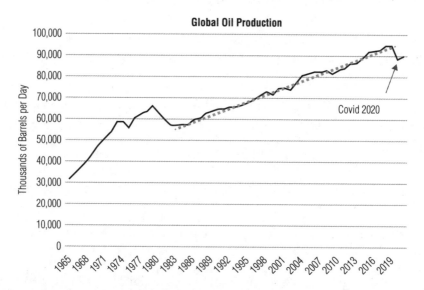

FIGURE 17.9 Yearly World Crude Oil Production

Crude oil production is going to struggle to regain its 2018/2019 highs due to a variety of factors ranging from subpar capital investment to lack of oilfield talent to shortages of needed materials like piping and even sand (for hydraulic fracturing in the United States).

Source: BP 2021 Statistical Review.

as we saw previously, running stronger than production. Prices spiked higher, too, which is normally a solid cue to the oil business to get busy finding and pumping more. But that didn't happen.

If we're already at peak, as the data suggests, then we've placed ourselves in quite a predicament. If we're lucky, the peak is still a couple of years away, but given events between Russia and Ukraine, along with statements from the few remaining oil powerhouses, that's the best we can hope for at present.

The optimal possible set of responses to Peak Oil should have happened two decades ago. But they didn't, and then the advance warnings given by all the dedicated "Peak Oilers" of the mid-2000s (myself among them) were not only ignored, but mainly ridiculed by a truly out-to-lunch set of critics and nearly all of the mainstream media.

Oil and GDP

We already showed that total energy use and GDP are quite tightly coupled. Now, let's take another look at the relationship between global GDP growth and oil consumption.

Since oil that's produced is rapidly consumed (approximately 50 days' worth of global consumption is above ground at any one time), we can use oil production as our measure of oil demand. Fortunately, we have access to very good data for oil production, which we can compare against global GDP growth, as in Figure 17.10.

What Figure 17.10 indicates is that GDP and oil consumption are very tightly linked. While economists would have you believe that an economy demands the oil it wants and then sets the rate of extraction, I would make the counterpoint that oil availability sets the stage for how much GDP can be made from it.

Although the 2018–2022 press was full of articles about "Peak Oil Demand" as if society would simply decide not to use as much oil sometime soon, we've instead seen a quite robust increase in demand (except for the wildly unusual Covid year of 2020, that is).

The Oil Production Output Gap

The very minute an oilfield is first tapped and begins to flow, its bounty begins to deplete. Depletion is a different concept from an output decline. What is being depleted is the total amount underground that can be gotten. A decline

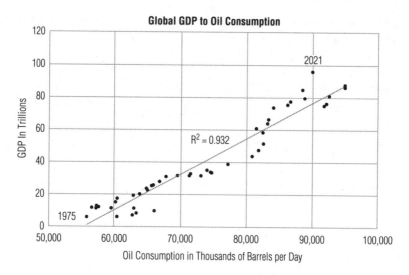

FIGURE 17.10   Global GDP Growth and Oil Production

Since 1975, global oil production and GDP growth have been very tightly coupled. The year 2021 stands out as well above trend, mainly because global oil production was below consumption, while excessive central bank printing created quite a burst of economic activity. Regardless, the "R-squared" stands at a robust 0.93, indicating that these two items are very tightly coupled.

Sources: Global GDP: World Bank and Global Oil Production: *BP 2021 Statistical Review.*

is what we're tracking in terms of an overall rate of oil production from a field. A field can be depleting even as its rate of production is rising.

But every field under production is depleting, and the longer they deplete the more they tend to decline as well. In order to make up for this reality, it's critical that more fields and wells are brought online all the time.

Estimates vary, but the rate of decline in existing fields is in the range of around 4–6% per year. That means around 3.5 to 5 million barrels per day of new production has to be found and then brought online each year. Year in and year out, no breaks.

Because of the massive hole in investment between 2015 and 2020, it was a rather easy prediction to make that the world would be facing oil shortages beginning around 2019 to 2020, a prediction I made back in 2017.[5]

I did not foresee the Covid pandemic back then, of course, which delayed the arrival by a year or so, but 2021 saw the predicted shortfalls arrive on time and as predicted. They will last for a minimum of five to seven years, and that's if and only if oil companies feel properly incentivized to risk a lot of capital.

Peak Exports

However, the most urgent issue before us doesn't lie with identifying the precise moment of Peak Oil. That is of academic interest and can only be identified in a rearview mirror anyway, but it's also something of a distraction, because the most economically important event around oil will occur when a persistent gap emerges between supply and demand. This is what began to unfold in 2021 and 2022. Should it continue (and I have every reason to expect it will), the response could be as swift as it is economically devastating for oil-importing countries.

Dallas geologist Jeffrey Brown developed a very simple and clever way to think about the supply and demand problem, which he calls the Export Land Model.[6]

Suppose we have a hypothetical country that produces three million barrels of crude oil per day, consumes one million barrels a day, and exports the balance of two million barrels a day. All things being equal, it can export those two million barrels year after year. But now, let's suppose that its oil field output is declining due to depletion issues at a modest 5% a year.

After 10 years, instead of two million barrels a day, this country can now only export 0.89 million barrels a day, or less than half the prior amount. The missing balance has depleted away, and it cannot export what it doesn't have. Now comes the kicker: Let's further suppose, quite realistically, that this country's citizens increases their internal demand for oil at a rate of 2.5% a year. What happens to exports in this case, where internal demand is rising and production is falling? Under this scenario, exports will plunge to zero in less than seven years.

This illustrates the miracle of compounding in reverse, where exports are eaten into from both ends by declining production and rising internal demand. It turns out that this isn't just a scenario, but a reality for many exporting countries. For example, in the case of Mexico, the number-three supplier of oil exports to the United States in 2009, production declines and demand growth will entirely eliminate its exports somewhere between the years 2011 and 2015 (depending on a variety of economic and petro-investment variables). When this happens, the United States will have to turn to the global market in search of a new number-three exporter to replace the lost imports. Unfortunately, global competition for oil supplies is likely to be quite stiff by that time.

When world production will peak is a matter of some dispute, with estimates ranging from 2005 to some 30 years hence. But as I said before, the precise moment of the peak is really just of academic concern. What we need to be most concerned with is the day the world's demand outstrips available supply. It's at that moment when the oil markets will change forever and probably quite suddenly.

First, we'll see massive price hikes—that's a given. But do you remember the food "shortages" that erupted seemingly overnight back in February of 2011? How about India banning rice exports in 2022? Those were triggered by the perception that demand exceeded supply, which led to an immediate export ban on food shipments by many countries. This same dynamic of national hoarding will certainly be a feature of the global oil market once the perception of shortage takes hold. When that happens, our concerns about price will be trumped by our fears of shortages.

The Ugly Power of Reverse Compounding

Remember all those exponential graphs from Chapter 5 (*Dangerous Exponentials*) and how time ran out in a hurry toward the end of the stadium example? In theory, there's nothing problematic with living in a world full of exponential growth and depletion curves—*as long as the world doesn't have any boundaries.*

However, exponential functions take on enormous importance when they approach a physical boundary, as was the case in the last five minutes of our stadium example and which *will soon be the case for oil.* We know oil is finite and have always known the day would come when we'd bump up against the roof of the oil production stadium. All the data I've been collecting and observing over the past five years strongly suggests that we've already bumped our heads up against oil's exponential boundary.

And here are some questions that this possibility raises:

- What if our exponentially based economic and monetary systems, rather than being the sophisticated culmination of human evolution, are really just an artifact of oil?

- What if all of our rich societal complexity and all of our trillions of dollars of wealth and debt are simply the human expression of surplus energy pumped from the ground?

- If so, what happens to our wealth, economic complexity, and social order when they cannot be fed by steadily rising energy inputs?

More immediately, you and I would be perfectly within our rights to wonder what will happen when (not *if*, but *when*) oil begins to decline in both quantity and quality.

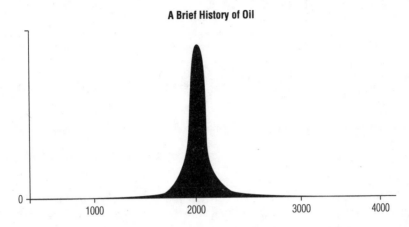

FIGURE 17.11   Global Oil Production on a 4,000-Year Timeline

- What will happen to our exponential, debt-based money system during this period?
- Is it even possible for it to function in a world without constant growth?

These are important questions for which we currently have no answers, only ideas and speculation.

To put our oil bonanza in some sort of appropriate context, Figure 17.11 shows oil extraction placed on a four-thousand-year timeline.

It's now up to us to wonder what we should expect in the future from a money system in which the most basic assumption might be in error. What if the assumption "the future will be not just larger, but exponentially larger than the present" is not correct?

Maybe shale oil will save us? Let's find out. . .

CHAPTER 18

Shale Oil

Full confession: Back in 2010 when the first edition of this book was penned, I did not even remotely foresee the shale oil story becoming so dominant. For some reason I assumed reason would prevail. I had analyzed and scrutinized the data and saw that the shale companies were losing money hand over fist and thought to myself, "Well, this will have to end soon."

I am ever hopeful that things will make sense and reason and rationality can be counted on, especially when it comes to money. What I did not foresee, at all, was the immensity of the losses "investors" were willing to bear in the shale oil industry. Hundreds of billions of dollars went there to die. I'd be more than fascinated to see a fully detailed accounting of those losses because I have my suspicions that more than a few of them were "officially absorbed," if you catch my drift.

A huge factor in that willingness to take losses was something else I didn't foresee: the Federal Reserve driving interest rates to zero and pegging them there, forcing many entities and individuals to recklessly "chase yield" wherever they could find it. The paltry 5% yields on offer from the shale patch were vastly better than anything that could be found elsewhere so . . . they piled in. Big mistake for them, but a lot of fun for the frackers and drillers!

Shale Oil—Amazing Technology, but Expensive Oil

I am truly in awe of what the shale patch drillers and frackers can accomplish. The technology is simply brilliant and deserving of a lot of respect.

When we say "shale" we are literally talking about a form of rock that is quite similar to the material used on old-style chalkboards. It's hard and dense, and a little bit brittle, so it shatters easily. But if you put even a thin piece up against your lips and tried to suck air through it, you'd get nowhere. It's pretty solid stuff.

One of the most important points to make about shale plays is that they are expensive plays, and shale oil will always be expensive oil compared to conventional oil.

Here's why.

Shale wells are more accurately called "tight rock" wells, because they might be in shale, or limestone, or even sandstone, but each rock type shares the characteristic of having really incredibly tiny pores that do not allow the oil or gas to flow easily.

Along comes fracking, the purpose of which is to shatter the shale, creating lots of tiny pieces, hugely increasing the surface area from which oil and/ or gas can escape the tight rock matrix and more easily flow into the well bore for collection.

In the good old conventional oil days, we might have drilled down a thousand feet, hit a gusher, and then had a well that might produce thousands of barrels of oil per day for 20 to 50 years.

And now?

With shale plays, the typical well goes down for 10,000 feet, turns sideways for another 10,000 feet, and then gets fracked in 20, 40, 80, even 100 or more separate times (called "stages") to thoroughly smash and fracture the shale so that gas and/or oil will flow to the surface. The typical shale well flows out at less than a thousand barrels per day for the first month and is down to 20 barrels per day within three years.

That's 1,000 total feet of drill and no expensive fracturing resulting in decades of high-volume oil flow in the first case, and up to 20,000 feet of drilling and a hundred frac stages in the second to create a well that will be largely depleted in a few short years.

Clearly, we can already detect that far more money, and *energy*, is required to drill and multi-stage frack a 20,000-foot well versus a 1,000-foot well that required no fracking. A shale well typically costs between $7 and $10 million to drill, and just think of all the steel piping and diesel required to run the rigs that drill the three- to four-mile-long wells—which is why shale wells produce expensive oil. It's not because of a lack of ingenuity or trying, that's for sure.

Looked at through our lens, shale wells deliver far less *net* energy than conventional wells of the past.

It is also true that the environmental impacts of the shale plays are high. First, there is the footprint of the drilling pads and collection pits to consider. Each drilled section requires a drill pad of one to two acres to be scraped flat, while open-air frac fluid collection pits dot every one.

And then there's the fracking fluid itself. Mixed with millions of gallons of water, this stuff is a downright toxic nightmare.

While we don't know everything it contains because the exact concoctions are protected trade secrets due to the so-called "Halliburton" amendment that specifically protects the oil and gas industry from having to reveal anything about what-all is in there, we do know it usually contains things like benzene and toluene and other highly toxic chemicals.

Even if the drilling is done right and no fracking fluid ever gets into the water table, the fracking process involves first injecting this soup into the bore hole under extremely high pressures, and then collecting all the flowback into an open-air pond before oil or gas collection begins.

At this point anything and everything in the fracking water—which includes the fracking fluid, heavy metals, and radioactive compounds like radium—liberated from the depths is free to evaporate and/or aerosolize and drift with the wind. And much of it does, creating enormous health issues for people and animals living downwind.

Last time I checked, there were more than 2,000 complaints about frac-damaged water wells which, sadly, will probably remain compromised for many generations to come.

The high dollar costs, the large environmental impacts, and the rapid decline rates make shale oil expensive oil.

Shale Oil—Game Changer or Retirement Party?

Given all the positive stories about shale oil and shale gas, many of which proclaimed "peak oil is dead" or that the United States should now be called "Saudi America," how is it possible for petroleum geologist Arthur Berman to proclaim the shale plays to be more of a retirement party than a revolution?

While I have a *lot* of admiration for the technology and the expertise and diligence of the people working in the oil sector, I have even more respect for geology. The United States began its love affair with oil by going after the conventional reservoirs that sat atop the ancient marine shales where 400 million years of ancient sunlight was laid down in the form of deposited plankton and algae.

Those conventional reservoirs eventually were pretty much all located and drilled (more will be found, just nothing like the heyday of prior decades). When I asked a former Shell senior executive about that assertion, he immediately agreed and told me, "Peak Oil is real and everyone in the business knows it."

What the shale revolution, or "retirement party," as Art Berman more accurately calls it, did was to drill straight into the source rocks themselves. What's left after you've drilled the source rocks? Nothing, that's what. There are no "pre-source" rocks to drill into next. There's no "grandparent layer" beneath those. We're at the bottom of the geologic barrel, scraping for the dregs.

Fledged on a Cliff

The very best month of production for a shale well is the first month, and things go very rapidly downhill from there. By the 36th month, the typical shale well has declined by 80% to 90%.

Because individual shale wells have these ferocious decline profiles, many of them summed together end up having the same profile that looks like a double black diamond ski slope. This means that in order to increase production from a shale field, more and more wells must be constantly drilled just to catch and then exceed the combined declines of all the prior wells.

Shale oil analyst Rune Livkern calls this "the Red Queen syndrome" after the queen in *Alice in Wonderland*, who remarked, "you have to run faster and faster just to stay in place!"

In any given shale oil basin—the Bakken, the Eagleford, the Permian—if drilling were ever completely halted within a single year, oil output would decline by a hair-raising 45%!

The shale plays, brilliant though they are in terms of technology, are a complete disaster because of how their fast-growing output lulled the entire nation of the United States into believing that they would somehow last forever. Instead, the math was kind of simple to run. Each well has to be spaced x feet from the next one and therefore occupies y acres, and there are only z acres in a given shale play. That means z divided by y = how many wells you can drill. Not too hard, right?

So, how many wells are left to be drilled? On February 3, 2022, one of the most important articles I've ever seen in the *Wall Street Journal* was titled "Oil Frackers Brace for End of the U.S. Shale Boom."

It noted:

> *Less than 3½ years after the shale revolution made the U.S. the world's largest oil producer, companies in the oil fields of Texas, New Mexico and North Dakota have tapped many of their best wells.*
>
> *If the largest shale drillers kept their output roughly flat, as they have during the pandemic, many could continue drilling profitable wells for a decade or two, according to a Wall Street Journal review of inventory data and analyses. If they boosted production 30% a year—the pre-pandemic growth rate in the Permian Basin, the country's biggest oil field—they would run out of prime drilling locations in just a few years.*
>
> *Shale companies once drilled rapidly in pursuit of breakneck growth. Now the industry has little choice but to keep running in place. Many are holding back on increasing production, despite the highest oil prices in years and requests from the White House that they drill more.*[1]

The choice is clear for the oil companies: either drill, baby, drill like they did before, in which case there are three more years of explosive growth to be had, or be more prudent and make money and stay in business for another decade or two. That's an easy choice, my friends. The U.S. shale companies are not going to be contributing much in the way of incremental new oil to the world from here on out.

That this article made its way into the front page of the *WSJ* rang a bell loud and clear for me. The shale party was over. It had sobered up. Gone was the raging frat-party atmosphere that permeated the industry from 2005 through 2015. Now, the entire industry knows what it's got and what it doesn't. The land rush, the speculative fever, the race to produce the most is over, never to return.

Which is a good thing. Drilling so quickly that associated natural gas was burned in such quantities it required satellite photos to appreciate, was maybe not such a great idea. Perhaps, now the United States can settle down and be a little bit more serious about what it's actually got and how it would like to use it.

International Shale

The United States is blessed with some world-class shale oil and gas basins, but it's hardly the only country with them. Argentina has a truly massive play called the Vaca Meurta (literally, "Dead Cow"), which seems to possibly hold life-changing amounts of oil and gas, and efforts are well underway to begin the long process of building out the infrastructure needed to develop that play. Of course, this is Argentina, corrupt and prone to changing the rules mid-game, so international capital is not exactly racing to the scene.

In Europe, people are far more ecologically sensitive; the continent is more tightly packed with people, so finding remote drill locations is all but impossible and, more importantly, people don't own the mineral rights to the oil and gas beneath their land as they do in the United States. All of these factors combine to make explosive growth of fracked oil and gas a remote possibility in Europe. It will happen, just not quickly is my bet.

China's shale plays turned out to be a bust, unfortunately for them, as did the once heavily promoted Monterrey shale in California. Sometimes they work, sometimes not, and you can't really know until you drill into them and give it a go.

The Middle East may well have the most extensive and best shale plays in the world, which would be fitting, given their geological luck with oil.

Shale basins exist all over the world as the map from the EIA shows in Figure 18.1

How much they will yield remains to be seen, although admittedly it could be quite a lot. Or it might be less than we hope. We'll just have to wait and see. But it won't be cheap, and it won't last forever, and by the time it gets going, the U.S. shale plays will be in terminal decline.

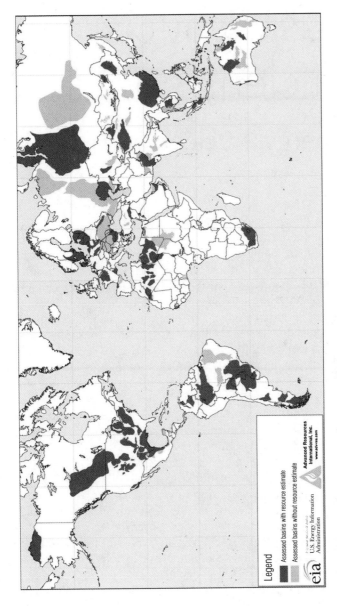

FIGURE 18.1   Shale Basins of the World

There are a huge number of as-yet unexplored and unexploited oil- and gas-bearing shale basins across the world. Some of them may prove to be monsters, and some will be duds.

Source: EIA.[2]

CHAPTER 19

Necessary but Insufficient

Clean Energy, Nuclear, and Coal

T he primary point of this book is that the economy to which we have become accustomed, along with our entire view of wealth in the forms of stocks and bonds, rests upon vast flows of energy (and other resources), the throughputs of which must not only be maintained but also exponentially increased each year. Without this constant growth in energy use, and every other resource, most of our creature comforts become much more difficult, if not impossible, to sustain. Having food, warmth, leisure, consumer goods— all on demand—is a wonderful thing.

The purpose of this chapter, then, isn't to completely cover the immense technical discussions that can (and should) surround energy, which economist Julian Simon rightfully called "the master resource."[1] Nor will we exhaustively cover all the various technologies and sources that could be alternatives. Instead, for our purposes, we will look at our energy predicament from a level that will permit us to address the question *How likely is it that other major sources of energy can seamlessly replace oil?*

A prevalent and hopeful line of thinking found all across the political spectrum suggests we will simply transition away from increased oil, coal, and natural gas consumption toward some combination of nuclear energy and/or alternative energy sources, such as solar, wind, or maybe even algae biofuels. While each of these energy sources will play an important role in mitigating the downslope of oil, none of them individually or in combination can ever completely plug the gap left by oil's slow departure.

Remember, the challenge here is not only to replace what will "go missing" as oil fields deplete, but also to increase the total energy supply of the world by a few percent each year as our exponential economy demands. Simple math, combined with the realities of time, scale, and cost, illustrates why this is improbable.

Simple Math

Half of all the oil ever produced throughout all of human history has been produced between 2022 and . . . 1992. That means someone who was 30 years old in 2022 had seen, in their short lifetime, half of all the amazing abundance of oil liberated and used. What they had experienced as the miracle of progress was really the miracle of the use of energy to foster economic complexity; a once-in-a-species liberation of energy that then liberated human minds to do wonderful and creative things besides farming and building shelter.

Energy itself comes in many forms. We don't value one source of energy over another for the form of the source itself, but rather to the extent each can do useful work for us. By putting different types of energy on an equal footing through a singular measure, we can compare them more easily. For our examples, we'll use a measure of power called watts.

Before we go any further, a reminder:

- A million is a thousand thousand
- A billion is a thousand million
- A trillion is a thousand billion
- A quadrillion is a thousand trillion

In 2021, the world produced and consumed 89.9 million barrels of oil per day (mbd), or 32.8 billion barrels for the year. Converting all of those billions of barrels into their energy content into watt hours (so we can easily compare across oil and sources of electricity), we discover that the world consumed around 53.6 quadrillion watt hours of energy in the form of oil. Coal provided the world with another 43.8 quadrillion watt hours, and natural gas another 39.2 quadrillion watt hours.

Assuming we wanted to get that same amount of watt hours from other sources, this would be the same as:

- More than 15,600 nuclear reactors running at the same efficiency as the United States' current 93 operating reactors (or roughly 15,100 more nuclear reactors than were operating worldwide in 2022).
- Nearly 15,611,000 new 1-megawatt wind towers running at their idealized output (assuming the perfect amount of wind blows every day of the year and no maintenance is ever required), or 52 million running under more realistic real-world conditions.
- At 2.8 acres to generate a GWhr of solar power per year, more than 380 million acres of land would have to be covered with solar panels (assuming enough locations even exist).

- More than 10 billion acres of farmland would have to be dedicated entirely to biomass energy production, representing 260% of the total amount of arable agricultural land in the world.

Those are some big numbers. Clearly, none of those approaches is workable alone, and even in combination it's difficult to get it all to pencil out. But that only gives us 2021 levels.

Now, let's suppose that the world wants to *increase* its total consumption of energy from petroleum 2.33% per year, which is what it has done over the past 55 years. You know, to keep the whole complex economic system increasing in complexity? Well, that's easy math, too. At a 2.3% rate of growth every 10 years you are adding more than 25% to the already massive amount of energy consumption already underway. Yay compounding!

Which means you have to take every one of those preposterous numbers above and make them all 25% larger every 10 years.

Again, China is the 800-pound gorilla in this story and is both by far the largest single-country consumer of energy in the world and has been compounding its use by an astonishing 6.3% per year, on average, between 2002 and 2021 (see Figure 19.1).

All of Europe used just slightly more than half as much energy as China in 2021 (52%), while the global economic powerhouse, the United States, used only 59% as much. Put another way, in 2021 China used as much energy as the

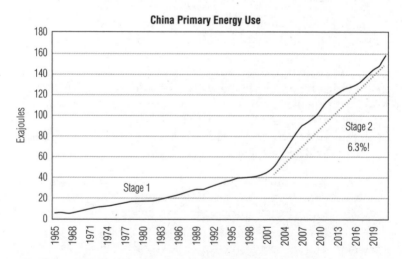

FIGURE 19.1   China's Total Energy Consumption

Ever since 2002 China's energy consumption has been compounding (growing) at the astonishing rate of 6.3% per year. There are clearly two stages to China's story: before 2002 and after 2002. The second stage has seen China expand its energy use for 20 years straight by an astonishing 6.3%, representing an 11-year doubling time.

Source: BP 2021 Statistical Review.

entire world did in 1965, and if it keeps growing at the rate of the past 20 years for the next 20 years, it will then consume as much power as the entire world does today. That's the magic of compounding at work again.

Again, we have to ask, what's the source of all that energy going to be? In 2021, the global mix of energy still saw fossil fuels representing 82% of the total primary energy mix.

In the stunning chart shown in Figure 19.2, much becomes clear. First, the shape of it—a hockey stick—shows that the world's increasing addiction to energy is clearly and unavoidably obvious. Compounding, there it is again. I told you we were surrounded by it.

Second, as fast as renewables have been growing, fossil fuels have been growing even faster in terms of amounts. In 2021, renewables, mainly wind and solar, grew by an astonishing 5.1 exajoules, an astonishing 14.7% expansion in a single year.

Fossil fuel use "only" expanded by 5.6%, but because that was 5.6% of a massive base, those fuels saw increased consumption in 2021 of 25 exajoules over 2020. In other words, fossil fuel use expanded by five times the *amount* that renewables did. Even if that amazing rate of growth is maintained, renewables won't catch up to fossil fuels for decades. And that's just to get to a 50/50 standoff.

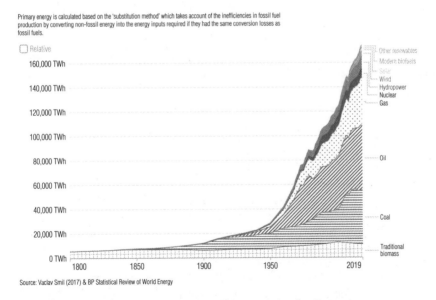

FIGURE 19.2 Global Primary Energy Consumption by Source

Global energy consumption "turned the corner" in the 1960s, creating a nearly perfect exponential chart. This is unsustainable.

Source: Hannah Ritchie, Max Roser, and Pablo Rosado, "Energy" (2020). Published online at **OurWorldInData.org**.

But I'm not hopeful that they will get close for two reasons: First, they aren't "renewables" so much as they are "replaceables." It takes energy to make energy and renewables don't just pass through a cosmic membrane full formed and ready to use: They require a huge amount of complicated and energy-intensive machinery, mining, and manufacturing processes to make them, principally, fossil fuels.

We have exactly zero (0) examples of renewables made entirely from renewable energy and resources. Once we begin to experiment with *that*, and we can successfully replace clean energy tech entirely with energy sourced from clean tech, I'll feel differently about the whole affair. Until then, these must all be viewed as fossil fuel–subsidized experiments.

The second reason is Europe.

The European Energy Disaster of 2022

In February of 2022, Russia invaded Ukraine. Europe sprang into action and immediately levied across-the-board sanctions against Russia. One thing they forgot to do in their haste was to top off their fuel supplies, which Russia critically supplied.

Both natural gas and oil were suddenly pinched off, and Europe had to scramble for LNG on the open market. Prices shot skyward, and a severe drought harmed commerce, farming, and energy production at the worst possible time. A heatwave struck and electricity use also spiked higher. France, in some of the worst timing ever, had roughly half of its nuclear plants offline due to delayed maintenance finally catching up with them in the form of cracks in critical cooling pipes.

Add it all up and electricity prices broke out to new record highs in the Old World, and specifically the UK, France, and Germany, week after week. By late summer, European leaders were already warning their citizens of the possibility of a freezing winter and rolling electricity blackouts. Millions of households were suddenly plunged into energy poverty.

Germany was as badly off as any other country, but it was further along in its efforts to transition to a low-carbon, renewable energy supply system than any other country. Between 2013 and 2020 Germany spent over 200 billion euros installing renewable energy projects. The share of German electricity from solar and wind vaulted from 8% to 31%.

So now renewables could be put to a real-world test. An energy crisis would be the perfect time for these projects to shine. How would they fare? They were saved (!), right? Nope.

They fared terribly, as it turned out. Within a few months of the gravity of the energy situation becoming clear, German politicians voted to reopen closed coal-fired power plants. A month later and those same discussions were centered on keeping the nuclear plants running instead of shutting them down as planned.

Wood-fired stoves disappeared from stores, firewood prices spiked by 500% in August of 2022, and it was reported to me (by my friend Michael Yon) that security guards had to be positioned to protect firewood from thieves. All this before summer was anywhere close to being over.

Immediately, calculations of the impact of reduced energy flows on the European economy began to surface. At first timid, they spoke of reduced growth. Then they spoke of flat growth. Then possibly slightly negative growth. Finally, the word recession came into popular use, followed by whispers that things could be a lot worse than *that*.

The truth is, as of this writing, nobody really knows, but we do know something those economists seem not to: Starving an industrialized continent of energy is certain to cause some or possibly a lot of that complexity to break down.

Germany in particular is central to a million industrial stories. The massive BASF chemical plant headquarters at Ludwigshafen on the Rhine River consists of 200 production plants and 125 production facilities, operated by 39,000 employees who ship out 1,900 truckloads and 400 rail carloads per day, as they make and move 20 billion pounds of chemical materials each year. In August 2022, there were announcements that the site may have to restrict operations or even shut down if Russian gas weren't restored to the country of Germany.

Can anybody predict what would happen to all the downstream activities if some or all of those chemicals from a single Germany facility (massive though it may be) were knocked out of commission for a while? No, and that's the point. We'd simply have to sit back and observe and see what emerged. Such is the nature of complex systems, and the intersection of humans and energy and industrial processes and political decisions make for a perfectly complex stew.

Europe in 2022/2023 will have provided enormously important lessons for those paying attention. My prediction (writing here in the fall of 2022) is that far more economic and social damage will occur than most expected or thought was possible. That's because most people don't appreciate the role of energy in creating the economy.

The Reality—Time, Scale, Cost, Limits

People who are hoping for a technological solution to our energy predicament sometimes overlook the realities involved in moving to a new energy technology. There are significant issues of time, scale, cost, and limits involved. Above, we've used some simple math to illustrate the *scale* of the predicament.

But the most overlooked and underappreciated aspect concerns the limits. Associate Professor Simon Micheaux (KTR Circular Economy Solutions, Geological Survey of Finland) has done the hard work of running a few calculations for us all.

In a research paper published on June 10, 2022, titled "Quantity of Metals Required to Manufacture One Generation of Renewable Technology Units to Phase Out Fossil Fuels," he found the following:

- A complete clean energy build-out would require 586,000 new non-fossil-fuel electrical power stations. There are only 46,000 total power stations at present (and mostly fossil fuels, of course).
- Hydropower would need to expand by 115% and nuclear would have to double.
- All known copper reserves would only cover 20% of the calculated requirements.
- Lithium reserves just 10%, leaving a 90% shortfall.
- Silver, zinc, manganese silicon, and zirconium all have adequate reserves.
- Vanadium has a shortfall of 96.5% (reserves just cover 3.5% of needs).
- Cobalt, also short by 96.5% (3.5% coverage).
- Nickel reserves will cover just 10% of need, leaving another 90% gap.[2]

It's clear that profound limits exist that will completely thwart the clean energy dreams and plans that have mostly failed to even question, if the materials and metals they require even exist. Just focusing on copper to illustrate the challenge, Professor Micheaux calculated that some 4.5 billion tons of the metal will be needed to complete that first-generation build-out of an alternative clean energy system. Copper is necessary to make electric motors and generators, and the gigantic cables that connect offshore windfarms (for example) to distribution systems.

Besides the obvious lack of copper reserves, let's assume some new reserves magically into existence. How long at 2019 rates of copper production would it take to mine the required amounts? Professor Micheaux calculated that to be 189.1 years. So, *time* is a factor as well.

If we wanted to speed that up to, say, 30 years, and again we're magically assuming the needed copper ore resources into existence here, could we even build enough mining equipment in time, hire and train enough workers, and find enough fresh water to operate the smelters? The *scale* of the project is dizzying. And how much would it cost, in terms of both money but also the energy required to mine all that copper?

When Professor Micheaux performed the same calculations for lithium, that effort yielded the preposterous time-to-mine result of 9,920 years. Cobalt at 1,733 years. Graphite at 3,287 years. Vanadium was 6,747 years. Germanium an eye-watering 29,113 years. Gut check time: Do you believe that market forces will somehow defeat those limits? What about government programs?

From time to time, I am accused of significantly underappreciating just how clever and resourceful humans are. Perhaps I do, but the scientist in me knows that cleverness cannot defeat the physical laws of the universe. And the former corporate executive in me knows just how difficult it can be to move from the lab, to a pilot plant, and then to full-scale operational delivery.

Historically, transitions from one energy source to another have been long, expensive, protracted affairs. Global energy use in the nineteenth century was dominated by wood, not coal, and it wasn't until 1964 that petroleum overtook coal as the main source of transportation energy. Even a 20–30% share of a national energy market by a new entrant takes several decades, possibly a century or more. At least historically this has been true.[3]

Part of the reason is that the old form of energy has an enormous installed capital base that must be phased out. For example, as our shipping fleets moved from wind power to coal, sailboats were slowly phased out over a period of decades as new coal steamers were individually brought online. Nobody wanted to dispose of their old capital simply because new technology was available; it wouldn't have made sense economically.

The same was true for the switch from horse-drawn carriages to automobiles. So, if we want to move from gasoline-powered autos to electric cars, a good guess would be that several decades of transition will be involved. The current crop of petroleum-powered vehicles will have one or two decades of useful life that their owners will want to wring out of them; service stations will have to be phased out, with their pumps and tanks removed; electric charging stations will need to be installed everywhere; and electric grids will have to be significantly upgraded to handle the new loads.

The rest of the reason that energy transitions take so long is simply the scale involved. Even if the world collectively decided 1,000 brand-new nuclear plants were exactly what it needed (and right away), it would still take decades to complete them all. Why? Because there aren't enough manufacturing facilities to build the reactor cores. So, those manufacturing facilities would have to be built first. Then, there aren't enough engineers trained in reactor assembly and operation, and training takes time. Further, all of the world's current uranium mines together wouldn't be able to supply the required fuel, so new mines would have to be identified and opened. That, too, would take a very long time as there would be permits to secure, endless red tape to wade through, and vast amounts of capital to raise.

In every historical case, energy transitions required decades to complete, and there's no reason to suspect that this time will be different. The only way to conceivably avoid this delay would be to override the markets and force the transition by government decree.

Perhaps we need the equivalent of a Manhattan Project times an Apollo Project times 10: a massive, sudden, and global decision to put enormous resources into bringing a new energy technology or sources onto the scene without relying on market forces to get the job done. So far there are no signs of that happening anywhere, except possibly China.

One example: A 2008 study by the National Research Council found that "plug-in hybrid electric vehicles will have little impact on U.S. oil consumption before 2030" and more substantial savings might be on the cards by 2050, reinforcing the notion that several decades separate the first launch of a new technology from its meaningful contribution to the energy landscape.[4]

The Nuclear Option

Even with significant current concerns about carbon in the atmosphere and recent technological advances in the field of nuclear reactor design, nuclear power still cannot step into the lead role and save us all from the effects of depleting oil. It will play a role, just not the lead role.

Here's why.

In 2004, nuclear power represented 8% of all energy consumed by the United States, while fossil energy represented 86%. By 2021, nuclear had fallen to 4% of the mix while fossil fuels were hanging tough at 82%. Worldwide, there were 440 nuclear power plants operating in 2010, but only 404 by 2022. In 2010, China had plans for or was already building 33 more nuclear plants to be ready by 2030, and a worldwide total of 61 were under construction in 16 countries. Most of those projects are behind schedule and over budget, as is typical of nuclear plants because of their immense complexity and the regulatory and environmentalist-caused hurdles that often change regulations mid-construction.

The very first question that must be asked before building a new power plant is, *Where is the fuel for this plant going to be coming from?* Power plants cannot run dry of fuel and need to be constantly fed, so sourcing the fuel is an extremely important task.

When it comes to fueling nuclear plants, there is a bit of an issue. The Chinese are already buying and stockpiling uranium for future use in their plants[5] because they apparently peered into the future and concluded fuel security was an issue, so they bought it in advance, just to be safe. The United States and France, the two countries with the most operating nuclear reactors, both hit a peak in uranium production back in the 1980s. Both countries only have very modest reserves of relatively low-grade uranium remaining within their borders.

The largest known uranium reserves in the world are located in Kazakhstan, Canada, and Australia.[6] By now, you'll find the story of uranium to be familiar, because it so closely parallels the story of petroleum. The highest grades and most convenient ores of uranium were exploited first and now those are nearly all gone, and the remaining ores are more dilute and/or more difficult to exploit. It's the same story as that of oil. Go after the easy, low-hanging fruit first.

High-grade uranium ore deposits, such as those still found in Canada, can be close to 20% in purity.[7] But most of the world's known deposits are in the range of 1% to 0.1%, with a few deposits even listed as "proven reserves," implying that they are worth going after despite having an ore purity grade of less than 0.01%, which is 2,000 times more dilute than the higher-grade ores in Canada.

In 2006, the 104 operating U.S. nuclear power plants purchased 66 million pounds of uranium, of which 11 million pounds came from domestic sources and the balance from foreign sources. From 2000 to 2010, the world's nuclear power plants had been running, in part, on the uranium from decommissioned U.S. and (former) Soviet warheads, with some 13% of the world's total reactor fuel coming from the "Megatons to Megawatts" program, which ended in 2013 and is unlikely to ever provide more fuel for use in nuclear power plants. In 2020, close to half of all uranium used by the United States was imported from (wait for it . . .) Russia (24%) and Kazakhstan and Uzbekistan (25%).

If the United States cannot currently meet its own needs for uranium domestically with only 93 operating reactors, where will the rest come from? If that's even an open question, then how much hope should we place on the idea of building and operating hundreds if not thousands more over the coming years? Even if the United States somehow managed to double its total number of operating reactors, it would still only be obtaining 16% of its total electricity needs from nuclear power. And even this assumes that power demand does not grow at all.

Nuclear, then, is a great technology with a lot of promise but until and unless the United States gets serious about progressing a thorium-fuel cycle reactor series, it will have to remain a vital but smallish piece of the equation.

For the world to move significantly to nuclear power above and beyond current levels, it will first need to figure out where the uranium to fuel the reactors will come from. The short answer is that it won't come from conventional mining, because that industry is having a hard time keeping up with the plants that are already in operation. It couldn't possibly service a doubling or tripling from these levels, let alone meet the 38-fold increase implied by the gap being left behind by the eventual loss of fossil fuels. That's 38-fold at present, and doesn't account for future growth in the use of energy.

Some hopeful nuclear power proponents then turn to the idea of fast breeder reactors (which create more fissile material than they use), or possibly those running on thorium (which is much more abundant than uranium), which could theoretically provide energy for the next thousand years.

Thorium truly has me excited in its promise, and both India and China are actively building pilot thorium reactors to test out the concept. As of 2022, there are no such public efforts to build thorium reactors in any Western countries.

As of 2017, there were only two commercial breeder reactors in operation, both Russia sodium-cooled and both relatively small. Several of the early experiments have already been shut down and/or decommissioned, but a small handful of experimental, demonstration, and pilot breeder reactors remain: two in India, and two in Russia.[8] The basic story here is that fast breeder reactors look very good on paper, but they have proved to be something of an operational nightmare, which is to say nothing of the intense national security risks that they pose by virtue of their production of plutonium if running on uranium, and uranium 233 (a fissile material useful for making nuclear bombs) if running on thorium.

Whether or not breeder reactors are a good idea is relatively insignificant when you consider that commercial reactors are not yet operating at scale. If we are going to entertain hopes that these complicated machines will contribute to our energy story, we must first admit that they can't possibly do this if they aren't built. This seems a trite concept, but you'd be surprised at how many people earnestly inform me that we are going to solve our energy predicament with breeder reactors.

With conventional Peak Oil firmly in the rearview mirror, and a peak in total (and more expensive nonconventional oil) arriving before 2030, it seems incredibly unlikely that the world will somehow manage to build hundreds of breeder and nuclear reactors within a few years, as would be required to offset the decline in the energy we get from oil.

Here's how the possibility of nuclear energy breaks down:

- **Time:** Decades. It will be at least 10 years (and probably more like 20) before the number of operating nuclear reactors in the world, currently standing at 404 (in 2022), could possibly be doubled.
- **Scale:** Enormous. The world's capacity to build nuclear plants depends on a limited number of engineers with the requisite training and skills, and there are a limited number of factories that can manufacture the specialty items needed to build a plant. More worryingly, it's not clear that the necessary fuel will be available from conventional mining sources. Dealing with the waste issue even at the current scales of operation has not yet been solved.

- **Cost:** Trillions and trillions of dollars. The price tag to build a modern 1-gigawatt nuclear plant was estimated to be $7 billion (in 2015) but the Vogtle plant being built in Georgia was $20 billion *over* the $14 billion budget and five years behind schedule in 2022, so perhaps the true cost is closer to $17 billion per reactor? Maintenance and fuel costs add millions of dollars more per plant. Merely doubling the world's nuclear plants would cost $2.2 trillion. Assuming we could get past the issues outlined in time and scale, and could build the roughly 200 nuclear reactors *per year* required to offset falling oil production, the price tag over just a single decade would be in the vicinity of $10 trillion.

- **Limits:** The good news is that there's enough Uranium to power current reactors for 90 years.[9] The bad news is in the word "current." If we double the number of reactors, then that drops to 45 years. So, nuclear too is a temporary "fix," at least as it's currently operated (see breeder reactors and thorium, above).

The Coal Story

I am sometimes asked if I am worried about the use of coal. No, I am not worried about it at all because I know that we're going to burn it all regardless of the consequence. So what's to worry about? Its use is inevitable.

The greenest of all countries in Europe, Germany, nearly instantly abandoned its abandonment of coal-fired power plants the instant they ran short of natural gas. Given the choice between being in the cold and dark or not, humans will always choose "not being in the cold and dark."

The question really isn't "will coal be used?" but "How fast will it be used?" I mean, sure, for appearances sake we'll use up all the natural gas we can because "it's greener," but the truth is that as soon as that runs down or becomes more expensive than coal, we'll switch back to coal. Back and forth until both are all gone. Unless . . . *unless* something changes in our story. That's why this book exists. To try and break out of this self-destructive cycle a lot of people seem to be intent on seeing through.

When he was president, George W. Bush gaffed on national television when he declared that the United States still has "250 million years of coal left."[10] Even if he were to have said what he probably meant, which was "we have 250 *years* of coal left," he would still have been wrong.

In truth, the only possible way to get to 250 years of coal is to start with the most optimistic possible estimate about U.S. coal reserves and then divide that number by *current* consumption, which is unrealistic because global consumption of coal is constantly growing. Realistically, if coal consumption continues to increase as it has done in every decade since at least 1800,[11] it's not possible to have anything close to 250 years of coal remaining.

As Albert Bartlett makes clear, one cannot reasonably leave out growth in consumption when discussing how long something will last. That would be like claiming that you had spent nothing in the past five minutes and that therefore the money in your wallet would last forever.

Bartlett dissected the innumeracy of our growth and energy policies for decades, and has pointed out some massive logical errors in our thinking, such as this statement taken from a U.S. Senate report: "At current levels of output and recovery, these American coal reserves can be expected to last more than 500 years."

Of this, Bartlett said:

> *This is one of the most dangerous statements in the literature. It's dangerous because it's true. It isn't the truth that makes it dangerous, the danger lies in the fact that people take the sentence apart: they just say coal will last 500 years. They forget the caveat with which the sentence started. Now, what were those opening words? "At current levels." What does that mean? That means if—and only if—we maintain zero growth of coal production.*[12]

He goes on to note that even the Department of Energy itself admits that perhaps half the coal reserves aren't recoverable, immediately dropping the estimate to 250 years. If we do that and assume that coal production increases at the same rate that it has for the past 20 years, then the known reserves will last for between 72 and 94 years; within the life expectancy of children born today. In terms of outlook, what's the difference between 250 years of coal left and 72 years? In a word, everything.

Coal is being used less and less often in places where natural gas can be substituted for the generation of electricity. Natural gas is clean and burns without making a lot of pollution; coal is the exact opposite. It's full of contaminants, makes a lot of CO_2, and leaves a lot of ash behind, which is a major disposal problem. So where and when it can be used, natural gas is preferred.

Despite all this, coal use has massively increased over the past 20 years, mainly because of China's use of coal and coal-fired power plants (see Figure 19.3).

The use of coal has been growing worldwide at very fast rates, largely driven by China but increasingly also by the base growth of power needs in other countries, principally also India, Asia, and Japan (post Fukushima). The world as a whole added anywhere between 50 and 100 net new coal-fired power plants in each and every year of the 2000s. The great energy crisis in Europe in 2022 saw Germany reopen mothballed brown coal (lignite) power plants against every better instinct of their green party, proving that when the chips are down, humans will use whatever energy they have.

Coal production

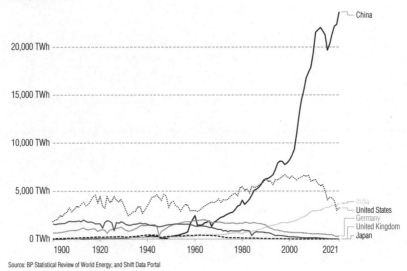

Source: BP Statistical Review of World Energy; and Shift Data Portal

FIGURE 19.3   Coal Use

In keeping with the idea that the United States has simply outsourced its dirty coal-based manufacturing to China, we see that shortly after China's coal use skyrocketed, the United States' own use began to decline.

Source: **OurWorldInData.org**.

As is true for all other energy sources and minerals and ores, the easiest to get to and best grades of coal were gone after and gotten first.

This brings us to the wrinkle in the coal story. Coal comes in several different grades. The most desirable grade is shiny, hard, black anthracite coal. It yields the most heat when burned, has a low moisture content, and is highly valued in the steel-making industry. After anthracite comes bituminous coal, offering slightly less energy per pound of weight, and then subbituminous, and then finally something called lignite (a.k.a. "brown coal"), which is low-energy, high-moisture stuff that really has no use besides burning. Lignite also leaves behind a lot of coal ash once burned. This is the stuff that Germany has lots of left and is now burning.

Next let's look at the United States' history with mining coal, separated out by the different grades (see Figure 19.4)

Look at the line labeled "anthracite" in Figure 19.4 and you'll observe a steadily declining line, which indicates that less and less of the most desirable form of coal is being mined. The reason we aren't mining more anthracite isn't because we don't want to, it's because we *can't*. It doesn't exist anymore and is pretty much all gone. Our entire "bank account" of anthracite, formed

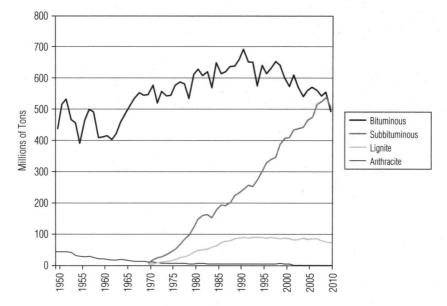

FIGURE 19.4   Coal Production by Grade

Source: Energy Information Administration.

over hundreds of millions of years, has been largely exhausted in a span of about 100 years.

Hundreds of millions of years to form; roughly a hundred years to consume. The point bears repeating: *When it's gone, it's gone.* You can't burn the same lump of coal twice. As with oil, more and more was extracted, and then, due to geological realities, less and less could be extracted.

Quite naturally, after anthracite went into decline, efforts then centered on to mining the next-best stuff—bituminous coal—and in Figure 19.4 we observe that a peak in the production of bituminous coal was hit in 1990. Was this because coal companies lost interest in the next-best grade of coal? Hardly. It simply meant we started to run out of that grade, too. Naturally, we then moved on to the next-best grade after that, subbituminous coal, which we see making up the difference to allow U.S. domestic production of coal to continue steadily growing. Most recently, lignite has been getting into the game, although we shouldn't expect to see lignite production really take off before the production of subbituminous coal peaks, which it someday will.

Now, here's the really interesting part. Remember when I said the heat content, or available free energy, of coal got progressively worse with each grade? If we plot the total energy content of the coal mined, instead of the tonnage, we get a very different picture (see Figure 19.5).

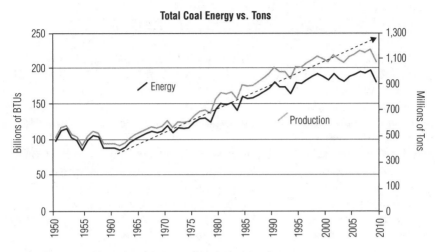

FIGURE 19.5   Plot of Coal Tonnage versus Coal Energy

Source: Energy Information Administration.

Where the tonnage has been moving up at a nice, steady rate of 2% per year, we find that the total energy content of mined coal leveled off around 1990 and has gone up by exactly zero percent since then. This implies that the United States is using more energy and spending more money to produce *more tons* of coal, but is essentially getting *less energy* back per ton for its troubles.

This finding mirrors the results of a 2010 study performed by Patzek and Croft, which determined that the net free energy from coal mined at all existing mining operations is nearing a permanent peak, possibly as early as 2011.[13] It's important to note that the study did not claim that the tons of coal mined will peak in 2011, but rather that the total *net energy* from those mined tons will hit a peak. This study wasn't about the *quantity* of coal that will be mined (or amount), but its *quality* (or net free energy).

After the peak, there will be slightly less and less available net free energy from coal. Of course, this shouldn't surprise anyone, because it's simply the story of extraction of a natural resource. Get the best stuff first, save the hard, poor-quality stuff for later. The highest grades of the most-accessible coal were exploited first, leaving the less-energy-dense, less-useful, and less-accessible reserves for later.

Despite a lot of column inches devoted to the idea that "coal is dead," I've yet to find any sign of that except for a downtick in the use of coal that is either completely tied to the price of natural gas (United States) or to a very temporary green ideal that people decided to give a try (Germany).

The Alternatives—Solar and Wind

Let me begin by stating, unequivocally that I am a big fan of alternative energy. Love it! I want to see more of it, a lot more. Solar, wind, tidal, geothermal, hydrogen and liquid ammonia to store it all, batteries, you name it, I am for it.

But it can't save the day. Yes, it has an important role to play at the edges, but it cannot be center stage. Yet.

When people think of alternative energy, they are primarily talking about means of making electricity from the sun, wind, or waves. Sometimes hydro gets lumped in there, but we're going to keep it out. It's an old, tried-and-true technology and there really isn't a lot of room for it to expand, given the limited number of viable river locations. It's vital and has a role, it's just a very different story from the so-called "renewables."

Again, "renewables" is in quotation marks because they require constant maintenance and eventual replacement and we have exactly zero examples of renewables creating the energy for their own replacement. If I were in charge, we'd have already run that experiment. I'd sign up a willing mid-sized city and give it a huge subsidy in terms of having all of its renewable energy wants completely supplied with a hefty margin to spare. But the deal would be that it's a one-time thing and they'd be responsible for 100% recreating and replacing their alternative energy supplies using *only* the power from those renewables. Best guess? There'd be a lot of failures and learnings along that path, but then we'd at least know what we were up against.

One of the current fads of thinking is electric cars, Teslas and their like. A lot of people seem to have placed a lot of their emotional health and future well-being on the idea that we can simply switch over and begin ferrying ourselves about on a transportation network running on electricity.

Currently, we're effectively nowhere in that story, the constant barrage of headlines to the contrary. Lawrence Livermore Laboratories each year puts out this amazing flowchart of energy consumption in the United States. It's a work of art (Figure 19.6).

Each block to the far left is a source of energy. The chart is in "quads," which is quadrillions of BTUs. Some of those sources get converted into electricity (next box to the right), and that electricity plus the other energy sources get used directly by residential, commercial, and industrial users and for transportation. The final boxes to the right show how much of that energy went toward performing useful work and how much was lost to the universe as waste heat (a.k.a. "rejected energy").

There's a line on there I want to draw your attention to and I know it's probably too fine to see so I've taken the liberty of blowing up a portion of that flowchart (Figure 19.7).

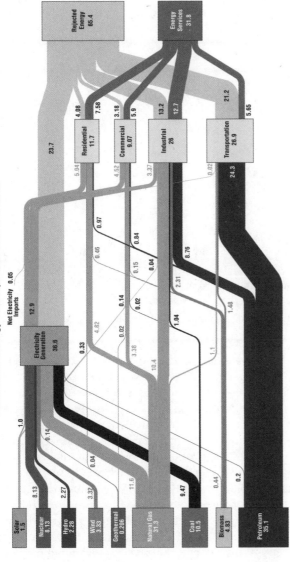

FIGURE 19.6 Energy Flow Diagram for the United States, 2021

Sources of energy are on the far left. The end uses (included "rejected energy," which is mainly waste heat) are on the far right.

Source: Lawrence Livermore National Laboratory and the DOE.

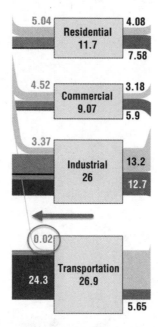

FIGURE 19.7   Zoomed-in Energy Flow Diagram for the United States, 2021

See that tiny line circled with the arrow pointing at it? That's how much of the total energy mix electrified transportation consumes. It's nowhere near being anything more than a curiosity. Someday perhaps, but not yet.

Source: Lawrence Livermore National Laboratory and the DOE.

See the arrow and the circle? Those are indicating the total amount of electricity in the United States that goes toward transportation. It stands at a tiny 0.02 quads out of 26.9 quads used for transportation and 97.3 quads of total energy use. For starters, electrical transportation is only 1/1345th of the total amount used for transportation. So, effectively it's a rounding error at present. Second, even if somehow 100% of all transportation could be electrified, that only takes care of 28% of current energy consumption. And even with that, the electricity still has to come from somewhere.

Look, I have an electric bicycle and I love it. Everyone should get one. I'll get a hybrid car with great range on my next vehicle purchase, but I am realistic about these efforts. They exist at the margins and are not yet ready for prime time. I'd feel entirely better about all this if the United States had gotten quite serious about electric transport and renewables and started in earnest about the time Jimmy Carter doffed a sweater during a presidential fireside chat (in 1977).

That would have been well in advance of and safely distant from a peak in net oil energy, but that didn't happen and here we are. Time to hope for the best but prepare for something else.

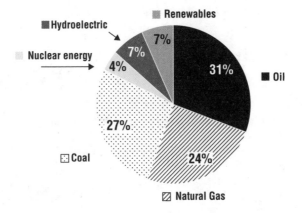

FIGURE 19.8   Global Energy Mix in 2021

Fossil fuels were 82% of total primary energy in 2021, and renewables just 7%, after trillions of dollars of investment.

Source: BP 2021 Statistical Review.

It's past time to face the facts honestly. According to the International Energy Agency's (IEA) 2022 World Energy Investment report, more than $4 trillion has been spent on renewable, or "clean," energy over the past decade and it now supplies 7% of the total of the world's primary energy generation (see Figure 19.8).

While 7% is a great achievement, we have to place it in context. No country can generate sufficient electricity from wind and solar to reliably power their country, even when coupled to some form of battery storage. Wind and solar are intermittent. Sometimes it's not windy, and sometimes it's cloudy. The most advanced countries so far can store a few minutes of national power consumption in batteries. Battery technology is not quite yet ready to plug those gaps for more than a few minutes at a time.

Even after decades of investing in solar and wind and other forms of clean energy, and after lots of gnashing of teeth and emotions expended on the matter, the reality of our use of fossil fuels over time is shown in Figure 19.9.

The problem with electricity is that it needs to be constantly supplied to be useful, especially to noninterruptible processes such as those found in hospitals and manufacturing. If we could ever find a convenient large-scale way to store electricity, it would certainly help, but so far success has eluded us in this matter. Again, if I could wave a magic-policy wand I'd put an enormous amount of national and global resources into the advance of batteries. The biggest game-changer out there isn't to be found in developing some new energy source, but in figuring out how to store electrical energy more effectively. If we could store electricity better, a host of issues would be immediately resolved.

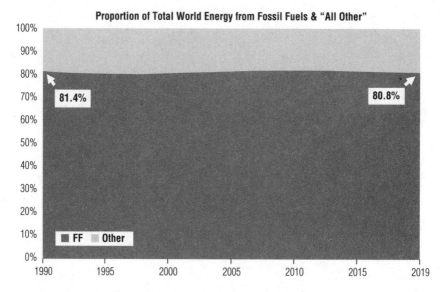

FIGURE 19.9   Fossil Fuel Use as a Percentage of Total

Fossil fuels were 81.4% of total primary energy in 1990 and after 30 years of aggressive clean energy investment they are . . . 80.8%.

Source: BP 2021 Statistical Review.

Right now, it's sad to say, most batteries in use are little changed in design from the one invented by Alessandro Volta in 1800. If ever there were an area that deserved a massive government investment, electrical storage would be it.

The other point to make here is that as of 2021, 95% of all energy used to transport things within and across the global economy was supplied by petroleum-derived liquid fuels. Even if we obtained massive amounts of electricity from alternative sources and figured out how to store it effectively, we'd still have to retrofit our entire transportation fleet to run on electricity. While this could certainly be done by a properly motivated society, the issues of time, scale, and cost of such an elaborate undertaking will remain significant foes.

Biofuels

Biofuels, such as ethanol and biodiesel, were both initially presented as viable energy sources and ecologically protective products. This introduction turned out to be both overly optimistic and flat-out wrong. The net energy returns from corn-based ethanol is a paltry 1.3, give or take a little, and requires the constant and unsustainable application of fertilizers and other industrial interventions to achieve the desired yields. If the United States were to try to completely replace its oil imports with corn ethanol, it would require nearly 550 million acres of farmland to be put to use,[14] representing 125% of all the cropland in the United States (which totals ~440 million acres). Anything that requires more than 100% of your arable land is not a viable solution.

In Europe, where a lot of biofuels are used, concerns have mounted about the destructive practices associated with such enterprises as Indonesian palm oil plantations, resulting in significant and legitimate controversy on ecological grounds. It turns out that the way the Indonesians produce the palm oil is to grow palm trees on peat bogs, which has the unfortunate result of both destroying sensitive ecologies and liberating more CO_2 than if oil alone had been burned.[15]

Where people initially thought biofuels represented a "green" alternative with the lowest (if any) impacts, now they are more aware of the quite significant environmental costs of biofuels that sometimes even exceed those of fossil fuels. We may someday discover a free lunch, but so far biofuels are not it, at least not at the scale required to run a global industrial society.

On another front, every year there are promising press releases made by the algal biodiesel[16] proponents, but I'm beginning to suspect that industry has got more cheerleaders than actual prospects. But as pleasing as the early signs are from this promising technology, here in 2022, we might note that virtually zero algal biodiesel is yet on the market, meaning an enormous build-out and scale-up of this technology will be required for it to have any meaningful impact. Again, there's a world of difference, and usually several decades, between the birth of an idea and full-scale implementation and adoption.

Here's how the alternatives break down:

- **Time:** Decades. Achieving even modest percentage footholds in our macro energy-use profiles will require a colossal investment. But it needs doing and should be done with all possible haste.
- **Scale:** Absolutely massive. Alternative energy technologies relying on wind, waves, or sun have extremely low (read: unfavorable) "energy densities," meaning that instead of installing a single power plant, thousands of individual units have to be installed over a much larger area. To simply construct the factories needed to build wind, solar, and other equipment will be a significant undertaking. Serious questions remain as to whether sufficient rare resources exist to build all the panels and windmills using current technologies.
- **Cost:** Hundreds of trillions of dollars, and they may never be stable enough to form the core of our energy future. But still, these investments should be made. Maybe somebody will make a fantastic battery discovery.

Natural Gas

Of all of the potential alternative fuels, natural gas is best suited to become a "bridge fuel" we can use to transition into a new future of less energy. Recent advances in shale bed drilling have opened up vast new supplies of natural gas.

If the reserve numbers are to be believed, there is ample supply of natural gas to "fund" a transition period. Of course, we'd have to tap that account wisely and preferentially use whatever there is to build a more resilient and efficient energy infrastructure, not waste it trying to increase retail sales and other forms of consumption. The EROEI is very high for gas wells, believed to be somewhere over 30.[17]

However, if we're seriously and credibly going to use natural gas, then we have to immediately begin the enormous task of retrofitting our energy and transportation infrastructure to use it. Cars will have to be modified, new natural gas fuel tanks must be installed, service stations will need new refueling equipment and storage tanks, pipelines will have to be built, and so on. However, converting a traditional internal combustion engine to run on natural gas is a snap compared to an electric vehicle that has to be built anew.

As before, there are issues of time, scale, and cost to be considered if we want to credibly exploit natural gas as a meaningful replacement for oil. It's certainly possible we can make the switch, but here in 2022, there is no sign that any such plans are even being considered, let alone approaching a scale of implementation that matches the urgency of the situation.

Yes, we could move toward natural gas as a prime energy source. But to do so, we would have to make the shift within a single decade, and no major energy transition has ever been accomplished in that short of a period of time. Is this possible? Sure, anything is possible. Is it probable? Not if we leave it up to "the markets," which seem to remain blissfully unaware of Peak Oil even as we have already passed the peak of conventional oil and appear ready to pass a peak of all types of oil in a frightfully short span of time.

I won't get excited by the prospect of a transition to natural gas until I hear a U.S. president get on television and announce the equivalent of a World War II–era effort to sketch out the predicament and dedicate massive resources to make it happen.

If there was one area where we might want to pressure our elected officials to support one energy transition over another, it would be for natural gas over corn-based ethanol. Hands down, natural gas is the winner due to its massively higher EROEI. Unless we get serious about making this transition, and soon, there's not much hope that natural gas will ever do more than play "catch up" with a receding oil horizon.

Hydrogen

Hydrogen definitely has a role to play, but it won't become the central role. Full disclosure, I am keen to place some of my own personal investment dollars into hydrogen technologies but haven't yet, as of this writing.

Hydrogen cannot play the central role because it is not a *source* of energy. There's no natural resource of hydrogen lying about to exploit. It is extremely reactive with oxygen (making water + energy + heat in the process). Any build-up of hydrogen in a given area creates an explosion risk, as two of the Fukushima reactor buildings, or the *Hindenburg*, can attest.

Hydrogen is more accurately described as a battery. Other sources of energy are used to make hydrogen, with large process losses along the way. The energy tax applied costs about 20–40% of the initial energy to create the hydrogen, and then another 40% energy tax when hydrogen energy is used for work. The general rule of thumb is that you will have to use two units of energy to get one back out of hydrogen.

The best of the hydrogen reactions splits water using surplus electricity from a hydro dam or wind, wave, or solar installation. Sometimes that surplus energy will otherwise be wasted, so getting a 1:2 return out of it is better than a 0:2.

Next best would be stripping hydrogen off of natural gas—not a very good idea at all because methane is already a wonderful fuel and we'd be best off getting all the energy we can out of it by simply using it directly.

Worst of all, we would be burning coal to make electricity to make hydrogen. That would basically just be spinning our wheels and wasting energy, because every stage of every process loses or loses some energy. It's just how things work.

Advances are being made almost daily in the field of splitting water, with some great progress being made in the efficiency of the electrolyzer, fuel cells, and storage and transport.

This is an area of great promise, as it solves that battery problem we discussed earlier. Hydrogen is a battery, a great one, but it has a tendency to be explosive so there's quite a bit of materials science and handling/processes to work out, which could take many years to perfect and broadly introduce to the world.

But the question about hydrogen and the role it will ultimately play rests on the source of the energy we will use to create the hydrogen. As outlined earlier, we cannot afford to lose 50% of the energy from clean energy sources because those intermittent and decidedly "nondense" energy sources are already struggling to provide high single-digit percentages of our total energy mix. If we're going to get serious about using hydrogen, the answer, which many won't like, is to use the output from nuclear reactors to split water to make hydrogen.

This is a war for our future, folks, and it's time to get serious.

Conclusion

Together, nuclear, coal, natural gas, and the clean-energy alternatives will definitely play a role in our energy future. But none is the energy savior some are hoping for (or even counting on). Perhaps, if we had started transitioning to these clean energy alternatives 20 or even 40 years ago, but at the current stage of development and scale, none of them is ready to take over the many roles of oil and, besides, nothing can provide exponentially more energy forever. That is just the basic reality of living on a finite planet with finite resources. So, one way or another, we'd have to figure out how to cure our addiction to growth, and that begins with replacing our system of money with a new one that isn't based on perpetual exponential growth.

Unfortunately, we did not even begin *mentally* transitioning away from oil in the decades before its imminent peak, let alone structurally or economically. In order to facilitate any kind of soft landing, several decades of preparation would have been required, given the realities of time, scale, and cost involved.

The International Energy Agency (IEA) dutifully put together a clean energy transition plan in 2021 detailing a "roadmap" for getting to net-zero carbon by 2050. To do this, we "only" have to (partial list only):

- Have no additional coal-fired plants approved after 2021.
- No new oil or gas field approved after 2022.
- Have most new clean technologies demonstrated at scale for heavy industry.
- Have 60% of all car sales be electric only by 2030.
- Have 1 TW of solar and wind installed per year by 2030.
- Have 50% of all heavy trucks sold be all electric by 2035.
- Have no more internal combustion engine (ICE) vehicles sold after 2035.

There are many more things on the list, but you get the idea. These things are simply not possible without the world governments coming together and all of society rededicating itself to the energy transition project as if our very lives depended on doing this.

We might, but the signs aren't looking very hopeful, so it only makes sense for prudent people to begin making other plans. You know, just in case.

The implications of this are profound. The economy you and I have come to know and love—the one predicated on a constant flow of ever-increasing quantities of energy—will have to operate on less energy. Even though having a few percent less energy instead of a few percent more sounds relatively minor, for an intertwined set of economic, financial, and monetary systems that are all based on perpetual exponential growth, the potential impacts are enormous.

CHAPTER 20

Why Technology Can't Fix This

B y now, some of you are certainly thinking that I've seriously underestimated the role technology and innovation will play in our future. Perhaps I have, but my background as a scientist keeps intruding into my optimism about the ability of technology to solve the predicaments we face.

In truth, I love technology and what it has brought us over the past centuries and will bring us in the future. I will stand up and applaud new discoveries and new advances as loudly as anyone when they are rolled out and deployed. But we need to be clear-eyed about what technology *can* do and, most importantly, what it *can't* do.

Fact 1: Technology Does Not Create Energy

Technology can help us do things more efficiently and effectively than in the past, and it can help us do far more with less. It can entertain and connect us in ways that we couldn't have conceived of only a decade ago. It can boost productivity. It can help us transform and use energy through innovative applications. It allows us to connect instantly with each other in new and exciting ways. But one thing it cannot do is *create* energy.

Energy can neither be created nor destroyed. So says the First Law of Thermodynamics. Energy can only be transformed from one form to another, such as when coal is turned into electricity, which becomes the cold air blown into a dentist's office in summer. Someday, perhaps and hopefully soon, fusion technology will create more energy than it uses. The magic goal line is to be above "unity," meaning that one or more units of energy are coming out for every unit of energy that went in. While in a narrow sense fusion has come close, for a fraction of a second here and there, the energy cost of building the machine, the people who work on it, or the spider web of suppliers who all have to be in place to manufacture the components has never been included in those calculations. Fusion scientists are getting closer all the time, but they are not anywhere close to a marketable working device here in late 2022.

Energy has certainly been *transformed* in quite brilliant ways, but the final accounting is always the same: Just as much energy exists afterwards as before the transformation; it's just that some of the energy is now lost to entropy, the form of diffuse heat that is useless for performing any more work.

This is where the Second Law of Thermodynamics comes in. It governs what happens to energy when it's transformed: Every transformation always loses at least a little energy (and sometimes quite a lot) in the form of diffuse heat.

Diffuse heat is the tax the universe places on all energy transactions. There's nothing wrong with diffuse heat—those of us in the northern United States happen to love it in our offices in February—it's just that diffuse heat cannot perform any work, and it's the work energy performs that we're mainly after. It bears repeating: *Every single time we convert energy from one form to another, we lose some of the initial energy content to the universe in the form of heat.*

For example, we might burn coal to turn into electricity, which we then use to split water so that we can capture and use hydrogen. Following this same set of transformations using the Second Law of Thermodynamics as our guide, we get the following:

1. When that coal is burned, about 40% of the energy it initially contained goes toward turning the electrical turbines, but 60% of its energy is lost to the universe as waste heat.

2. The electricity travels to the site where the water will be split, losing 7% of its energy along the way in the form of nicely warmed transmission lines that gently radiate their heat into the universe.

3. The electrolysis is performed, splitting water into oxygen and hydrogen, with 80% of the energy in the electricity captured in the form of pure hydrogen and a final 20% lost as heat.

At every step, the universe demanded and received its tax in the form of diffuse heat. In this example, the final efficiency of converting coal into electricity and then hydrogen is 30%: $0.40 \times 0.93 \times 0.80 = 30$. In other words, the act of converting coal to hydrogen loses 70% of the energy to the universe. These universal energy losses are as unavoidable as death and taxes.

The universe always tends toward randomness as it ceaselessly strives toward its goal of someday reaching one very average and uniform temperature. This is the process of entropy described in the Second Law of

Thermodynamics. Entropy represents the amount of energy in a system that is no longer available for doing any work. At each stage of our conversion of coal into hydrogen, entropy (randomness) increases. Entropy, then, is the name of the tax that the universe places on all energy transformations.

Entropy is the reason your coffee cup starts hot and gets cold, but never starts warm and gets hotter all on its own. Cold molecules are slower-moving, closer together, and more orderly than heated molecules. They have less entropy than warmer molecules. It is the rule of the universe that high entropy always runs toward low entropy and never the opposite, just as running water always heads toward the sea. All molecules with higher disorder (heat energy) seek to share their wild exuberance with molecules that have less disorder, never the other way around. So, your coffee cup starts hot but grows cooler, until it has shared as much of its entropy as it can and becomes the same as the room temperature. If entropy ever ran in reverse, you'd be as surprised as if you saw a river flowing uphill or a jumbled pile of books fly up onto a shelf in perfect alphabetical order.

The second law states that as we transform energy, we always start with a concentrated form, like diesel fuel or a stick of wood, and after we've transformed it into something else, we're left with whatever work that energy performed plus heat—random, diffuse heat. Our unavoidable entropy tax.

Think of the Second Law of Thermodynamics as a frictionless slide (meaning you can't shimmy back up the slope to a higher spot), where at the top of the slide is beautiful, wonderful, concentrated energy, and at the bottom is diffuse heat. At the top of the slide, we might put diesel fuel and at the bottom we might put a plowed field and a hot engine. Once diesel has taken its one-way trip down that slide, whatever it did is all it's ever going to do.

When energy takes a trip down that frictionless slide, it's a one-way trip. Water never flows uphill and burned hydrocarbons never magically reform themselves out of exhaust fumes. Every form of energy gets only one turn on the slide.

Given this, I like to think of the concentrated energy we have been given as a one-time free gift of energy perched at the top of a frictionless slide. Our choice is whether we're going to do something truly useful with that energy when we push it down the slide, or simply turn as much of it as we can into useless heat as fast as possible. Either way, we only get to do it once.

In all of history never, not once, have we observed the law of entropy violated. If we did, it would be the most spectacular news in scientific (and human) history, and many people would scour the findings with great excitement to be sure they were true.

Nearly every year, someone claims they've invented a perpetual motion machine that produces more energy than it consumes. Without fail, these claims make a big splash and then quietly disappear within a few months, never to be heard from again. The inventors of these magical devices demonstrate a remarkable ability to secure gullible media interest, and sometimes even deep-pocketed investors, but not one of them in all of history ever produced a surplus-energy-perpetual-motion machine that actually works as claimed.

If you find the Second Law of Thermodynamics a bit esoteric and want to observe a more direct and observable law of nature that has also never been violated, consider the law of gravity. Not once has anything dropped on Earth ever floated upward instead of accelerating downward.

Even our most spectacular technology has not found a way around gravity. If we could just defeat that one stubborn law, then perpetual motion would be ours as we could float large objects higher and capture their energy on the way back down.

The latest high-tech gizmos may intrigue and impress us, but they are as firmly straitjacketed by the laws of energy and entropy as you are glued to the earth by gravity.

Our first step toward understanding the limits of technology is to fully appreciate that technology can find, produce, and transform energy, but it cannot create it. Once we really understand that fact, we're in a better position to appreciate its offerings and shortcomings.

Fact 2: Transforming Energy Is Expensive

Once energy has taken the trip all the way to the bottom of our frictionless slide, it's given up all it can to perform useful work. Technology may permit us to push things back up the slide, but only at an energy cost. By now, you should be guessing that this cost is "diffuse heat." Any time we decide to concentrate a form of energy, we lose some energy to heat.

For example, you may have heard about making fuel oil from the air. The Navy announced such a racket to great fanfare in 2021 which sounded swell, but the devil was in the details. By "air" they meant CO_2 in the air, a molecule all the way at the bottom of our frictionless slide, with nowhere further to fall. At great energetic expense, the Navy process first split the carbon and with further effort, hydrogen was split from water, and finally with even more effort the carbon and the hydrogen were chemically reacted to create a long-chain hydrocarbon resembling jet fuel. The catch? Where they might have gotten three units of useful work energy out of the jet fuel, they had to spend five units to create it. So, a net loss. Maybe not a deal breaker if you are the Navy and have idling onboard nuclear reactors and need jet fuel. But it wasn't a means of magically extracting jet fuel from the atmosphere, as many articles ignorantly hinted.

Put another way, if we want to create one unit of concentrated energy, we will have to start with *more than one unit* of less concentrated (but still useful) energy, with the extra balance representing the portion that will be "donated" to the universe as heat. Pushing things back up the slide is possible, but only if we're willing to pay.

Concentrating energy takes energy. More has to be put in than you get back out.

This is why the much-advertised "hydrogen economy" is not a solution to the predicament of not having enough energy. Hydrogen is energy-expensive to make (because water too is at the bottom of the frictionless slide), and there's simply no way to make it without using and losing energy along the way. We might make it from natural gas, or from electricity, but we lose energy and create waste heat with every step of the conversion process. The more hydrogen we make, the less energy we have. Hydrogen might still make a lot of sense economically and/or politically and could be a huge benefit where and when too much energy is being created to otherwise use (as often happens with wind farms when it's especially windy out).

There's nothing that technology can do to circumvent this reality. Transforming energy is expensive; it costs energy. Heat is lost, the entropy tax is unavoidable. This isn't techno-pessimism—it's the law: the Second Law of Thermodynamics, to be exact. The universe always applies its tax.

Fact 3: Energy Transitions Take Time

If Peak Oil arrives on or before 2030, as seems likely at the time of this writing, then very few years remain to try and engineer some sort of a smooth transition to alternative and/or clean energy sources. Energy transitions take time—a lot of time—and that is a function not so much of technology, but of human behavior and the economics of already-deployed capital.

For example, note in Figure 20.1 that it took 60 long years after coal was introduced for it to claim just *half* the market share from biomass, even though it was a denser and hotter fuel source than biomass and therefore superior.

Oil is vastly superior to both biomass and coal, and yet it took 50 long years for oil to equal coal's energy output. After 80 years of sustained growth, natural gas has yet to equal either of those energy sources, but it is rapidly making up for lost time.

The point here is that these transitions took decades, typically five or more, to happen. The reason is because even with favorable market forces it takes time to swap out old capital based on a prior form of energy and to replace it with a new energy. Sailing ships weren't instantly abandoned when steamers came along, they were used to the very end of their useful life. Steam

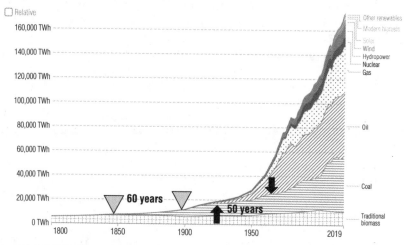

Global primary energy consumption by source

Primary energy is calculated based on the "substitution method" which takes account of the inefficiencies in fossil fuel production by converting non-fossil energy into the energy inputs required if they had the same conversion losses as fossil fuels.

Source: Vaclav Smil (2017) & BP Statistical Review of World Energy

FIGURE 20.1 Energy Transitions Take Time

The gray textured triangles mark the appearance of coal and indicate that it took 60 years for coal to become half of the energy mix. The black arrows mark the appearance of oil and that it took a full 50 years for it to become one-third of the energy mix.

Source: **OurWorldInData.org**.

locomotives were slowly replaced by diesel locomotives as they aged out. This is rational and logical, and we should expect the same measured pace of adoption to be true for every energy transition. They take time.

In other words, even if clean energy were vastly superior and demanded by "market forces," we should still expect that it would take 50 to 60 years for those to get to just one-third of the total energy mix.

At the pace of renewable installations that occurred between 2015 and 2020, estimates of the length of the energy transition ranged from 30 years to more than 400 years.[1]

Why Technology Can't Fix This

Technology can help us exploit what energy we do have more cleanly, cheaply, and more efficiently, but, as I said, it cannot create energy. And when we do transform energy, we lose energy to the universe along the way in the form of diffuse heat.

Therefore, it's appropriate to view the fossil fuel stores of the earth as if it were a gigantic pile of food that our species can only eat once and when we do, it will be gone—a once-in-a-species bequeathment to use however it saw fit. Our species decided to grow into it exponentially and use it up as fast as possible.

Because economic order, complexity, and growth all require energy, and because our original allotment of energy cannot be increased by technology, technology alone cannot "fix" the predicament of needing more energy than we have. Technology has an enormous role to play in helping us to use our energy more wisely and with greater efficiency and utility, but these efforts will only somewhat delay the eventual day when our giant pile of free food is gone. At this pace, at some future point in time, we'll once again be on a daily energy budget supplied by sun.

Between here and there, it's up to us to decide what to do with this once-in-a-species energy bonanza. Shall we increase our prosperity by creating enduring works of architecture and lavishly funding our best and brightest minds to stretch the limits of what's possible? Or shall we use energy's one trip down the frictionless slide merely to promote the most rapid economic growth and ostentatious consumption?

Both are choices we could make, and in either case, nature will be indifferent. It will carry on whether we use up our energy stores wisely and elegantly, or squander them on trivial pursuits.

Technology is the prevailing religion of the era, and far too many people place a lot of faith in the idea that technology will solve any and all problems of the future. Perhaps, but then again perhaps not.

PART V

Environment

CHAPTER 21

Minerals

Gone with the Wind

These next few chapters won't be a grim recitation of the various environmental stresses and issues that currently plague the world, though they are numerous and distressing.

There are many incredibly detailed sources chronicling the depletion and mismanagement of the earth's resources, perhaps none better than Lester Brown's *Plan B* series (currently in version 4.0) from the World Watch Institute. I would direct all interested readers to that fine work.

Instead, we're going to tell a story around our dependence on and use of natural resources, especially what are called nonrenewable natural resources such as hard rock ores. That story, when coupled with the energy story, illustrates just how unsustainable our entire economic reality is.

I do not intend to diminish the importance of environmental issues, or to intentionally or unintentionally subjugate them to money and the economy. Rather, the main point to which I adhere is this: *The most immediate "environmental" impact we will feel in our own lives will be transmitted to us **first** via the economy.* If the economy fails us, then we will lack the resources to protect and preserve the environment anyway, as we will be worrying about survival, which inevitably trumps all other considerations. We should strive to stabilize our condition first, and then set about repairing what we can.

Quantity and Quality (Again)

The story of energy basically boils down to two "Qs," quantity and quality. We noted that oil global discoveries peaked in 1964, which means that someday, inevitably, the *quantity* (amount) of oil coming out of the ground will someday peak as well. Discoveries precede output. A peak in the former indicates a peak in the latter.

Further, we noted that the issue isn't just how *much* energy is coming out of the ground; it's also the *quality* of that energy, with quality being an expression for the net free energy returned from those exploration and development activities.

This same story of quantity and quality applies to all other mineral resources, as well as any other primary sources of wealth that come from the earth. Our economy as we know it is an industrial economy that really only began in earnest when we started harnessing the energy of coal to do work. The industrial economy began about 150 years ago, during which time the world has undergone a truly breathtaking transformation—but not all the good kind.

Where abundant mineral resources were once lying around for the taking, now every last major deposit has been mapped, and lesser and lesser grades of ores are being pursued at higher and higher costs, both energetic and monetary.

One hundred and fifty years, it should be noted, is a relative blink of an eye. When we think about the fact that Cleopatra was born closer in time to the launching of the space shuttle than to the building of the Great Pyramids of Cheops,[1] suddenly 150 years doesn't seem like all that much time. It's not, really, and that's the point. And yet, even after this relatively brief but intense burst of activity, we're already running out of high-quality mineral ores.

One of my favorite images is a grainy black-and-white 1800s-era photo showing two dapper gentlemen reclining on what appears to be a large rock in a streambed. In fact, that "rock" happens to be an immense copper nugget, an enormously concentrated form of mineral wealth that was just sitting there in a stream, waiting to be discovered. Other copper nuggets were found scattered about the earth around the same time that copper wiring was coming into high demand.

Before long, all of the large copper nuggets were swept up and used, so smaller and smaller nuggets were pursued, until finally all of those were commercially depleted, too. Then people moved on to the highest-grade copper ores, beautiful blues and greens, which also were soon exhausted. And so on down the ore purity ladder we crept, exhausting the better plays before moving onto the next lower and less play. Those initial plays were brilliant copper plays, often with ore grades of 10% or more in purity.

In the United States, one of the largest copper mines is the Bingham Canyon Mine in Utah. It's 2.5 miles across, three-quarters of a mile deep, and used to be a rather sizeable hill that has since been hauled away, crushed, smelted, and transformed into a very large hole. The ore grade at Bingham Canyon is quite low, only 0.2% when all the waste rock is factored in. Now think of a hole in the ground that's nearly 4,000 feet deep and imagine trying to get the ore and waste rock up and out of that hole **without using gigantic diesel trucks**. Think of the energy involved in hoisting rocks and earth thousands of feet into the air just so that we can get at the remaining dregs of copper in the earth's crust.

Where our financial markets might tell us that this is a reasonable thing to do, perhaps because copper is at $5.00/pound, while diesel fuel is only at $4.85/gallon, it doesn't make a lot of sense on an energetic basis. Once we convert that highly concentrated diesel fuel into waste heat, humans will never be able to use that energy again to do anything else.

Perhaps bringing rocks up from 4,000 feet down so that we can extract a relatively tiny proportion of copper from them is really not the best use for that energy? Perhaps there are more pressing priorities, like rebuilding our soils, or insulating existing homes? This is one way financial markets can lead to perfectly rational *economic* decisions that also happen to be perfectly irrational *energetic* decisions.

The other point I want to be sure to communicate here is the stunning sense of pace in this story. From giant nuggets lying in streambeds to 0.2% ore grades in only 150 years. That's an astonishingly short amount of time and a very quick romp through ores that were deposited over hundreds of millions of years.

What about the next 150 years? What do we do for an encore? How about the next 150 years after *that*? When put in this context, it's sobering to consider just how fast the mineral wealth of the earth has been exploited and how relatively few years remain until all of the known deposits are completely exhausted.

Actually, that's an overstatement. The deposits will never be completely exhausted, as that would likely require far more energy than we actually have. As we recall from Chapter 16 (*Energy and the Economy*), one gallon of gas is equivalent to between 350 and 500 hours of human labor. How much is 350 to 500 hours of your labor worth to you? My prediction is that once petroleum energy begins to be priced at something closer to its intrinsic worth based on the work it can perform, which is vastly higher than a few bucks per gallon, most marginal mining activities will cease. We will never get around to removing those last few flecks of mineral wealth.

Instead of thinking of the dollars associated with chasing after 0.2% copper ore, I want you to think of the energy use, because those are what are going to shape the future.

Remember from the chapter on exponentials just how difficult it is to appreciate nonlinear curves? Another nonlinear curve relates to the amount of energy required to go after and produce metals and other minerals that must be extracted from depleting ore bodies. Figure 21.1 and Figure 21.2 illustrate the declining quality of mineral ores.

This is important; where 10 pounds of rock need to be mined and refined to get a pound of copper from 10% ore, it takes 500 pounds to get a single pound of copper from 0.02% ore. The energy required to blast, haul, crush,

Ore Grade	Pounds of Ore to Produce One Pound of Mineral
20%	5
10%	10
8%	13
6%	17
4%	25
2%	50
1%	100
0.70%	143
0.50%	200
0.30%	333
0.10%	1,000
0.08%	1,250
0.06%	1,667
0.04%	2,500
0.02%	5,000
0.01%	10,000

FIGURE 21.1   Ratios of Mined Ore to Produce One Pound of Mineral or Metal

and refine 500 pounds of ore is exponentially more than that required to do the same for 10 pounds of ore.

It's clear that the energy requirement of chasing after depleting ore bodies is very much a nonlinear story. Assuming the ore is coming from mines that are a similar depth and distance from the processing mill, each percent decrease in the ore concentration requires a full doubling of the amount of ore that is removed for processing to obtain the same amount of the desired material. This is ore that must be smashed or blasted away from surrounding material, transported, crushed, and refined. Every step is energy intensive.

One trait humans share with all animals is that we go after the easiest, highest-quality sources of materials first. That's just natural. You go after the lame impala before the healthy adults.

Those ores that are more concentrated and nearer to the surface (or markets) are preferentially exploited first. We tend to farm the best soils first, harvest the tallest trees, and go after the most concentrated ore bodies. It's a

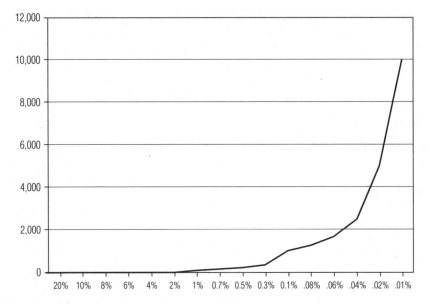

FIGURE 21.2   Pounds of Ore to Create One Pound of Refined Mineral

process called "high grading," and it simply means doing the obvious: using up the best and most convenient stuff before the other stuff. Which means that by the time we're chasing the less-attractive ores as a second order of business, there's a very good chance those ores are inconveniently located, perhaps deeper in the ground or in a more remote location, or both, and/or in more dilute form. Because of this, as we go forward, the energy required to chase the lesser ores will be even more than is implied by a simple chart comparing the ore percentages to processing amounts.

Quite simply, the key point here is that getting more and more minerals from depleting ore bodies in the future won't require just a little bit more energy, it will require exponentially more energy.

Economic Growth and Minerals

The economy, which I've attempted to convince you is due for a massive shake-up due to energy considerations alone, also depends on ever-increasing flows of materials running through it. That's what an exponentially increasing economy implies—more stuff in ever-increasing quantities. The predicament is that sooner or later this will no longer be possible, because there's a limit to all resources. Even the most pie-in-the-sky optimists can be made to admit that eventually there will be limits, although some cling fast to the belief that those limits are still very far off in the future, maybe even too far off to concern ourselves with at this time.

One of the favorite devices used by such optimists is to state that we have many remaining decades of resources x, y, and z "at current rates of consumption." The problem with that, as I hope you can now immediately appreciate, is that an exponential economy cannot be satisfied with "current rates of consumption" because that amounts to the same thing as saying "zero growth," which simply won't do!

Our particular type of economy is based on ever-increasing amounts of everything flowing through it. More money, more debt, more gasoline, more cars, more minerals, more profits, more buildings, more clothes, more and more of everything.

So, if you ever hear the phrase "at current rates of consumption" in regard to a nonrenewable natural resource, this is a sure sign the person wielding the statistics has painted an erroneously rosy picture of that resource, either accidentally or on purpose.

To illustrate the importance of mineral wealth to economic growth, consider what goes into our cars and trucks. Automobiles are a perfect starting point because mobility is extremely important to people everywhere on the globe. We can easily appreciate how economic growth translates into more cars on the road, and cars use up lots of different minerals in their construction and operation.

To manufacture a car or truck, the mineral elements that are shown in Figure 21.3 are needed.

A Tesla weighs 4,647 pounds and has a similarly long list of input materials. A Tesla Model S has:

- 410 pounds of aluminum
- 100 pounds of copper
- A 1,200-pound battery containing lithium cobalt, nickel, and aluminum
- Also, rubber, plastics, glass, steel (made with coking coal), titanium, boron, and computer chips

It's questionable whether enough lithium even exists to make all these vehicles, but it's a sure bet we're working our way through the easiest and cheapest lithium first. It has been calculated that 500,000 pounds of ore must be mined and processed to make the lithium for a single Tesla battery. Leaving aside the environmental impacts and monetary cost of such an activity, think of the energy required.

Even if we assume 100% recycling of the materials in a car or truck, electric or otherwise, one thing we can't get around is that each year, with economic growth, there are more cars and trucks plying the global highways

Metal/Element	Purpose	Pounds in Car
Steel (Iron Ore)	Frame mostly, engine	4,960
Petroleum	Plastics: body and interior, rubber tires, paint, fabrics, gas and lubricating oils	980
Aluminum	Also in the frame, lighter than steel	240
Quartz	Silica to make glass	170
Glass	Windows	85
Copper	Wiring, starter motor	70
Carbon	Used to make iron ore into steel, tires	46
Rubber	Tires	44
Silicon	Ceramic components	41
Lead (Galena)	Battery	24
Zinc	Galvanizing agent	18
Manganese	An alloy with steel that is resistant to wear in axles, pistons, crankshafts	17.6
Nickel	Stainless steel plating	9
Magnesium	Alloy used to strengthen aluminum	4.4
Sulfur	Used in battery	2
Asbestos	Brake pads	1.2
Molybdenum	Strengthens steel and lubricants	1
Vanadium	Used to form alloys that are fatigue-resistant	1
Oxygen	Combustion in engine	Varies
Antimony	Makes car upholstery fire resistant	Trace
Barium	Coat electrical conductors in the ignition system	Trace
Cadmium	Electrolytically deposited as a coating on metals to form a chemically resistant coating	Trace
Clays	Used to make spark plugs in engine	Trace
Cobalt	Makes thermally resistant alloys (superalloys)	Trace
Fluorospar	Used to manufacture aluminum, gasoline, and steel	Trace
Gallium	Mirrors, transistors, and LEDs	Trace
Gold	Electronics	Trace
Mica	Fills the shocks	Trace
Nitrogen	Ceramic materials (spark plugs) and in battery	Trace
Platinum	Catalytic Converter	Trace
Palladium	Catalytic Converter	Trace
Rhodium	Catalytic Converter	Trace
Strontium	Phosphorescent paint on dials	Trace
Tin	Solders	Trace
Titanium	Makes metallic alloys and substitutes for aluminum Paint, lacquers, plastics, rubber	Trace
Tungsten	Fliament of light bulbs, spark plug	Trace
Zirconium	Alloy of steel and glass, light bulb filaments	Trace

FIGURE 21.3   Types of Metal or Element (by Weight) in a Typical Automobile

Source: McLelland, "What Earth Materials Are in My Subaru?"[2]

than the previous year. As of 2019, there were 1.4 billion motor vehicles in the world.

More cars and trucks mean that more of those things in Figure 21.3 must be extracted from the earth. More copper, steel, aluminum, and everything else in that list must come out of the ground to be converted into vehicles. The same is true for cell phones, computers, televisions, and everything else that includes some form of mineral wealth.

For its part, the U.S. economy depends on the importation of 100% of its needs for 20 critical, economically important elements or minerals. It imports more than 50% for another 28.*

The implication of this is clear: The U.S. economy now requires more mineral wealth than can be secured from within its own borders, and in several cases, it has entirely depleted its natural endowment of mineral wealth after only 150 years of running its industrial economy.

The End of an Era

Several high-quality studies have already peered into the future of our known mineral resources and determined that some of them are now past peak, and several will be entirely exhausted within just a few decades. Maybe they're wrong and we've got 100 years left. But what then? What sort of a world are we leaving behind where every single high-quality resource has already been extracted and used up? Is this really the world we wish to leave behind?

It's startling to realize that nearly all of these mineral resources were in fully pristine, untouched condition just 150 years ago. Where the earth once spent hundreds of millions of years concentrating these ores into a relatively few seams and pockets around the globe, humans managed to eat through a significant quantity of those in only 150 years. But that, too, underplays the situation. The amounts of minerals extracted each year have been steadily climbing through time. If we assume a 2% rate of increase in yearly extraction, this would mean—using our handy Rule of 72—that world extraction and use of mineral resources will double every 36 years. Double! And then double again!! Remember, with each doubling, as much is consumed during that sole doubling period as in all of prior history combined.

Now would be a good time for a gut check—ask yourself if that seems either likely or doable. Heck, is it advisable even if it were doable? If, like me, your answer is, *No, this is neither likely nor doable*, then it makes sense to begin planning for a future that will be very different from today.

---

*Please refer to the Appendix for a list of the minerals that the United States must fully or partially import.

Reduce, Reuse, Recycle

There can be no doubt that an important response is the careful stewardship of our remaining resources. By reducing, reusing, and recycling our nonrenewable natural resources, we will be able to extend and hopefully blunt the day of reckoning. Unfortunately, however favorable or well-executed this strategy might be, it won't be sufficient to prevent seismic shifts in the superstructure of our economy.

However well-implemented, a strategy of reduce/reuse/recycle won't be able to mitigate any of the following:

- *The impact of the loss of materials for which no substitutes exist.* There are a variety of extremely critical rare elements for which no substitutes are known to exist for certain applications. Their loss will necessitate finding acceptable workarounds that may be less advantageous than the original—an example of technology going backward.

- *Materials that are combined or used in ways that prevent their easy extraction and reuse.* One of the many uses for cobalt is as an alloy material to make stainless steel. Once it is mixed in dilute amounts with the steel, it would take an enormous amount of energy to recover that cobalt to use it in a different way. In fact, economically and energetically speaking, it's really not an option; the cobalt in the steel is far too dilute, so in every practical sense, the cobalt is effectively locked into the steel. When mined potash is spread on a field in Iowa as fertilizer, and then washes down the Mississippi River and into the Gulf of Mexico, it's far too diluted to be recovered (although it's plenty concentrated to support algal blooms).

- *Materials lost through dispersion.* When steel rusts, it's essentially lost forever, because it's in too dilute a form to be economically recoverable. Over time, our activities have the effect of taking relatively concentrated ores, using a lot of energy to concentrate and purify them to exceptional levels, and then carefully spreading them evenly over the surface of the earth, rendering them forever unrecoverable.

Gone with the Wind

The bottom line is that our activities tend to disperse our mineral wealth in ways that often prevent their reclamation and reuse. In many cases this is a one-way trip that isn't amenable to recycling or reuse.

After (just) 150 years of industrialization, we can already see the end of several key mineral resources *just a few years or decades out.* And even these projections blithely assume the energy is there to complete the task of depleting the known reserves, an assumption I'm not willing to make.

With the depletion of certain key minerals, things will change, possibly dramatically. Am I saying that I expect the economy to come to a crashing halt if a key mineral is exhausted? No, absolutely not. But I am saying that it will no longer work the same way it did before, and that's what this book is about—alerting you to some seemingly quite obvious and predictable changes clearly headed our way.

CHAPTER 22

Soil

Thin, Thinner, Gone

In January 2009, an architect who'd arranged for me to speak in his community was driving me from San Francisco to an event in his hometown of Sonora, California. As we passed through some of the most fertile farmland I had ever seen, I remarked on the bounty I could sense just outside the glass as we drove by at 65 miles per hour. Row after row, field after field, dark soil beckoning now and again from freshly turned operations spoke of the immense agricultural treasure as we zoomed our way east.

Then, all of a sudden, the flat fields turned into row after row of neat, tidy houses, all squished together as if the prior 40 miles of flat expanse were irrelevant and space was suddenly hard to come by. "Hey, what's going on here?" I asked. He briefly dipped his head and brought it up to say, "I'm embarrassed for my profession. We should, of all professions, know better than to build on farmland, but there's no awareness yet in my colleagues of the tragedy that what you see represents."

This silent tragedy, converting rich soils into tract housing, is happening all across the United States and elsewhere in the world and is, again, driven by financial—not necessarily thoughtful—decisions.

Civilization has always grown up around and depended on the thin layer of soil that covers the earth, and we're as dependent on it today as we've ever been. Without soil, food won't grow. We would do well to remember that without primary wealth, there's no secondary wealth, and without *that*, nothing else really matters, certainly not your stocks and bonds.

Do We Heat or Do We Eat?

In 2010, a United Nations (UN) commission reported on the state of the world's food situation and made these statements:

. . . satisfying the expected food and feed demand will require a substantial increase of global food production of 70 percent by 2050.

Much of the natural resource base already in use worldwide shows worrying signs of degradation. Soil nutrient depletion, erosion, desertification, depletion of freshwater reserves, loss of tropical forest and biodiversity are clear indicators.[1]

One-tenth of the world's land mass is suitable for growing crops, while another four-tenths is only suitable as range land due to the thinness of the soil, steepness, dryness, or some combination of those factors. The remaining half of the world's landmass is unsuitable for any sort of food production at all. The UN report examined the issue of how we will manage to feed 9.5 billion people by 2050 (a 46% increase from 2010), given that virtually *all* the world's available farmland is already under production. Increased demand is expected to require an enormous increase in crop production.

Even under a circumstance of energy sufficiency, the math was questionable in 2010. By 2022, the core issue was laid bare by the European energy crisis that saw natural gas prices skyrocket by a factor of 10× in a few short months. The prospect of an imminent shortage roiled the European energy markets, upending decades of relative calm for both natural gas and electricity prices. In "perfect storm" fashion, a punishing drought limited both necessary river barge traffic and forced power plants to limit operations due to water levels that were too low and river temperatures that were too high, while France had forced shutdowns of roughly half of its vaunted nuclear power plants due to critical maintenance issues.

Faced with skyrocketing energy bills and a lot of uncertainty, governments were predictably slow to react, and by the time they had begun to fashion some economic relief packages in August 2022, 21 separate ammonia fertilizer factories in Europe had either shut down or severely curtailed operations. People who needed to heat their buildings were willing to pay a higher price for the scarce natural gas than the fertilizer producers setting up a strange choice: *Do we heat, or do we eat?*

Economically, it was not possible for the fertilizer plants to operate, so they shut down. If the governments of Europe had been functioning at all, they would have made sure that these plants remained open, as crop yields are exceptionally dependent on continuous fertilizer application. But they sat by and watched, and actually said very little publicly about the closures. The press too didn't quite manage to appreciate or convey the seriousness of the situation, remarking on the closures as if they were reporting on nail salons going out of business.

Europe in 2022/2023 was the first major test of a major industrialized continent facing an energy shortfall, and its official response and reactions were quite underwhelming and economically destructive. But it taught us one thing quite clearly: When faced with the prospect of cold citizens (due to a lack of gas for heating) and hungry citizens eventually facing vastly higher food prices, if not food shortages, politicians chose warmth over food. I predict they will make a more nuanced and different choice in the future after they are schooled in the importance of fertilizers to crop yields.

Puzzlingly, the summer of 2022 saw politicians in several major food-producing European countries actually target their farmers with punishing new rules and additional costs in the name of climate change. The Netherlands implemented new nitrogen reduction rules that sparked massive and sustained farmer protests. Italian, German, Polish, and Spanish farmers also joined in protesting both the new nitrogen rules and high fuel costs. It's something of a mystery as to why so many European governments decided that out of all the moments in history to make things tougher for farmers, 2022 was the year.

Whether this was due to sheer incompetence or reflected the inertia of policies crafted during very different and more abundant times we are left with the same conclusion: The government's actions made things worse. Was this intentional as some believe (a.k.a. The Great Reset and "Build Back Better"), or was it due to profound ignorance?

Hard to say—maybe it was a bit of both—but it does not bode well for our future chances of avoiding a disruptive set of outcomes. We need clear-eyed and rational decision making and leadership, not ignorance or veiled policies with vague aims that aren't well thought through or grounded in reality.

For now, because our global industrial agricultural practices are fully dependent on fertilizers—with most estimates saying that yields would plummet by 40% to as much as 100% if not for chemical fertilizers—any reductions in the use of fertilizers will have to accomplished very carefully with and a lot of planning and coordination.

The Important Difference Between Soil and Dirt

Our modern, industrial agriculture system feeds more people while employing fewer people than at any time in history. Even more remarkably, crop science has delivered ever-increasing yields on a per-acre basis at ever-lower costs. As impressive as this is, by now you probably won't be surprised to learn that such gains come with hidden costs. Life is always more complicated than it seems at first. One of the most important costs has been incurred by the soil itself.

There is an important distinction between soil and dirt made here:

Soil is alive. Dirt is dead. A single teaspoon of soil can contain billions of microscopic bacteria, fungi, protozoa and nematodes. A handful of the same soil will contain numerous earthworms, arthropods, and other visible crawling creatures. Healthy soil is a complex community of life and actually supports the most bio diverse ecosystem on the planet.

Why is it then, that much of the food from the conventional agricultural system is grown in dirt? The plants grown in this lifeless soil are dependent on fertilizer and biocide inputs, chemicals which further destroy water quality, soil health and nutritional content.[2]

In our quest to grow more food, more cheaply, on the same amount of land, year after year, we have been strip-mining the soil of its essential nutrients and qualities and converting it into lifeless dirt. What would happen if modern farming suddenly had to make do without fertilizers, pesticides/herbicides, and other petroleum inputs? Yields would fall, substantially, of that there's no doubt. Increased yields have less to do with better technology and understanding, and more to do with the forceful application of external energy, which is what fertilizers really represent. It takes energy to make ammonia—a **lot** of energy. It takes energy to mine and process phosphate rock from the very few places it exists naturally and ship it to and spread on fields across the globe. Ditto for potassium mineral fertilizers.

The real tragedy is that by converting rich, biologically active soil into lifeless dirt we grow poorer-quality foods with fewer nutrients in them, as it is the rich tapestry of soil microorganisms that liberates these nutrients. The plants feed the microorganisms by exuding sugars from their roots, and the microorganisms symbiotically feed the plants nutrients. Chemical fertilizers break that cycle and create dependency on their continued application—once again, at a tremendous energy cost to produce ship and apply. What happens when there's not enough energy to both fertilize fields and keep all our houses and buildings warm and/or cool?

Industrial agriculture is marvelously cost-effective, but also remarkably brittle. It completely depends on and is built around a perpetual inflow of chemical fertilizers to replace the nutrients that are stripped, as well as petrochemical inputs in the form of herbicides, fungicides, and pesticides to counteract the deleterious effects of soil sterilization and monocropping.

There's very little difference between Walmart and an industrial farm. Both are extremely cost-effective, and both are desperately fragile. If anything disrupts the just-in-time delivery systems around which their methods of profitability are built, either operation will experience profound difficulties. If there's a gap in the ability to deliver shipping containers from China to Walmart's operational distribution centers, wares rapidly vanish from the shelves. It may be a cost-effective way to do things, but it's not resilient.

Similarly, if an industrial farming operation is deprived of the chemical inputs required to enforce growth in its crops, yields will immediately decline. Various studies of the impact of fertilization have proven that anywhere from 40% to 100% gains in grain crop yields are dependent on the application of fertilizers.[3] Sufficient supplies of fossil fuel products are essential to the success of both of these ventures.

Exporting Nutrients

The United States exports some 80 million tons of agricultural products each year (primarily grains), which represent a massive amount of water, as we'll see in Chapter 23 (*Parched*), and vital nutrients that were mined (by the plant's roots) from the soils and shipped overseas. Without the nutrients being completely recycled back into the soils, the farmland quite rapidly becomes depleted of the vital elements plants use to support their biological functions and growth, and which our bodies use to promote health and vigor.

One puzzle you might have read about recently comes from the observation that plants that are grown and tested for their nutrient content some decades ago contained far more nutrients than plants harvested today. The quoted evidence below was assembled by Dr. Donald R. Davis and reveals the following patterns of depletion in food nutrition and soil nutrients:

- In wheat and barley, protein concentrations declined by 30–50% between the years 1938 and 1990.
- Likewise, a study of 45 corn varieties that were developed from 1920 to 2001, grown side by side, found that the concentrations of protein, oil, and three amino acids have all declined in the newer varieties.
- Six minerals have declined by 22–39% in 14 widely grown wheat varieties developed over the past 100 years.
- Official U.S. Department of Agriculture (USDA) nutrient data shows that the calcium content of broccoli averaged 12.9 milligrams per gram of dry weight in 1950, but only 4.4 milligrams per gram dry weight in 2003.[4]

There is no mystery to these results. If you constantly harvest minerals from the soil and then truck them away without replacing them, eventually the soil will become depleted and there will be less of those minerals available to plants.

In this sense, then, many farmers are in fact "mining" the soils upon which their livelihoods depend. Without closing that loop somehow and getting those nutrients *back* into the soils in measures equal to the rates at which they're harvested and transported away, the practice of farming on those soils is thoroughly unsustainable. Sooner or later, those soils will become utterly sterile, suitable only for the type of farming that uses massive amounts of energy (somewhere along the line) to transport and replace those nutrients by some other means.

The High (Energy) Cost of Low-Cost Fertilizers

The three key nutrients mandatory for crop growth are nitrogen (N), phosphorus (P), and potassium (K), which you'll see listed together on the front of a bag of fertilizer as "NPK." Virtually all of the world's nitrogen is made using natural gas to supply the energy (and hydrogen) needed to convert gaseous nitrogen into ammonia, a form of nitrogen biologically available to plants. (The gaseous form of nitrogen that makes up more than 70% of the atmosphere is inert and useless to plants.) It's an enormously energy-intensive process: A pound of ammonia fertilizer requires the energy equivalent of a pound of diesel fuel to create it.

Therefore, the extent to which plant yields are dependent on nitrogen fertilizers is really the extent to which farming yields are dependent on fossil fuels (principally natural gas).

As long as there are ever-increasing amounts of natural gas to dedicate to making nitrogen fertilizers, then the system we currently use should continue to function. But if this *isn't* the case—if it turns out that natural gas becomes limited in some way (which indeed it someday will)—then we need to seriously think about how we go about growing food. As in a complete and total overhaul of the entire system, probably with lower and more sustainable yields per acre as the outcome.

Until and unless we figure out a practical way to return harvested nitrogen back to the land in a usable form, the whole operation should be considered a temporary circumstance of fossil fuels.

Currently, the number-one eventual destination for applied farming nitrogen is the ocean, which is where we send most of our sewage. Right now, we can "afford" to do that because we have the energy to waste, but in the future, it will be a sure bet that we'll have to find ways to close the poop-loop and return these essential nutrients to the land and the soils upon which we depend.

The story of phosphorus is even more urgent, if not alarming, as our only source for this utterly essential element is from mined rocks. Again, we "mine" phosphorus from our farming soils and send it out to the sea to become hopelessly diluted, never to be recovered. Once thought to be virtually inexhaustible, rock phosphate has been mined in ever-larger quantities over the years to support our exponential need for more food, and we can now see that a peak in this important mineral resource is plainly in view.

> *Our supply of mined phosphorus is running out. Many mines used to meet this growing demand are degrading, as they are increasingly forced to access deeper layers and extract a lower quality of phosphate-bearing rock (phosphate is the chemical form in which nearly all phosphorus is found). Some initial analyses from scientists with the Global Phosphorus Research Initiative estimate that there will not be sufficient phosphorus supplies from mining to meet agricultural demand within 30 to 40 years. Although more research is clearly needed, this is not a comforting time scale.*[5]

This is the exact same story we've already seen for petroleum and other minerals. There is a fixed quantity of this vital product. It's being mined in ever-larger amounts, and it's depleting rapidly. That it will someday run out isn't in doubt; such a fate lies in the future of any finite material that's consumed. But "running out" isn't really our most immediate concern; "peaking" is. If farming yields must grow to meet future demand (more people), and those yields depend on phosphorus, then the peaking of phosphorus is going to put enormous pressures on efforts to increase yields.

Modern farming practices represent the effective mining of nutrients—a one-way trip from the soil to the sea—which we combat by mining or creating replacement nutrients elsewhere and then spreading them back on the land, using a lot of energy in the process. Right now, our approach to nutrients could be illustrated by a giant, one-way arrow that begins where the fertilizers are mined, crosses some farmed land, and briefly touches before heading out to sea.

This is completely and totally unsustainable.

Soil Erosion and Desertification

Even if all the soil (and its critical minerals) were staying in place, instead of being dispersed out to the ocean, there is another way in which modern farming practices aren't sustainable. Much of the soil itself is being lost, and this, too, is a concern. Fertile soil builds up only very slowly, often requiring 100 years of natural processes to create a single inch, and it is being lost at a rate that far exceeds its rate of accumulation. Some of it is lost slowly through simple erosion over time, and sometimes it is lost rather dramatically, as was the case in the U.S. Dust Bowl in the 1930s, when a single dust storm on April 14, 1935, was calculated to have contained 300,000 tons of topsoil, twice as much material as was dug from the Panama Canal.[6] That soil was lifted from the ground and deposited far to the east, with much of it ending up in the Atlantic Ocean.

Desertification is another destructive process that is often initiated and accelerated by the actions of humans. The process usually involves overgrazing of already marginal, dry lands, which destroys the meager plant cover that protects what little soil there is. Eventually a windstorm comes along and blows that soil away, and then nothing is left to absorb the sparse rains when next they come. The Amazon Basin is being strip-cleared to create agricultural lands and there's concern that if it goes too far, a tipping point will be reached that breaks the hydrological cycle and what was once rainforest will "tip" into being an arid desert.

In every case, it doesn't have to be this way. The groundbreaking work by Allan Savory shows that with intelligent and thoughtful management, humans moving animals about can actually reverse the process of desertification, build soils, and create more abundance. But it involves working with nature, and not against it.

Unfortunately, that's what's possible. What's currently practiced is completely and thoroughly unsustainable. The only question is if we'll change before or after disaster and famine strike.

Conclusion

Modern industrial agriculture is unsustainable. Instead of building up our primary wealth—soils—we're rather steadily, and sometimes spasmodically, eroding and depleting them. Current farming yields are truly magnificent, but they require enormous energy inputs to create the fertilizers and run the irrigation pumps. Sooner or later, the energy won't be there to create the fertilizers and irrigate the fields, and we'd do well to begin supporting local sustainable farming practices as if our very lives depended on them.

Farming on arid land isn't sustainable. Farming in a way that depletes ("mines") the soil isn't sustainable, nor are methods that cause soil to be eroded faster than it's created. Taken together, these facts about the fate of our soils and available farmland lead me to a stark conclusion: The percentage of our disposable income spent on food is going to continue going up in the years to come.

The whole story of farming on an industrial scale is one of low costs and even lower sustainability. The low costs are illusory and will eventually result in much higher costs, as we'll eventually have to cope with the expense of restoring millions of acres of dirt back into soil.

In order to farm sustainably, soils must be minimally maintained at their current depths and levels of fertility. In a world of surplus energy, these defects can be hidden by "nutrient subsidies" hauled in at great energy costs from far away. But when the energy subsidy is withdrawn, the true state of our croplands will be revealed.

CHAPTER 23

Parched

The Coming Water Wars

W hen you were young, perhaps your mother admonished you to turn off the tap while brushing your teeth to conserve water. That's good advice, and I don't want to diminish it, but the coming water predicaments will be driven more by the food on your plate than by the few gallons you might send down the drain. Water tables all across the globe are falling fast because aquifers are pumped at rates far faster than they are being recharged.

As Lester Brown explains:

The link between water and food is strong. We each consume, on average, nearly 4 liters of water per day in one form or another, while the water required to produce our daily food totals at least 2,000 liters—500 times as much. This helps explain why 70 percent of all water use is for irrigation. Another 20 percent is used by industry, and 10 percent goes for residential purposes. With the demand for water growing in all three categories, competition among sectors is intensifying, with agriculture almost always losing. While most people recognize that the world is facing a future of water shortages, not everyone has connected the dots to see that this also means a future of food shortages.[1]

While turning off the faucet as you brush your teeth isn't a bad idea, residential water use comprises only 10% of the total. Even if we could cut our domestic water use by 100%, we'd still have 90% of the water issue left to deal with.

As with Chapter 21 (*Minerals*), my purpose in this section isn't to write exhaustively about water issues. For that I refer you to other excellent sources for the details.[2] Instead, I want to simply illustrate that the exact same dynamics of exponential depletion and exponential growth are as relevant to water use as they are to petroleum and mineral extraction.

It's the same story all over again: Exponential growth is driving extractive behaviors that are creating water issues, problems, and predicaments all across the globe. No longer can clever engineering deliver all of the desired water to some places in the world; even now, there simply isn't sufficient water to meet the level of desired consumption.

Therefore, the story with water is simply that we're placing exponentially increasing demands on what, in many cases, is essentially a fixed supply. Understanding what drives water demand in many areas is no more complicated than tracking their population growth.

An additional 80 million people are added to the planet each year (equivalent to approximately eight New York Cities annually). They all need to eat, and food takes a lot of water to grow; they want electricity, which takes water to produce (in a thermal cycle power plant); and they all want to take showers and consume manufactured goods, all of which consume water.

A single pound of wheat takes a thousand pounds of water to grow, and this 1:1,000 ratio, coupled with population growth, is one of the key drivers for increasing water demand across the globe.

Running Dry

The water with which we are most familiar is above ground in the form of ponds, lakes, rivers, and reservoirs; that form of water has the wonderful characteristic of recharging and replenishing itself from the rain and snow falling from the sky. We can easily view the water levels in rivers and reservoirs and see for ourselves whether they are rising or falling enough to be cause for alarm. Over just the past 40 years, as the world's population has more than doubled, many of these rivers and reservoirs have gone from being sufficient to being nearly depleted.

The mighty Colorado River no longer roars into the sea, and in 2022 water authorities struggled with the effects of a mega-drought that caused water levels in both Lake Powell and Lake Mead to plunge to levels requiring emergency rationing.

The Yellow River in China is in the same condition. All over the globe, once-mighty rivers now limp toward the ocean, often drying up entirely during the dry season before they reach the sea. While there's some latitude to push things a bit further along with conservation efforts and altered-use practices, the surface water of the world clearly cannot stand any more "doublings" in demand. Already, practically every major river has been dammed, diverted, sluiced, and sliced up into apportioned allotments that are too numerous to sustainably support. Some minor rivers have disappeared entirely and formerly vast inland water bodies such as the Caspian and Salton seas are drying up. The conclusion is clear: Sooner or later, fresh water will be a major limiting factor to population growth and economic expansion.

What Lies Beneath

Because we can see it, we often tend to think of surface water as the main story, but really the relationship between surface water and the totality of the water we use is very similar to an iceberg's dimensions above and below the water.

The most important sources of water for most cities and agriculture lie in aquifers hidden deep beneath the ground, which means that it's difficult for most people to readily appreciate on the true state of things down there.

If we do take a look at the data, what we nearly always find are the effects of rapid and increasing rates of depletion. Many of these aquifers recharge so slowly, often over the course of tens of thousands of years, that Lester Brown rightly calls them "fossil aquifers."

In the United States, the massive Ogallala aquifer lies under eight western states, supplies 21 million acre-feet of water for irrigation every year, and some regions have already been placed off limits for further agricultural extraction. Once as large as Lake Huron but below the ground, the crop lands on top of the Ogallala are responsible for fully 1/6th (!) of the entire world's grain production. Where the Colorado River captures all the runoff to the west of the Continental Divide, the Ogallala captured all the runoff that went east. Not being able to make it all the way to the Mississippi drainage due to higher elevations in the way, the water sank beneath the ground and collected over tens of thousands of years. When (not *if*, but *when*) it is pumped too dry to be of economic use, a vast amount of productive farmland will immediately revert to low-output arid scrub land. In this sense, extracting water from deep, ultra-slow-recharging aquifers is no different from mining: Once the ore (or water) has been removed, it's as good as gone forever, at least on a human timeline. This is where our intuitive sense of water might lead us astray. Instead of thinking of it as an infinitely renewable resource, we need to be aware that an enormous proportion of the water we use is effectively a nonrenewable resource, at least on any relevant human timeline. Aquifers like the Ogallala are more like a non-interest-bearing bank account gifted to us by a distant relative. Because it won't last forever, a prudent person would have a strict budget and a solid plan for what to do on the day the account runs dry. Water politics are so emotionally charged and complicated that, well, there really isn't a plan in place. While people argue over it all, water continues to be drained.

Ancient aquifers all over the globe are being pumped at unsustainable rates and will therefore someday fail to provide sufficient water to local populations. The problem areas are seemingly endless and intractable, and very few of these locations have any sort of credible plans for what to do when the water runs out.

Exporting Water—The Food Story

World food harvests have tripled since 1950, and irrigation is responsible for a large portion of those gains. I was surprised to learn that every pound of harvested wheat required one thousand pounds of water to grow. In a sense, this 1,000:1 ratio means that when the United States exports wheat, it's really exporting water. A million tons of grain is the same as exporting a billion tons of water, which explains why many water-starved countries prefer to buy their grains rather than growing them on their parched soils.

Without the use of aquifers, much of the drier agricultural land in the world, such as the wheat fields in Saudi Arabia (estimated to produce 700,000 metric tonnes of wheat in 2022), would have to be abandoned altogether.

And agriculture in the more temperate regions would have to revert to dry land farming practices—which means depending on rainfall alone, rather than irrigation—and this would also lower yields, often dramatically. This is an inconvenient reality at a time when future food security is already an open concern of world leaders and population is slated to grow by approximately 40% over the next 40 years.

To quote Lester Brown again, "Knowing where grain deficits will be concentrated tomorrow requires looking at where water deficits are developing today."[3] The drier and more populous nations are already struggling with severe water issues today. So, as we ponder the predicament of falling water tables, we might also ask what the impact of these will be on our ability to support even a few more decades of exponential growth, let alone an endless amount of it. Given the enormous litany of water issues that are already upon us, I find it quite improbable that we will be able to support even one more economic doubling without running into serious issues.

The Food Bubble

Because water is so indispensable to agriculture, and the more populous and dryer regions are so heavily dependent on ancient aquifers to meet their irrigation needs, some stark conclusions are apparent. Again, from Brown's *Plan B*:

> *Many countries are in essence creating a "food bubble economy"—one in which food production is artificially inflated by the unsustainable mining of groundwater. At what point does water scarcity translate into food scarcity?*[4]

David Seckler and his colleagues at the International Water Management Institute, the world's premier water research group, summarized this issue well:

Many of the most populous countries of the world—China, India, Pakistan, Mexico, and nearly all the countries of the Middle East and North Africa—have literally been having a free ride over the past two or three decades by depleting their groundwater resources. The penalty for mismanagement of this valuable resource is now coming due and it's no exaggeration to say that the results could be catastrophic for these countries and, given their importance, for the world as a whole.[5]

As is the case with so many of our modern predicaments, we don't have thousands of years of experience to help guide us through what happens next. What happens when the aquifers that supported the emergence of exponentially larger populations above them are depleted? Nobody knows, so our imaginations will have to fill in the blanks.

The story of water then is another tale of an unsustainable set of practices playing out right before our very eyes and getting surprisingly scant attention, given the stakes involved. The mystery here is why so many clearly unsustainable practices are running at once without more urgent and intelligent conversations taking place at the national and global levels.

Energy and Water

Because water is a liquid and flows so easily, effortlessly coursing down rivers and sliding through pipes, its other primary characteristic often gets overlooked: It's heavy. A cube of water measuring just slightly over three feet on a side weighs a ton. It is wonderful that huge amounts of water will flow so readily down an incline, such as 100-mile-long culvert that's graded properly. However, if you want water to go the other way, there's an enormous energy price to pay.

In certain states in India, where the irrigation pipes now have to reach deeper and deeper each year to draw up precious water, irrigation now accounts for more than half of the electrical energy used. Unsurprisingly, bringing water up from great depths is enormously energy intensive, and irrigation is one of the major uses of energy in farming, consuming 13% of the direct energy used to grow food.[6]

As aquifers deplete and are drawn down to lower and lower depths, the energy—and cost—required to push water up to the surface increases. In the future, we'll see twin pressures on food-growing costs: the direct increase in petroleum prices on things like fueling up tractors and making fertilizer, and the costs of pumping water up from ever-greater depths. Of course, once an aquifer runs dry, then it's game over for productive farming in that area.

The other primary use for water that often goes overlooked is the production of energy itself. Nuclear and coal-fired plants both require enormous amounts of water, used in the cooling cycle, to operate. If we express the amount of water required on the basis of kilowatt hours, we find that it takes two gallons of water to produce a single kilowatt hour of consumed electricity. Surprisingly, hydroelectric plants "consume" the most, as their reservoirs lose a lot of water to evaporation. For all new thermoelectric plants (coal, nuclear, etc.) the average is approximately 0.5 gallons per end-use kilowatt hour. This may not sound like a lot, but it means that more than half of all the water consumed in the United States is consumed by electrical power plants. If we want more electricity, we'll need to use more water.[7]

The Future of Water

Once again, if we take a hard look at the facts as they stand, we come to the conclusion that the correct question isn't *How do we manage our water resources to permit endless perpetual growth?* but rather, *How can we best manage the water we've got?*

Fresh water isn't evenly distributed across the globe, and neither are these water-based problems—some places are in much worse shape than others. Some are in fine shape. So local mileage will vary, as they say. If you're thinking about whether to move or to stay where you are, please place water at the very top of your list of important criteria. In farming they say, *Too much water will scare you, but too little will kill you.*

The future of water is already upon us, as evidenced by the number of farm operations and regions systematically losing their water access by expropriation or selling their water rights to cities. When economics sets the rules, farmers lose, because the monetary value of the crops that can be grown with a given amount of water is a fraction of the value at which water can be sold to residential and industrial customers. Because of the period of time we've all just lived through, many make the assumption that it's perfectly okay to prioritize water for uses other than farming because you can always buy your food grown somewhere else. Given the looming energy predicament, this assumption may not be a good one for much longer.

We're already at the point where water is a limiting factor for societies and economies all across the globe. With eight billion souls (and counting) living the way we do, all the fresh water on the face of the earth, and even that beneath the surface, is barely meeting our needs. What happens when the world's population goes to 9.0–10.5 billion, as the UN suggests is likely by 2050? At a simple level, this nearly 12% to 30% increase in population implies that we'll need 12% to 30% more water in the future. Is this realistic? The depletion of ancient aquifers suggests it is not.

The future of water is one of profound and growing scarcity. It's a future where "water refugees" will need to move from regions where the local aquifers can no longer support the populations above them, and where nations will squabble and possibly go to war over water rights and access. It's difficult to imagine how this water scarcity won't translate into crop and food scarcity.

CHAPTER 24

All Fished Out

A s a child, I loved fishing with my grandfather. I can't recall us ever talking about anything, but there was no need for words; he was a man of few words, he loved me unconditionally, and we were *fishing*. He took me to the Branford public pier on Long Island Sound, and there we routinely caught many different types of fish. As I remember, the waters were teeming with life—an abundance, sadly, that is gone.

Once again, this chapter isn't designed to be a long recitation of the many challenges that our oceans are facing—there are too many to list—but I'll continue to make the simple point that we're already up against hard limits with respect to what the oceans can provide. More growth? Another 10, 20, or 30 years of increasing exploitation of the ocean's riches? It's not going to happen. They're already fished out.

Ninety Percent Gone

A recent study published in the esteemed journal *Nature* concluded that the combined weight of all oceanic large fish species has declined by 90%.[1] If something supposedly renewable is being harvested at a rate that causes its mass to shrink alarmingly, then it's a poster child for the concept of "unsustainability."

As Lester Brown put it in *Plan B 3.0*:

After World War II, accelerating population growth and steadily rising incomes drove the demand for seafood upward at a record pace. At the same time, advances in fishing technologies, including huge, refrigerated processing ships that enabled trawlers to exploit distant oceans, enabled fishers to respond to the growing world demand. In response, the oceanic fish catch climbed from 19 million tons in 1950 to its historic high of 93 million tons in 1997. This fivefold growth—more than double that of population during this period—raised the wild seafood supply per person worldwide from 7 kilograms in 1950 to a peak of 17 kilograms in 1988. Since then, it has fallen to14 kilograms.[2]

As population grows and as modern food-marketing systems give more people access to these products, so does seafood consumption. Indeed, the human appetite for seafood is outgrowing the sustainable yield of oceanic fisheries. A 2020 study concluded that 82% of all tracked fishery stocks in the world were in varying states of depletion, and just 18% were healthy.[3]

Cod, bluefin tuna, swordfish, shark, herring, and innumerable other species are in rapid decline and are in danger of collapsing or becoming extinct. This isn't some future issue that we might worry about; it's happening right now.

While overfishing puts serious pressure on oceanic health, probably the worst problem of the lot right now, there are other problems as well, ranging from destruction of estuaries, loss of coral reefs, oceanic "dead zones" caused by pollution runoff, and the buildup of toxic metals and other industrial pollutants in the top species.

> *Sperm whales feeding even in the most remote reaches of Earth's oceans have built up stunningly high levels of toxic and heavy metals. [R] esearchers found mercury as high as 16 parts per million in the whales. Fish high in mercury such as shark and swordfish—the types health experts warn children and pregnant women to avoid—typically have levels of about 1 part per million.[4]*

What sort of signal should we receive from the fact that whales— mammals, like us—now carry toxic loads of mercury so far beyond what the EPA would allow in humans that they would probably require whale meat to be buried in a special leakproof hazardous material container to prevent the release of mercury?

The Oxygen You Breathe

I was taught in middle school that the oxygen I breathe comes from trees. That's not entirely wrong; it's just not entirely accurate either. The source of half the world's oxygen is not majestic trees in the Amazon, but microscopically invisible one-celled creatures that live at the ocean surface, tossed hither and yon by majestic waves and currents.[5] Called "phytoplankton," which is a fancy way of saying "photosynthetic organisms that are really small and live in the ocean," these little "trees of the ocean" are responsible for more than half the oxygen you breathe; they are the very base of the food pyramid in the ocean.

On land, plants form the base of the pyramid, and these plants are eaten (for example) by the rabbits, which are eaten by the foxes. In the ocean, phytoplankton are the plants, which are eaten by slightly larger plankton and larvae, which are eaten by . . . well, you get the picture. There's an entire ecosystem and food chain in the ocean that exactly mirrors the one on land in its basic pyramid shape, but it is eons older in terms of its layers, complexity, and structure. Life started in the sea and has a billion or more years of a head start on terrestrial life when it comes to complexity (e.g., interrelationships, dependencies, feedback loops, and the like).

This is all well and good and perfectly ignorable until we read things like this:

> *The microscopic plants that support all life in the oceans are dying off at a dramatic rate, according to a study that has documented for the first time a disturbing and unprecedented change at the base of the marine food web.*
>
> *Scientists have discovered that the phytoplankton of the oceans has declined by about 40 per cent over the past century, with much of the loss occurring since the 1950s.[6]*

While we don't know if this finding will hold up, or what might be causing it if it is real, it's a trend that has been tracked by scientists for quite a long time.[7,8] If such findings are true, we should be just as focused on why half of the world's supply of oxygen is disappearing as why our GDP is not growing as rapidly as we might like.

The very air you breathe is dependent on a form of life that you almost certainly have never seen with your own eyes, and something seems to be amiss with it. Whether the cause is global warming, nutrient imbalances, or an upset in the normal predator–prey relationships is utterly unknown at this point. Wouldn't it be good to know what the cause is? Without (hopefully) belaboring the obvious, human pressures on the oceans, in whatever form, are a ripe candidate for speculation and inquiry.

The Great Thiamine (B_1) Mystery

In 2018, something truly shocking came to my attention. An environmental biochemist at the University of Stockholm reported that wild seabird colonies were suffering from some sort of paralytic disease or poisoning. Birds weren't eating, some had difficulty breathing, and others were completely paralyzed. Over the past 60 years, seabird populations have declined by approximately 70%. He suspected thiamine deficiency.

Then in 2021, staff at a U.S. national fish hatchery observed the following:

> *Disoriented little fish caught the attention of staff members at the Coleman National Fish Hatchery in Red Bluff, California, in early January 2020. Looking down into the outdoor tanks, called raceways,*

the facility's employees noticed that among the dark, olive-colored clouds of live fish, there were occasional slivers of silver from the undersides of tiny fry that were struggling to swim. The fish would roll onto their sides, sink to the bottom for a moment, spring back upright, swim a few strokes, and then roll over again.

Many were dying, too. While a few hundred mortalities daily in a facility containing millions of fish is normal, something was defi- nitely amiss.[9]

After some sleuthing, they discovered the little fish were desperately short of a vitamin called thiamin, which is also called vitamin B_1. Further, they discovered that other oceanic and freshwater researchers the world over had noticed the same thing and had been studying it for years, so it wasn't contained to their particular patch of nearby ocean.

The lack of thiamin had been definitively fingered as the main culprit behind massive bird die-offs and poor fish breeding and survival statistics. The entire food chain was impacted, top to bottom. Because this deficiency is found in both salt and freshwater systems and is global, our list of causes now has to span some sort of environmental toxin or disrupter.

Continuing from the article:

Scientists are floating various explanations for what's depriving organ- isms of this nutrient, and some believe that changing environmental conditions, especially in the ocean, may be stifling thiamine production or its transfer between producers and the animals that eat them.[10]

The consensus is that humans are somehow responsible, but nobody knows just how yet. Have we accidentally introduced an environmen- tal chemical that blocks thiamin production? With over 500,000 produced human-made chemicals, this is plausible. Have we overfished a small species that's necessary to first ingest B_1 from plankton before passing it up the food chain? This too is possible.

Whatever the reason, the very thought that human activity could some- how decimate a necessary and vital nutrient within and across the entire globe is sobering. Perhaps our excessive focus on economic growth at any cost is turning out to be too expensive after all?

The Bottom Line

All the data coming from the oceans says that even at a population of eight billion, humans are exerting unsustainable pressures and demands upon the world's oceans. There is much we don't understand about our saltwater resources, probably because, like aquifers, they are out of our direct sight and therefore our appreciation. Our role in collapsing the thiamin cycle world-wide certainly indicates that we don't really have a clue what we're doing or what the impacts will be. But how could we? Life and ecosystems are complex systems, and therefore they have emergent behaviors.

But one thing that we can be sure about is that, by definition, unsustainable practices must someday stop. As we head toward 9 or 10 or more billion people, what are the chances that we'll be able to sustainably harvest 10% or 20% or 30% more fish from the oceans? The answer is somewhere between zero and none.

We're already at limit, and probably beyond, when it comes to the oceans. The story of perpetual economic growth, then, will have to be told without getting more resources from the oceans. They are all tapped out and headed toward collapse, with reductions in certain key areas and species upon which we already depend for much of our protein.

For any who care to look, signs are present that we have either hit or are rapidly approaching hard, physical limits all around us. This isn't a case of pessimism; this is simply what the data is telling us at this time. Whether or not you choose to heed the warning signs and adjust your life to the implications of this information is for you to decide.

In my own lifetime, a mere blink by historical human standards, I've personally witnessed what seems like the complete demise of shore-based fisheries. I went back to fish off that pier in Branford, Connecticut recently, and it was not the place of my boyhood leisure. Where there had been abundance was now a salty ghost town.

In many places, there's nothing left to catch. The water is beautiful on the surface, but underneath it's a desert, stripped bare of life.

When I consider just how rapid this depletion of the ocean's resources has been, I think back to our stadium example—as far as the oceans are concerned, the water is already swirling up the staircase to the bleachers.

CHAPTER 25

What Do You Mean We're Running Out of Sand?

Strange but True

The case I've been patiently laying out for you is that our economic system is unsustainable. It requires that we constantly do more and more with a finite amount of resources. It is 100% fraudulent to say that infinite growth on a finite planet is both possible and desirable. It's painfully easy to locate examples of natural resources being used up either too quickly to be replenished (as in the case of underground aquifers) or being used up at a faster and faster pace without a plan for how we'll replace them when they are all used up (e.g., fossil fuels).

Sometimes such big ideas are too much to absorb and it's better to tell a smaller story that sheds light on the bigger picture. So, let's talk about sand.

Sand is the second most commonly used commodity in the world after water. It is used as an additive to cement to make concrete, it is laid under patios and roadways, and it is melted down to make windows, smartphone screens, and computer chips.

It is absolutely *critical* to our entire way of life and the world is facing a severe shortage of the sort of sand that's best for making concrete. Who ever thought we could run out of sand? I certainly didn't.

While the numbers are a bit iffy because there isn't any global sand tracking done, it is estimated that humans use roughly 40 to 50 billion tons of sand each year. It's a huge number. With that amount of sand, you could build a wall 100 feet tall by 100 feet wide that goes entirely around the earth. Every year.

But sand is in such short supply in some parts of the world that "sand pirates" are now a thing, who will show up in the middle of the night with guns and a dredge to steal your beach. Sadly, people have been killed trying to defend their sand.

While it might seem like the Sahara Desert is chock-full of endless amounts of sand, and it is, it's the wrong sort. Tumbled smooth by the wind, desert sand resembles little golf balls under a microscope and therefore makes terrible concrete that crumbles easily. Instead, the world is hungry for sand carried to the ocean by rivers, smashed and dashed and full of angular edges that catch on each other and make for strong, durable concrete.

The demand for concrete is enormous. Between 2011 and 2013, China poured more concrete than did the United States during the entire twentieth century. And the right kind of sand was needed for every bit of that effort.

Question: *If we're already running out of sand, and we know that vast amounts of concrete will need to be replaced over the coming decades (see Chapter 15, about concrete), what will the global economy use for its next cycle of concrete replacement, let alone expansion?*

The answer, of course, is that we won't be using sand. Not like we used to. It won't exist in sufficient quantities. We'll have to figure something else out, and it's a rock-solid guarantee that it will be more expensive than scooping buckets of sand from natural deposits and placing them into trucks to be hauled off and used.

I find the story of sand to be quite sobering. If we're already running out of *sand*, of all things, what else are we running out of? How can we persist with the fantasy that the model of continuous economic growth makes any sense at all when it's clearly already running out of the most basic and obvious of things like soil nutrients, fresh water, oil, and sand? It clearly doesn't add up.

PART VI

Convergence

CHAPTER 26

Where Have All the Insects Gone?

Silence of the Lamps

Perhaps you've noticed: The windshield of your car no longer gathers insects, even during long trips through the countryside in summer. This is an emergency.

When I was a kid, the family would drive each summer from Connecticut to a spot in upstate New York, a distance of about 300 miles. I mostly recall our wood-paneled station wagon because of how hard it was to reach the windshield from the ground. I'd have to crawl up on the hood, sometimes blisteringly hot, at every gas stop because it was my job to clean bugs and insects off the windshield we'd gathered since the last stop. It took some effort, I can tell you, especially the big fat explosions of yellowy stuff that had dried on there.

These days? Now, I can drive those same 300 miles in August without hitting a single insect. My windshield is completely clean.

More people are aware of this phenomenon now and it's even been in the news quite a bit. The *New York Times* has run long and thorough articles on the insect apocalypse, bee colony collapse, and loss of butterflies, notably the monarch. What's missing, typically, is an appreciation for just how awful this really is.

Similar to the missing aquatic thiamin story, the insect collapse is broad-based. It was a group of amateur entomologists in Germany that first raised the alarm. They had been carrying out insect population surveys for decades, setting various traps in wild areas and then literally weighing the haul and dutifully and carefully recording the data.

Eventually, they noticed that the weights were down significantly and heading lower every year. They spoke with scientists and the concern grew from there.

Anybody over the age of 50 can tell you that once upon a time if you left your window open without a screen with a light on, on a summer night, your room would rapidly fill with all manner of insects, some of them frankly large and alarming. Gigantic beetles with huge horns flying as if blindfolded, moths of every size and shape, walking sticks and crane flies, things large and small. Now there are practically none. A porch lamp was a fascinating summer evening event when I was a boy and I truly miss those winged wonders of my youth.

As a person trained in biology and ecology, I can assure you wiping out the bottom of the food chain is a very bad, terrible, no-good idea. The loss of insects of every type spanning across every family, order, and species and from multiple continents should alarm each of us. It means, once again, that something we're doing is having a global impact and that, once again, there's too little apparent concern among the public to do much about it.

I am convinced, beyond a reasonable doubt, that the neonicotinoid ("neonics") class of insecticides is largely responsible. I wrote a long piece on the subject back in 2015 ("Suicide by Pesticide") after the EPA under Barack Obama decided to punt and not regulate these nasty awful chemicals despite literal mountains of science telling us just how terrifyingly awful they are.

They are not pesticides so much as they are *biocides*. Neonics are so toxic that a coated seed kernel has enough on it and will absorb enough toxin from that coating during germination that the adult plant will be lethal to a hungry caterpillar. The coating on a single seed contains enough poison to kill a sparrow outright. The half-life of neonics in the soil and water is a mind-bending 1,000 days, meaning that after nearly three years, half of the amount first applied is still in the ecosystem working its damage. Since it's applied every year, it accumulates rapidly.

First introduced in quantity to farmers in the mid 1990s, but really taking off with the introduction of Clothianidin in 2004, ecologists and beekeepers began noticing alarming signs by 2006.

Germany took note of the science and banned the entire family of neonics in 2008. In took until 2015 for the U.S. EPA to do . . . well, nothing really at all. They finally ruled, after dragging out the process for years, to restrict new uses of neonicotinoids. All the old uses and applications were grandfathered in, despite strong evidence that these compounds were directly responsible for a massive insect apocalypse. There were farming dollars and corporate profits to consider, you see.

The lessons we might draw from this sad and ongoing tale are that: (1) for many in power, money is more important than life, (2) even when confronted with overwhelming evidence that something needs to change, it still probably won't happen, and (3) there seems to be almost no appreciation for how complex systems work and that they need to be treated with respect and humility.

Oh well. So, there are fewer insects. What's the worst that could happen? seems to be the mindset. And there's the rub—nobody knows, but it's basically terminating the arrangements of a 450-million-year-old food chain in less than a decade. That seems . . . unwise, to put it mildly.

These days it is possible to leave a porch light on all night and only accumulate a single lonely moth. It is truly the *Silence of the Lamps*.

Remember, it's the pace of change that matters most.

CHAPTER 27

The Bumpy Path to 2030

The next 20 years are going to be completely unlike the last 20 years.

—Chris Martenson, 2008

I penned that statement in 2008. It is now clear, here in August of 2022, that these words were prophetic. Europe is going through the greatest energy crisis of any major industrialized nation ever. It is being shocked by the fastest price hikes for natural gas and electricity costs ever witnessed. The price charts are perfectly exponential and are truly shocking to observe. And it's not yet winter.

My crystal ball that allowed me to foresee these difficulties was the framework I've just shared with you. It's really not that difficult once you set aside the noise of irrelevant data ("Solar is now cheaper than coal!" "Electric car sales are up 43%!") and focus on the big picture of net energy and can link that to how complex systems use energy to foster greater complexity and more order.

The road to 2030 is now laid before us. It's going to be a rough and bumpy ride. For those who can follow the logic and think for themselves—that is, break away from the inherent centrism of popular culture and press—this is not necessarily bad news. Hey, bad luck can strike anyone at any time, but, as they say, chance favors the prepared.

Far too many people are completely unprepared for what's coming. They lack the framework to appreciate what's really going on and/or they may lack the emotional ability to adjust to the emerging reality in time to have a better go of it all.

> *It is not the strongest of the species that survives, nor the most intelligent that survives. It is the one that is most adaptable to change.*
> —*Not Charles Darwin (quote often misattributed to him)*

If I've assembled and interpreted the data correctly, the road to 2030 is going to be exceptionally bumpy and dangerous. But that will just be the first part of the journey. Figuring out how to equitably and fairly share the dwindling pool of nonrenewable natural resources is going to require a level of diplomacy and political sophistication that seems to be utterly lacking in the current crop of Western leaders. Hopefully, better men and women will rise to power, and I suppose they will, but I can't see the existing political and educational institutions as contributing positively for years to come. They are too fully invested in the past and trying to preserve a status quo that is unsustainable.

Remember the difference between problems and predicaments. Any time or effort trying to find a solution to a predicament is time and effort that is wasted. We cannot afford to waste either time or energy, but that's exactly what's happening at present.

Humanity is on the cusp of *major* change—the kind where any time or resources we dedicate to mitigating the risks will prove to be the best investment we could ever make.

As someone who has done a lot of recreational rock climbing and some over-the-horizon boating, I have a strong appreciation for the difference between "sort-of" prepared and *actually* prepared.

When you're 600 feet up a rock wall, you either have a critical piece of gear or clothing with you, or you don't. Trust me, being stuck that high up without rain gear because it was too nice a day at the bottom to justify hauling it up can result in a very memorable experience. Once you're out of sight of land, if you get into boating trouble, you either have an emergency locator beacon (or any other piece of needed gear or spare parts) with you, or you don't. If you do, the rescue crews can find you instantly; if not, they may never even know you're in trouble, let alone where to look once you've been reported missing.

It is my central belief that our future contains exceptionally high risks that could usher in political and social unrest, a collapsing dollar (and other fiat currencies), hyperinflation (or hyper*deflation*), and even full economic collapse.

But it's important that you understand that these are merely risks, not certainties. My background as a pathologist trained me to view the world as a collection of statistics and probabilities; nothing is ever black and white to people in my (former) profession. People who smoke four packs a day are at higher risk of certain diseases but are not certain to die of anything in particular. Cancer exists on a continuum of aggressiveness, which we segment into stages, but even then, there are no guarantees as to the outcome of an individual case. Similarly, when I look into the future, I don't have any certainty about what might come next; instead, I see risks to be weighed and mitigated.

It's also important to note that I don't get rattled easily. I undertook no preparations for Y2K, and I don't fret about flying or driving or being near secondhand smoke. I rock climb and shoot and eat meat.

The Foundation

Exponential growth defines the human experience of the past few hundred years. With the advent of effective medicine and abundant energy, exponential population growth became so embedded in our collective reality that we designed both monetary and economic systems around its presence. Without such robust economic growth, "the system" threatens to collapse. Remember 2009? Global GDP shrank by a mere 2%, debt growth briefly went into reverse, and the banking system very nearly collapsed and was said to have been only hours away from meltdown.[1]

All growth requires energy, and if there happens to be abundant surplus, both growth *and* prosperity can result. However, if there is insufficient surplus to "fund" both, then you can only enjoy one or the other. When, not *if*, this condition arrives, it will not be a problem to solve, but a predicament to manage.

The Economy

To review, our understanding of the economy began with the fact that money is loaned into existence, with interest, and this results in powerful pressures to keep the amount of credit, or money, constantly growing by some percentage each year. Anything growing by some percentage over time is the very definition of exponential growth. Money and debt have been growing exponentially (almost perfectly) for several decades.

Keeping this dynamic in mind, we dove into the data on debt, which is really a claim on the future, and saw that current levels of debt vastly exceed all historical benchmarks. The flip side to this (a significant sociological trend in its own right) is the steady erosion of savings that has been observed over the exact same period of time. Combined, we have the highest levels of debt ever recorded, coincident with some of the lowest levels of savings ever recorded. We also saw that our failure to save extends through all levels of our society and even includes a notable failure to invest in infrastructure with a huge repair and replacement bill due for reinforced concrete alone.

Next, we saw how when credit bubbles burst, they result in financial panics that end up destroying a lot of capital. Actually, that's not quite right; this quote says it better:

> *Panics do not destroy capital; they merely reveal the extent to which it has been previously destroyed by its betrayal into hopelessly unproductive works.*
>
> —*John Stuart Mill (1806–1873)*

We learned that a bursting bubble isn't something that's easily fixed by authorities, because such attempts to "limit further damage" are misplaced. The damage has already been done; the capital has already been betrayed. It's contained within too many houses, too many strip malls sold for too high prices, and too many goods imported and bought on credit. All of that's *done*. What is left is figuring out who is going to end up eating the losses. Papering over the losses only makes them disappear for a while only to emerge larger and more destructively in the future.

Then we learned that the most profound financial shortfalls of the U.S. government rest with the liabilities associated with the entitlement programs that are underfunded by somewhere between $50 trillion and $200 trillion, neither of which are payable under the most optimistic of assumptions. A number of other governments around the globe are suffering similar shortfalls and constraints.

Throughout the past several decades, the economic numbers we reported to ourselves were systematically debased until they no longer reflected reality. They were (and continue to be) fuzzy numbers. Bad data leads to bad decisions, and this entrenched practice of lying to ourselves is another reason why we find ourselves in our current predicament. The longer we continue these lies, the worse the eventual outcome is likely to be.

Energy

Next, we learned that energy is the source of all economic activity—it's the master resource—and that oil is a critically important source of energy. Our entire economic model rests upon continuous growth and expansion. This means that it's built around the flawed assumption that unlimited growth in energy supplies is possible, which, unfortunately, is an easily refuted proposition. Individual oil fields peak, as do collections of them. Peak Oil isn't a theory; it's simply an observation about how oil fields age.

We explored the tension between a monetary system that *must* grow and an energy system that *can't* grow. All complex systems, of which the economy is a textbook example, owe their order and complexity to the energy that flows through them. Remove the energy, and by definition (and universal law), order and complexity will be reduced. Starving our economy of fuel risks crashing it.

The amount of fossil energy we have at our disposal is fixed. Like a trust fund that earns no interest, it can only get spent once, and then it's gone. Technology can help us to utilize that energy more efficiently, but it cannot create new energy.

The Environment

Finally, we noted that the environment, meaning the world's resources and natural systems upon which we depend, is exhibiting clear signs that we're approaching its limits. We're in the position of needing to exploit the poorest-quality mineral ores, peaks in critical resources are being noted at a faster and faster pace, and we're scouring the globe for the last few concentrated sources of primary wealth. Heck, we're even running out of sand, if you can believe it.

We're also depleting water in fossil aquifers at unsustainable rates, farmers are mining soils of essential nutrients, and our oceans' rich ecosystems are suffering. The natural world provides all the primary wealth out of which all secondary and tertiary wealth is fashioned. When the primary wealth is gone, there can be no secondary or tertiary wealth. None.

It's impossible to observe the decline in primary wealth and come away with any other conclusion besides "this is unsustainable." Anything that is unsustainable will someday stop.

"Unsustainable"

Putting it all together, we come up with a story that's very simple and virtually airtight: *Our present course is unsustainable.*

Perhaps we can console ourselves with the idea that somehow we won't reach the limits of our resources during our individual lifetimes, but we cannot argue that finite energy resources can last forever.

Many theoretical thinkers—including economists—reject the idea of limits, but individuals armed with the proper facts almost never do. The landmark modeling work done for *Limits to Growth* in the early 1970s was spot-on in virtually every respect, but economists and the media trounced on it because it did not fit their preferred view of a world without limits.[2] To economists at the time (whose ideas unfortunately still hold sway), resources just show up on time and as needed in response to "market demand," and any intrusions on this tidy arrangement are often rejected out of hand.

If we had taken the time to heed the lessons in *Limits to Growth,* we would be in far better shape today, but we didn't. In addition, we failed to take seriously the lessons offered by Oil Shock I, also in the 1970s. And so, here we are, with a lot more water in our stadium and the shackles still firmly affixed to our wrists.

Convergence: The Timeline

If all we had to do was face any *one* of the predicaments outlined above—debt, bubbles, crumbling infrastructure, Peak Oil, depleted resources, fertilizer shortages, ruined croplands—I'm confident that we would collectively do our best, respond intelligently, accommodate the outcome, and carry on. But, if we allow for the possibility of facing several of these predicaments *at once*, the concern mounts considerably. A timeline stretching from 2020 to 2030 reveals a truly massive set of challenges converging on an exceptionally short timeframe.

In 1798, Thomas Malthus postulated that the human population's geometric growth would, at some point, exceed the arithmetic returns of the earth, principally in the arena of food. To paraphrase, he recognized that the chart line of human exponential growth would someday cross the world's available resource line. Because this has not yet happened, some have claimed Malthus was not only wrong, but was wrong forever. This is the same logic as saying, "people have said I will someday die, but I haven't, here I am, so they must be wrong and I'll never die."

The key events shaping our lives between here and 2030 will be:

- The global recognition of Peak Oil and the near certainty of the national hoarding this will provoke on the part of the dwindling number of oil-exporting nations.

- The unplanned and uncontrolled loss of systemic complexity due to Peak Net Energy from oil, which will be detected by most as economic stagnation and decline.

- The continued use of money printing by nations to try and combat the loss of economic vigor caused by lower throughput of surplus, or net, energy within their respective economies.

- Massive inflation resulting from all that printing with the eventual destruction of many fiat currencies including the euro, the yen, and the dollar, which will further erode public trust and cohesion.

- Resource wars over access to everything from oil to water to lithium to copper to fish and eventually to food.

- Increasingly difficult food production due to a host of factors ranging from extremely expensive fertilizer inputs to unstable weather patterns in key growing regions (too hot, drought, too much rain, etc.).
- Food hoarding by food-exporting nations as a means of being able to provide for their own people.
- Increasing social unrest, beginning in the poorer countries; riots and toppled governments as the result of food and fuel costs that spike into territory that shreds social cohesion.
- Higher and higher costs to simply maintain and replace the current built infrastructure, especially in the United States, which has deferred maintenance for decades.

Any one of these events will prove to be a difficult strain on the global economy, but what happens if two of them arrive simultaneously? What about three? It's not hard to appreciate that potentially enormous risks lie along this timeline.

Even if these are managed well, they will be disruptive. Just take the loss of sufficient natural gas in Europe in 2022/2023. It resulted in massively higher electricity costs and caused the shutdown or limitation of output for 70% of all of Europe's nitrogen fertilizer production. Unless managed extremely well, this could easily result in the deaths of millions of people due to the combined difficulties of too little food (because it is unavailable or too expensive, or both), economic hardship, and cold.

If these many predicaments and problems are managed badly, they could lead to economic collapse and mass population decline. The data we have from the early 2020s is that the complexity of the issues is completely outside the ability of the current crop of leaders to conceptualize or manage. For example, in Europe, politicians simply sat by and watched as energy-intensive industries shut down, including fertilizer, glass, and aluminum. Had they appreciated that those industries are kind of like insects in biology—the base of the food chain with a lot of higher organisms and complexities built off of them—they would not have idly sat by.

Perhaps I should define collapse. To me, an "economic collapse" means that an economy declines and remains that way permanently, losing one or more key set of services along the way. It could mean policing, banking, reliable food delivery to cities, or the ability to make computer chips. Once that capability is lost, it's gone for a very long period of time, perhaps forever, as when the world lost a Concorde jet (Air France Flight 4590) on July 25, 2000, and saw the end of supersonic passenger transport for decades. While there are plans to bring back such flights, we'll see if those ever come to pass. Perhaps this next fiat currency "everything bubble" will crash and mark the end of many wondrous things we once took for granted.

Each of these key trends or threats will take years, if not decades, of careful planning and adjustment to mitigate. And yet we find them all parked smack-dab in front of us, without any serious national discussions or international efforts, as if they weren't really actual concerns. With every passing day, we squander precious time while the problems grow larger and more costly to remedy, if not becoming thoroughly intractable.

The mark of a mature adult is someone who can manage complexity and plan ahead. In my opinion, with few exceptions, the current political and corporate leadership of most countries are neither managing nor planning for the future that is rapidly arriving.

This Time *Is* Different

I can hear the critics now: *Doomsayers have been predicting the end of the world since the beginning of time, and the doom has never happened.*

Or perhaps, "*What's the difference between the story you have laid out and the one Thomas Malthus expounded upon back in the late 1700s?*"*

For starters, we have access to a **lot** more data than Malthus could ever dream of. Whereas he had access to a limited number of physical books to refer to, anybody with access to the internet has access to all of the information in the world.

Second, in Malthus's time, the laws of thermodynamics were incomplete and rudimentary, and even full acceptance of germ theory was another 90 years in the future. To compare our understanding today to that of Malthus would be like comparing an old rotary phone to the latest smartphone.

Both of the listed objections fall under the same logical fallacy (inductive): "Because this thing hasn't happened before, that thing can't (or won't) happen in the future."

Hopefully, it's not too much of a stretch to suggest that we've progressed in our understandings of things somewhat since Malthus's time, and that the remaining natural, untapped abundance of the earth is heavily diminished since 1798.

---

*In 1798, Thomas Malthus postulated that the human population's geometric growth would at some point exceed the arithmetic returns of the earth, principally in the arena of food. To paraphrase, he recognized that the exponential growth of human numbers would meet with the constraints imposed by a finite world. Because this has not yet happened, some have claimed perpetual victory over the entire concept of limits. It should be noted that Thomas Malthus had no way of knowing that oil and coal would dominate the energy landscape for the next 200-plus years.

Lastly, I am not predicting doom, although that's one possible path to be sure, but I am predicting massive change. Whether someone experiences it as a crisis or an opportunity has less to do with facts and data, and more to do with psychology.

What truly is different this time is that collectively, as a species, we have never before faced *declining* energy flows. Never. So, we're about to enter completely uncharted waters. Anybody who says we know how to manage this is either lying or ignorant. All we have are snippets and fragments from history to tell us what happens to localized cultures that run low on food or fuel, but these are poor analogues to our own globalized, just-in-time, highly complex, multibillion-person system of economic organization and delivery. This time, there's nowhere to go, nowhere to run, and my theory is that it is registering in our collective intuition and that's making the human herd skittish and prone to erratic decisions.

PART VII

What Should I Do?

CHAPTER 28

The Good News

We Already Have Everything
We Need

The good news is that we already have everything we need to create a better future. All of the understanding, resources, technology, ideas, systems, institutions, materials, and concepts are already available, invented, in place, and ready to be deployed in service of a better future.

We could do a lot better if we just decided to deploy our remaining energy and resources smartly. Whether we will or not is the open question. We might decide to be dummies instead of using common sense. When it comes to groups of people choosing the wrong path, well, that's something of a tradition.

Fundamentally, this book and my work are about exposing the choices and options we have. As dire as things seem, the future has not yet happened. Hope remains that we can respond intelligently to the current predicaments, and even create something better for ourselves along the way.

Yet, it's also true that our stadium is rapidly filling with water, time is running short, events are speeding up, and the mistakes we make going forward are going to be irreversible and costly. There's a lot less room for error than there was a few decades back, when we had plenty of time and surplus net energy to make mistakes and fumble around with our handcuffs. But now that the water is swirling up the last row of stairs to the upper bleachers, our choices matter a great deal more and will have to be made quickly with imperfect information.

There's no time to waste making wrong choices anymore. It's as if future historians are sitting up straight with pen poised over notebook, carefully watching to see what we do to determine how our efforts should be scored and recorded.

Technology

To begin this conversation, we don't need to develop any new technologies (although it will be nice when they come along).

That's the truth, the whole truth, and nothing but the truth.

We already know how to build highly efficient machines and dwellings that use tiny fractions of the energy of those currently in use. We've known how to build a "net zero" house since the 1970s, but mostly have opted not to.

That's the real story. We are simply not being intelligent and using/ deploying the technology we already have. This reveals that it's not a shortfall in new technology causing our issues and predicaments, but a failure of the narratives shaping our policies and actions.

It's also true that we're making bad choices by failing to change behaviors that can be easily changed. It's possible to drive your kids to soccer practice in a vehicle that weighs far less and uses far less energy than a 6,000-pound SUV. Billionaires do not need private jets and 500-foot yachts. Manufacturing and food growing can be conducted close to where their products are used and consumed, instead of being located many thousands of miles away. These are all choices that can (and should) be modified.

By doing so, we will preserve some energy for the future, which will grant us both the gift of time and the gift of having more options in the future. The only thing standing between us and making these better decisions is a near-complete lack of vision from our leadership.

I will be among the first and loudest to applaud when new high-capacity batteries are developed, but we don't *need* them in order to immediately begin using existing technology to consume less electricity. Here's an example: Electricity is still consumed in large quantities to heat water for home and commercial use. It's anywhere from 25 to 30% of a home heating budget. Solar hot water panels are a proven, decades-old technology that works and is economically sound at virtually any energy price. Despite this, such panels are relatively rare in some countries, the United States especially. Other countries, such as Israel and China, have made them mandatory because they make so much sense. Why use fossil fuels to heat water when the sun will happily do it for free? You spend a small amount of money on the solar hot water heater system and minimal money on maintenance, and you get hot water for the entire 25-year lifespan of a typical solar hot water system.

So, what is stopping us from making the installation of solar hot water panels a top priority, beginning immediately? The limitations that exist have nothing to do with technology that's been proven for 50 years. It's a failure of narrative. Socially and politically, we simply don't (yet) have the story in our heads that this is something we *need* to do.

We already know how to build houses that face the sun and use almost no energy, we know how to build smaller and more fuel-efficient vehicles, we know how to live, work, and play near where we live, and we have all the technology we need to live far more sustainably than we currently do. So, what is holding us back? I submit that there's nothing rational or logical or even economically sensible about our lack of action on these matters; the cause lies elsewhere.

Food

We know healthy soils produce more and better food than ruined, nearly biologically sterilized *dirt*. Elementary logic tells us that flushing vital and irreplaceable nutrients into the sea is neither sustainable nor good for the oceans.

Eventually we're going to have to find some way of recycling farm nutrients back to the farms. We understand how to build soils and we know that growing crops in arid regions using pumped groundwater is an energy and hydrological mistake.

We don't need any more studies, additional insights, or new books to be written on these subjects. We already know enough to do better. We don't need deeper understandings of what we need to do—although I will applaud them as they come along; we already have everything we need. What we *do* need is the mental commitment to make such changes a priority and to choose sustainable paths.

As much as possible, food needs to be grown and consumed locally, in alignment with local water availability, and strategies for recycling the nutrients back to the farms need to be implemented.

You can help start this process by demanding local foods, which is always the first step. By supporting local farmers, your demand will drive local supply and help to secure the food you and your community need in both the short term and the long term.

Even better, plant a garden! Start growing your own food in a garden plot, or a window box, or even just a single pot on the porch. Solutions to the issue of food, although daunting in scale, are easy to conceptualize and are already underway to some extent in virtually every community.

Energy

The prescription here is simple: *We need to be as conservative in our use of our remaining fossil fuels as we can possibly be.*

This means *stop wasting energy.* Not stop *using* energy; stop *wasting* it. That would be an excellent first step. Given that fossil fuels are a "one and done" arrangement—you only get to burn them once—we need to develop and nurture a brand-new appreciation for just how valuable energy really is. We really ought to see our fossil energy sources as the one-in-a-species bonanza and the irreplaceable resources they truly are.

Currently, fossil energy sources are "valued" by the abstraction we call money, which does an incredibly good job of masking their true worth by concealing how valuable they really are and that they are in limited, finite supplies and depleting.

The idea that gasoline, a nonrenewable resource, is only considered to be "worth" a few dollars a gallon, when it capably performs the same amount of work as a human laboring for hundreds of hours, is just silly. It should be valued more highly, and if it were, I'm confident it would be used more wisely. Even if a gallon of gasoline were "just" 200 hours of labor, and was valued at $20/hour, then that pencils out to a value of $4,000/gallon as compared to today's price of $4/gallon. Am I proposing that we undervalue (and therefore underappreciate) gasoline by a factor of 1,000? Yes, I am.

If we want to preserve the order and complexity of our economy, and, by extension, our society, then we need to begin by better appreciating the role of energy in delivering and maintaining *both* order and complexity.

Especially now that we've gone and overlapped critical markets and resources. In a drought-ridden area, the need to product hydroelectricity, water for farmers, water for other electrical production, and water for residential and industrial consumers all compete with each other. How does one choose between food and power, or more widgets or showers? It's complicated.

Or consider natural gas, which powers innumerable processes, meaning that choices might have to be made between producing fertilizer, running a peaking powerplant, or heating a residential home. This is precisely the situation Europe faced in the fall and winter of 2022. A snappy headline writer came up with the phrase "heat or eat?" Which do you choose? Clearly, "markets" cannot sort out the best use of anything, as that defaults to the highest price—which is a quite meaningless concept, especially in a world where central banks print up money out of thin air by the trillions.

It is this connection between the economy and energy that's entirely missing from the current practice of mainstream economics. It's almost as if the current practitioners of economic theory (with relatively few exceptions)[1] are entirely unaware that the economy would have no form, no function, and no "life" without energy. An economy would quickly lose all of its interesting and fascinating functions without energy. This intellectual disconnect explains why we're so deeply mired in the predicaments in which we find ourselves, and it explains why I view the risks to our future so seriously.

As Max Planck, the famous physicist, once said, "A new scientific truth does not triumph by convincing its opponents and making them see the light, but rather because its opponents eventually die, and a new generation grows up that is familiar with it."[2]

In other words, science advances one funeral at a time.

Historically, new ideas do tend to run into stiff opposition from the establishment. There are too many economists and other people in positions of power who seem to have no idea of the connections between the economy, energy, and the environment. When reality finally convinces enough of them that it needs to be taken seriously, in what sort of a world will we be living and how many options will remain?

Luckily, we don't have to wait for economists to arrive at the truth before we begin to act more rationally and use our fossil fuels as if they were an extremely valuable, nonrenewable, one-time energy inheritance.

Economy and Money

We can already tell that our debt-based, backed-by-nothing fiat currency is performing badly, and as its resource props are pulled away, it's likely to perform even more poorly in the future and eventually wobble and fall. To counter this, we will need new forms of money, possibly several, that can operate tolerably well in a world without growth, along with people to manage them.

Fortunately, several new forms of money already exist, including mutual credit arrangements (such as LET systems),[3] demurrage money,[4] and various forms of cryptocurrency capable of being backed by something tangible. Bitcoin, for example, is backed by scarcity—only 21,000,000 of them can ever be mined, and no small number of them got accidentally tossed into landfills. Others are backed by gold, and I see no reason future versions couldn't be attached to barrels of oil that come out of the ground (and you'd need to use them to consume that oil) giving them actual intrinsic energy value.

If we were to put more of these kinds of currency into play alongside our current form of money, then we would have a more resilient ecosystem of money, where if one form gets into difficulty of some sort, there are others waiting to pick up the slack. If a single currency is like a concrete channel designed to carry the maximum amount of water, multiple currencies are like wetlands designed to maximize the buffering of the water levels in times of both drought and flood.

Also, every form of currency rewards some behaviors and punishes others. Debt-based money is very good at motivating people to pay off the debts. But what if we had other forms of money that rewarded building soil, or being a great member of your community, or thinking and building for the long term? If we had these in place, we'd be far more resilient.

The very first step, however, needs to begin with the idea that you cannot possibly borrow more than you earn forever. The implication of this is that the U.S. government will need to cut spending to bring it in line with the actual economic realities that will result from "too much debt" and a looming resource predicament. If it doesn't the U.S. dollar will implode, or explode, at some point in the future and become another museum relic for future people to scan past on their way to the more interesting exhibits.

Population

We cannot beat around the bush on this "third-rail" topic any longer: We need to stabilize world population at a level that can be sustained. If we don't, then nature will do it for us, and not pleasantly, either. This means balancing world population in perpetuity with available and sustainable resource use. We may not know what this stable level is just yet, and more study is certainly needed, especially in light of declining energy resources. But we should do everything we can to avoid badly overshooting the number of humans that can be sustainably supported on our planet while carelessly avoiding an examination of the role of petroleum in supporting those populations.

According to the work of professor William (Bill) Rees, humans are operating well past Earth's sustainable carrying capacity, which is a function of two things: the number of humans on the earth and their standards of living.[5] According to this work, every organism has an ecological footprint, and humans now require the equivalent of 1.4 Earths to sustain themselves. There are only two ways to solve this problem: reduce the number of people or lower living standards. If those are our options, would we prefer to have fewer people in the world enjoying elevated standards of living, or more people in the world with reduced standards of living? In other words, would we prefer prosperity or growth? Saying "both" is the same thing as saying "growth," because in the battle between growth and prosperity, growth always wins and prosperity loses.

A New Narrative

I am often asked, "How do I convey this difficult information to someone I love (work with, live next to, etc.)?" The answer is to understand that people rarely (and in some cases never) change how they see the world because of information. For hundreds of thousands of years before writing came along, 100% of all our information was stored and conveyed in the form of stories.

Narratives are wired deeply into our biological wiring. Hollywood tells stories. Good books tell stories. We tell ourselves stories and live into them.

Because of this, what we need more than anything is to reshape the stories that we tell ourselves. Because you've read this far you are one of the rare people who can absorb information and then usefully slot it into their brain. That makes you quite a rare breed, as I've come to learn over the years. Your role, should you choose to accept it, will be to help other people see the challenges and predicaments in a new light, and that means helping a new story come to light.

The main problem for most people? It's that we're "between stories," as Charles Eisenstein has brilliantly said. It's an uncomfortable place. It's a power vacuum of sorts, and it's a place of great uncertainty and, like an unexplored territory, little is known and only can be revealed as it emerges over time during one's wanderings.

The old story of endless growth on a finite planet is winding down. Nobody yet knows what the new story might be. Whatever it is, it won't be a continuation of the past. We're going to have to change, like it or not.

More bluntly, the easy times are over, and a period of disruption has begun. It may be many years or even decades before things truly settle into a new equilibrium (of sorts—there really isn't any such thing in this ever-changing universe).

The concern that most people intuit is that complex systems don't change smoothly from one state to the next. Instead, they have tipping points. A tipping point is a critical moment in time when the old gives way to the new, suddenly and irreversibly (at least from a human lifetime perspective, and sometimes forever).

Easter Island tipping over from a forest ecology to a grassland ecology is an example. Perhaps one too many trees was cut down and then that was that. The forest ecosystem was gone and replaced by grass. There's nothing "wrong" with a grassland ecology, it's just very different than a forest ecology. Each has a very complex arrangement, and a forest is far more complex and has thousands of different components such as monkeys and birds and snakes and insects and plants/shrubs/vines/trees. By comparison, a grassland is a simple affair. Ditto for the Black Sea now being full of jellyfish instead of anchovies.

There are concerns that the complex hydrology of the Amazon basin, now a rainforest, could tip into being a desert if too many trees are cut down. It rains a lot in the Amazon. Where does all that moisture come from? Substantially from the trees themselves. Remove the trees and the rains no longer fall in sufficient quantities to support the trees. Once that cycle is broken and the whole system tips into "desert mode," how does one reset the system back to "rainforest mode"? Nobody has the slightest clue.

Right now, the "growth is essential" story is firmly lodged in our national and global narratives, and so that's what we get—policies and actions that chase growth. If instead we shared a story that placed "long-term prosperity" as our highest goal, then we would probably get different results.

One thing is sure: Waiting for politicians to arrive at this new story on their own is a bad strategy. If we look back through history and note whenever the status quo was challenged and changed, we'd see that such change was never initiated by those in power. Every single social gain of note—labor rights, civil rights, women's rights, the environmental movement, or any other that you care to think of—began on the periphery of society and was brought, kicking and screaming, to the center.

If it seems as though I'm suggesting that a social movement is needed, it's because I am. The story that I have told in this book needs to be spread far and wide. Others need to tell it in their own way, because we will need many teachers to get the message into every corner and down every side street. We need a tipping point of awareness about the true nature of the predicaments we face.

We each need to be responsible for helping to change the story so that we can have a better future. The alternatives are unacceptable.

The Good News . . .

Again, we don't need anything we don't already have in order to turn this story around. We know what the issues are, and we know what we have to do. It's as simple and as hard as this: We need to change our stories, away from a blind obedience to infinite money and endless growth and toward a store where "enough" is enough and stewardship becomes cooler and sexier than consumption.

Eventually we will do this, but with every passing day, our energy surplus shrinks, our other resources deplete, debts continue to climb, our environmental predicaments grow larger, world population continues to swell, and our range of potential reactions become fewer and ever more expensive. Our choice is to decide whether we wish to continue ahead with our foot on the gas pedal and risk hitting the wall at top speed or give ourselves a sporting chance by applying the brakes now.

Yes, we have everything we need to make the right choices, but as a collective whole, it seems quite likely that we won't choose enough of them in time to prevent disruptions from occurring.

So, the good news is that we have everything we need and creating a world worth inheriting is as simple as deciding to do the right things from here on. Which brings us to the bad news.

CHAPTER 29

Closing the Book on Growth

It is time to close the book on growth.

Exponential economic growth is in its final days. The only question is whether we recognize this early, on our own terms, or later, as a consequence of a series of regrettable collapses resulting in enormous suffering to humans and ecosystems.

The economic predicament, as I've laid it out, goes like this:

1. Over time, debt-based money grows exponentially due to interest, and this is an immutable feature of the system.

2. Due to nonproductive loans that can't be serviced with interest flows, the accumulation of debt also "goes exponential" over time. To combat this, central banks lower interest rates until they run out of room (at the zero bound).

3. Debt is a powerful motivator, and therefore exponential debt drives exponential economic growth and behaviors.

4. Any growth, but especially exponential economic growth, requires ever-increasing amounts of energy to sustain its order and complexity.

5. Because energy cannot, through any combination of known technologies, grow exponentially into the future forever, economic complexity will continue to expand until that process chews through all the energy, at which point it all collapses.

The only sure conclusion from this line of thinking is that someday our current model of economic growth will end and something new will take its place. It's only a question of when.

Of course, simple logic concludes that nothing can keep growing forever, and I suspect most people have always known, perhaps deep down, that our current model is unsustainable. The growth paradigm's end is now apparent as the world economy and financial systems lurch from crisis to crisis, each larger than the last, increasingly unresponsive to the magic money incantations and spending potions that seemed to work in the past.

What happens when an economy that *must* grow is being fueled by an energy source that *cannot* grow because it is dependent on depleting mineral resources (or are in limiting supply)?

My prediction has always been that the economy would begin to wobble and collapse, debts would prove to be unserviceable in total and begin to default, and monetary policy would lose traction and cease to be effective, as it is finally revealed that money is merely a tertiary abstraction from real forms of wealth. My secondary prediction has always been that the monetary and fiscal authorities would attempt to solve this predicament by printing money out of thin air and spending wildly in an attempt to keep things moving along.

So, whether the final economic and monetary insults are felt by people as deflationary or inflationary is still an open question, but one heavily weighted by human tendencies toward inflation.

Sooner or later the growth must stop; the only unknowns are when and under what terms. That isn't an indictment of capitalism or any particular "-ism" at all. I'm an equal-opportunity critic who indicts any particular "-ism" that seeks perpetual growth. Ditto for any political party, religion, economic model, or any other social organizing structure that falls into that mindset. It really does not matter to me in the slightest whether someone calls their perpetual growth paradigm Marxism, Capitalism, or Socialism, or whether they hail from a country located south of the equator or north of it. Perpetual growth of resource consumption is mathematically impossible.

Again, quoting Professor Simon Micheaux, this time from a 2021 research paper titled "The Mining of Minerals and the Limits to Growth:"

> *Current thinking is that European industrial businesses will replace a complex industrial ecosystem that took more than a century to build. This system was built with the support of the highest calorifically dense source of energy the world has ever known (oil), in cheap abundant quantities, with easily available credit, and unlimited mineral resources. This task is hoped to be done at a time when there is comparatively very expensive energy, a fragile finance system saturated in debt, not enough minerals, and an unprecedented number of human populations, embedded in a deteriorating environment.*[1]

Well, when you put it *that* way, Professor, it all sounds rather . . . impossible. Indeed, it actually is impossible, yet whole nations have **converted to clean energy** as their one and only defined energy policy.

While I tend to focus on the economy because this is where the most immediate impacts to all of our daily lives will surface and be felt the most acutely, the warning signs have been blinking for some time in the fields of mining, petroleum engineering, oceanology, ecology, farming, climatology, fishing, and every other specialty that taps into or studies the earth—our primary source of wealth.

Your challenge, then, is to accept the implications of the data that I've presented—that hard, physical limits aren't some vague conditions of a far-off future; they are concrete and immediate concerns. The next challenge is to accept that it's possible there won't be any grand plan put forward by wise leaders in time to prevent a host of interrelated disruptions to our lives.

We are between stories. However, one thing is clear: It's time to close the book on growth. It is an uncomfortable time, but we also get to be part of writing a new story.

Is there anything that *can* be done, that you might do to thrive in the future and live a life of abundance and joy? Yes, lots of things, which brings us to the final chapters of this book, on building your resilience.

CHAPTER 30

What Should I Do?

Okay, time to take a deep breath. It's not as bad as it seems. There's a better future out there if we decide to do things differently. But it's also time to take personal action. Time to take the warning signs seriously and begin preparing yourself, your family, and your community for potentially very hard times.

While I've just laid out a big heap of data and strung some facts together, what prevents most people from taking action is not a lack of compelling data, it is their own emotional blockages. I know because I went through the same full range of emotions when I first grappled with all this. Anxiety, fear, disbelief, bargaining, anger, avoidance, even a case of "fuck it," which is similar to depression in that it demotivates.

So, the first invitation, and for many the very first step, of moving toward action is to allow yourself to feel whatever comes up and let it have its way with you. We all need to grieve the many losses—be those a species or our own beliefs and dreams about the future—so we can get on with the many tasks ahead. (As a side note, if you've ever found yourself trying to communicate any of these concepts to friends, family, or colleagues but have gotten absolutely nowhere—except possibly frustrated—that's almost certainly because they are not yet able or willing to confront the emotions involved in dismantling their existing belief systems.)

> **PRO TIP** If you ever find yourself facing an emotional backlash from someone after trying to present them with data, you are up against an entrenched belief system, not a rational person.

That was a hard-learned lesson of mine, and it only came to me slowly and painfully. Perhaps you can learn from my mistakes. My new rule is "go slowly" with someone who cannot emotionally face the implications of all this data. I raise this because it is entirely likely that your spouse or close family members, or possibly neighbors or community, will be resistant to preparing (or "prepping" or "being a crazy survivalist" or however they deflect in order to defend) and yet you'll still want to prepare, even without their support.

The advice I have is to try to find common ground, and to absolutely not require them to see the world the way you do. A few great ways to accomplish this include:

- Saying that buying additional clothes, food, and perhaps installing a wood stove are great ways to dodge inflation and save money.
- Exploring the idea of being able to support others in their time of need, should that ever happen.
- If they are worried you might be taking them into the woods to live a life of isolation, tell them that social capital is one of the most important assets we have and you are counting on them to maintain close friends and family (while you build up a deep pantry).
- Find the common ground of wanting to provide and secure a loving and abundant homestead for your children or grandchildren "just in case."

Simpler, Harder, and More Expensive

Until and unless we humans find another *source* of high-net-energy fuels, this prediction is easily made: The future will be simpler, harder, and more expensive. The "simple" part scares me the most because so much of our daily comfort is built on top of a heap of complexity.

In 2021, "shortages" became such a dominant theme that entire social media communities developed around them to track them. Companies instituted defensive buying to deepen their inventories. Oil companies in Texas reported being short of piping of all sizes, sand for fracking, and electric motors and specialty tools. Trucking companies ran short of the anti-pollution additive DEF, while automobiles and light trucks could not be manufactured due to computer chip shortages. By 2022, shortages were a way of life.

By the summer of 2022, the biggest and most frightening of all shortages developed rather suddenly in Europe—an energy shortage. This quickly morphed into electricity bills that were 3 times and even 10 times what they were the year prior. Natural gas prices spiked so high that energy-intensive companies such as those making fertilizer, glass, and aluminum curtailed or even shut down production entirely. Suddenly, extremely expensive nitrogen fertilizers (which are made from natural gas) weren't applied by farmers the world over. The yields of farms growing our food sank. Small businesses shut down all over Europe.

The point of raising all this is to illustrate that these sorts of chaotic and disruptive outcomes are *precisely* what you'd predict from a future with less energy.

There will be fewer businesses and consumer choices, so things will be *simpler*. These illustrate the areas where you probably want to plan ahead and make some basic preparations. How will you heat and cool your home? Where will your water come from, especially if there's an electricity outage of more than a day? How long could you survive on the food in your home and community?

With supply chain difficulties, rampant inflation from the feed-through costs of higher energy prices, and various shortages (especially of balanced government, corporate, and household budgets), things will simply be *harder* to get done. And everything will cost more—a lot more—so things will be *more expensive*.

Those are trends I would predict to generally persist from here on forward, barring some miracle new energy discovery, or a huge shift in the narrative of **more** that still infects our cultural decision-making. More, *more*, **more**. Everything **has** to grow, right? Well, no, and until that changes there's really no hope of any of these difficulties sorting themselves out. There is no fairy godmother and her magic motherly wand to wave over and clean up our many messes.

But as long as humans insist on chasing growth at the expense of prosperity, expect your life to get harder, your living standards to go down, your wealth to be robbed by the process of printing/inflation, and the economy to shed complexity in the form of fewer products, fewer jobs, and fewer job types.

Becoming Resilient

All of which means it's time for you to get busy and become resilient. The topic of becoming more resilient is an entire set of books all on its own and it's what my website (https://peakprosperity.com) is devoted to, so be sure to visit there for up-to-date information and a vibrant community of intelligent people who are taking action.

Our economy, as I've outlined, is brilliantly complex and cost efficient, but it is also brittle. It has too many nested dependencies. If the globalized economy runs in reverse, even for a short while, it will completely unravel for some countries, mainly those that cannot self-produce their food, their fuels, or mission-critical manufacturing components. Put bluntly, it might break down. Becoming resilient, then, is about becoming as self-reliant as you possibly can (within reason, of course) and making yourself less dependent on an increasingly undependable world.

Re·sil·ience

noun

1. the capacity to recover quickly from difficulties; toughness.
2. having multiple, redundant means of meeting one's needs; having buffers and stored resources; and the ability to switch easily and rapidly between different materials, sources or processes.

All we can really do here is cover some of the basics to get you started. But for most people, that's the most important part: getting started. The gap between what you know and the actions you aren't taking is where anxiety, dread, and fear live. So, let's eliminate that gap.

Your needs for resilience will be completely different from mine (probably) or even your neighbor's. Your situation might include being younger, or older, having fewer or greater or different skills sets, more or less financial capability, or living in an area with entirely different amounts of water or food-growing capabilities. You might see things in a more or less positive light and therefore weight both the severity and the timing of the economic, energy, and ecological challenges very differently from someone else. Maybe you think things won't be that bad after all, or perhaps you're worried about a Mad Max future. My job isn't to try and steer you in either direction because, after all, I might be wrong (*but I'm not confused*, so I am preparing for a future of scarcity and shortages of basic things).

The Bare Minimum

There are a huge number of variables that will make your specific needs and responses different from mine, and that's expected. You might be older or younger, or have more or fewer monetary resources, or live in a drier or hotter or colder environment. In other words, I don't have a magic and specific list of things that everybody and anybody needs. Except these, which *everyone* should have:

1. A minimum of three months of food per person in your household stored, covering about 2,000 calories per day per person.
2. A plan for where to go in case where you are currently living becomes unsafe.
3. A minimum of three months of emergency funds in cash safely stored outside of the banking system.

4. A deep pantry and a deep basement, filled with the things you normally consume to combat both potential scarcity and inflation (see #1).

5. Three weeks of stored water and a water filter sufficient to create clean drinking water for you and your family with enough replacement filters to last a year.

6. The ability to keep yourself warm in winter should your heating systems fail or be too expensive (blankets, sleeping bags, wool sweaters, etc.) and the means of keeping cool in summer that's not A/C.

7. The ability to defend yourself and your family from violence.

That covers the bottom layer of Maslow's hierarchy of needs, which is physical survival. Truthfully, everyone should have those basic precautions anyway, *especially* people who live in areas prone to natural disasters.

Our just-in-time globalized economy is fantastically efficient and allows us to live in places that would otherwise be completely untenable. No major city can support itself in terms of food, fuel, or water without everything continuing to function as they currently do. I live in a region where if snow removal by gigantic gasoline or diesel-powered plow trucks were to stop during a snowy season, the roads would become impassable until the spring thaws. If our electricity were to cut out, things would become quite grim for my region in about a week, depending on the temperature.

Where to Live

These days, I live on a farm with my partner, with cows and chickens, a big garden, a large and improving field, in a place with abundant water. Because our property is quite large by eastern standards, we currently own a lot of trees, which we feel will become more and more valuable as energy becomes more and more expensive. We've even got a spring that flows year-round and comes out of a pipe here at the base of the hill with astonishing pressure, 24/7 all year. Our goal is to grow as much food as we can in the space we've got while constantly improving the soil and the natural abundance all around us. We have a wide range of skills and material goods that will help us through most economic or social storms. I set this as context, so you know I am walking the talk.

But not everybody can or wants to live out in the country. Because of my line of work, I personally have met and know of thousands of people who are preparing for the future by becoming resilient. In many cases, they are well beyond my own levels of preparation when it comes to personal security, solar energy installations, food production, and many other areas. They've done this in urban, suburban, rural, desert, and mountainous areas all over the globe.

Again, each person has to decide what sort of a future they are preparing for and how much effort they want to expend getting there. So, blanket statements about where to live and how to go about preparing are difficult to make, but not impossible. Here are a few blanket statements I am comfortable making:

- If you live in an area without adequate water to grow food, it's not a good place to set up for the long term.
- Cities already on the decline (Oakland, Las Vegas, New York, San Francisco, Chicago, New Orleans, etc.) will be bad places to live for people who value living without having to constantly be on the alert. As energy costs make everything expensive, cities will be packed with increasingly desperate people. Personally, I would move out of any city or area already struggling with violence, squalor, homelessness, open-air hard drug use, and has poor leadership struggling to comprehend the true roots of their predicaments. Things can only go downhill from here, so leave any place that is starting from a position of hardship.
- Everyone should plant a garden or have a very good relationship with a local farmer(s) for meat, dairy, and vegetables.
- Everyone should safeguard their tertiary paper wealth by moving a good portion of it into primary and secondary forms of wealth. This means hard assets and/or the means of production.
- If you rely on medications, you should do what you can to ensure that you have as much of a supply as is necessary for you. This is especially true for any that cause physical dependence, or upon which your life absolutely depends.

There are no right or wrong answers, or actions, since none of us knows precisely what will unfold or when. Instead, we must prepare as if for a trip across open water—right now it seems calm enough, but . . . you never know. Once the waters turn rough, you'll only be able to make use of whatever preparations and training you happen to have brought along—no more and no less.

If it helps, think of these steps as the insurance you hope you never have to collect on, like life insurance or vehicle collision insurance. If you own a home, you probably have fire insurance, because you know life is risky and you want to mitigate what risks you can. Even though homeowners have a 99.9% chance of ever needing their fire insurance, they get it anyway. The same thinking regarding resilience applies here. You hope to never use it, but you get it anyway because that's the prudent thing to do.

My philosophy on preparing is simple: *Get started*. Begin by doing whatever is easiest and fastest as a means of taking that first step. It doesn't matter what your initial actions are, as long as you get started. Any actions you take will begin to allow an alignment to develop between your thinking and your life's activities.

One immediate benefit of getting started is relief from worry.

Insufficient, but Necessary

Let's be perfectly honest: No matter how grand the steps we might take to prepare for a potential environmental, social, or economic disruption, they are almost certain to be insufficient. Yet at the same time, they're still necessary.

They'll be insufficient because being perfectly and completely prepared is infinitely expensive. Even trying to maintain a specific standard of living may become too costly to bear. But actions are still necessary, even if insufficient, because they help us align what we do with what we know.

In my experience, when gaps exist between what you know to be true and your actions, anxiety (if not fear) is the result. So, while the state of the world may contribute to your sense of anxiety, it's a lack of action that lets it fester.

If not now, when? If not you, who?

—*Hillel the Elder*

We take actions because we must. If we don't, who will? We change the world by changing ourselves. We reduce stress, fear, and anxiety in our lives by aligning our thoughts and our actions, being realistic about what we can preserve, and setting our goals and plans accordingly.

Set Targets

When considering preparation, the first question is usually, "How much?" Here I recommend setting a realistic goal, given the amount of money and time you have to devote.

My family's goal has never been to be 100% self-sufficient in meeting *any* of our basic needs. Instead, our goal has been to increase our self-sufficiency to something—*anything*—greater than "none." For example, until we got our solar photovoltaic panels, we were 100% dependent on the utility grid for our electricity. Now we're just a tiny bit less dependent, perhaps 97%, but we can manufacture and deploy our own electricity if necessary, and that's no small feat.

How big is the difference between being 0% self-reliant and 3%? It's huge. With our 3%, we can charge batteries, have light at night and, most important, prevent our fully stocked freezer from thawing during a power outage. We have some control over our electricity, the most critical energy source to our daily lives.

Similarly, there's an enormous difference between being 0% and 10% self-sufficient for food production. At 0% self-sufficiency, you rely entirely on the existing food distribution system. At something over 0%, you may grow a garden, foster local relationships with farmers, plant fruit trees in the yard, keep a few chickens, and/or maintain a deep pantry, which means you can always meet some of your own food needs. Developing even a limited percentage of your own food sufficiency doesn't take a lot of money, and it requires just a little bit of time. And it allows you and your family to develop skills and connections that will very likely make a huge difference at some point.

So why not set a realistic target that makes sense for you and your family, and then find a way to get there?

Being in Service

Our household is not preparing for ourselves alone. We are preparing for people we haven't even yet met. When we set food aside, we do so with the idea that we may be feeding others. When we buy sleeping bags, we buy more than we could need or use.

Reducing our own anxiety was reason enough to prepare, but an equally important objective was to be in a position to serve our community should that need arise in the future. Were a crisis to occur, we would fully expect to find many unprepared people scrambling around in a desperate bid to meet their needs, somewhat paralyzed by the situation and unable to react effectively. We feel it is our duty to reduce (not add to) the confusion and unmet needs and help out as many others as we can.

Some think of personal preparation as a selfish act, perhaps involving such things as guns and bunkers, but that's not at all what this is about; in fact, it is the opposite. My experience in life tells me that being a good community member means putting your own house in order first. If you do, you'll have a stable foundation and be in a better position to add valuable resources and skills to community efforts. It's like putting on your oxygen mask in an airplane emergency. You put yours on first before helping your kids put theirs on.

A strong community begins with strong households. It's like a fractal pattern: The whole is reflected in the parts. A strong community cannot be fashioned from weak households. My expectation is that communities will rally in the face of a disruption, an act I witnessed several times during hurricanes I lived through when I was in North Carolina. But some communities will fare better than others, and the difference between them will be determined by the personal resilience of their respective citizen populations. Your challenge here is to first get your own house in order, and then work on ways that you can help to increase the resilience of your local community and personal networks. If your community has no backbone, no cohesion, you might want to reconsider living there.

You must be the change you wish to see. If it is your wish to live in a resilient community, you must become more resilient yourself. In order to best assist your seatmate, you must put on your own oxygen mask first.

Step 0

Many people, when daunted by the potential magnitude of the coming change, immediately jump to some very hard conclusions that prove to be incapacitating. For example, they may have thoughts such as, *I need to go back to school to get an entirely different degree so I can have a different job!* or *I need to completely relocate to a new area and start over, leaving all of my friends behind!* or *I need to abandon my comfortable home and move to a remote off-grid cabin!*

These anxious conclusions may feel so radical that they're quickly abandoned as unfeasible. As a result, nothing gets accomplished. Nearly everyone has hidden barriers to action lurking within.

My advice here is crisp and clear: *Find the smallest and easiest thing you can do, and then do it.* It doesn't matter what the first step is. If that thing is buying an extra jar of pimentos because you can't imagine life without them, then buy an extra jar next time you're out shopping and put it in the pantry. I'm only halfway joking. I call this "Step 0" to symbolize something minor that might precede Step 1. The point is that small steps lead to bigger steps. If you've not yet taken Step 1 toward personal preparation and resilience, I invite you to consider taking Step 0 first.

Other Step 0 examples might be taking out a small bit of extra cash to store outside of the bank in case of a banking disruption, buying a bit more food each week to slowly deepen your pantry, or going online to learn something more about ways you can increase your resilience around water, food, energy, or anything else you deem important to your future. It doesn't much matter what it is, as long as you take an action that has meaning to you.

The goal of Step 0 is to break the ice now and get things rolling. My motto is, *I'd rather be a year early than a day late.*

The Importance of Community

Of all the steps I've taken, building my community has developed the most important element of my resilience. Whatever the future holds, I'd rather face it surrounded by people I respect, admire, and love in my local community, people I trust and know I can count on. That's my measure of true wealth.

I would recommend working with people you trust or with whom you already share basic values. The closer they live to you geographically, the better. Next door is best. I have no interest in living in fear, and my plan is to live through whatever comes next with a positive attitude and with as much satisfaction and fun as I can possibly muster. So, it has always been important to be in community with others who share this outlook.

It's incredibly helpful to find people to join forces with as you step through the basics of self-preparation. I encourage you to consider seeking like-minded locals with whom to form such a group, if you haven't already done so, and to encourage others to do the same.

You are only as secure as your neighbor, and together you are only as secure as your town, and your town is only as secure as the next town over. But it all begins at the center, like a fractal pattern, with a core of resilient households being at the center of it all.

What's the First Thing I Should Do?

The answer is simple: *Get started!*

The sooner you get started, the sooner you'll begin to feel happier, more in control, and ready to face the future with your eyes fixed on the opportunities that will arise and options that exist.

CHAPTER 31

Build Up Your Capital!

None are so poor as those who only have money.

T he road toward becoming more resilient begins with broadening your definition of "capital." If you can build up the four forms of capital outlined in this chapter, you'll be far more resilient than you were before, and way ahead of someone who is rich in just one of them.

You are probably already well acquainted with financial capital. That's money in the bank, it's stocks and bonds and other representations of currency and asset ownership. Nearly 100% of Wall Street, academia, and media's efforts are spent keeping you squarely focused on financial capital to the exclusion of all other forms of capital. Their messages are clear: "Money is the only thing that matters!"

But aren't your time and your health also forms of capital you "own"? Yes, they really are. And so are anything and *everything* that brings you joy and happiness and contentment to your life. By this definition, you have many different types of assets and forms of capital, and each of them needs to be tended to if you want them to increase, which at this point you really, *really* should.

If you are rich across multiple forms of capital, then you are more resilient than someone who may be stupendously well-endowed in one form of capital. For example, someone who has a billion dollars is as rich as Croesus (well, not actually, his wealth would have been if all you have is financial capital), but even if you have millions to your name, you are *not* resilient. My line

Home	Health
Wealth	Community

FIGURE 31.1 The Four Forms of Capital

of work has brought me before rich people who are terrified and brittle, and poor people who are incredibly blessed with a fullness of life and happiness.

Some of you may be familiar with these forms of wealth as having been broken down into eight categories. Truthfully, people have found those hard to remember—heck, even I have to strain sometimes to pull numbers 7 and 8 out of my brain. So, I've simplified them into four forms of capital, shown in Figure 31.1.

1. **Home** includes everything in your home, all the items in the pantry and your basement and/or garage. It includes how well insulated it is, and how many redundant means of heating and cooling you have installed and operating.

2. **Health** includes the state of health of your body, and your emotional health and spiritual depth.

3. **Wealth** is your money, of course, but also your knowledge and your time. If you have financial freedom (where passive income supports your lifestyle) and you have time to spare for your passions, and your skills allow you to make the most out of any situation and life, then you have real wealth.

4. **Community** is your social capital and the state of the culture in which you live. I don't mean the culture of "France" or "the United States" but your *local* culture. For example, New Orleans has a very different cultural capital depth than Concord, New Hampshire. Your social capital is not just how many people you know, but how well you know them.

Let's look at each of these in more depth.

Home

Material capital consists of the tangible things that meet our needs, infuse our lives with beauty, we can see and touch, and either provide value to us or insulate us from future costs. Things like buildings, roads, art, fences, bridges, power facilities, factories, cars, wells, and tractors.

On our property, this includes things like solar hot water and PV systems, generators, honey extractors, backup heating and water systems, and quality hand tools—the list goes on.

This topic could fill an entire book on its own. In this section, we'll provide guidance on how to develop the foundational aspects of material capital, and note that detailed recommendations (such as specific products to consider) can be found at **https://peakprosperity.com**.

Your home is going to be your primary fortress against whatever might come. You'll want to take advantage of the relative calm that exists now, when goods and services are plentiful and affordable (at least compared to what they will be in an energy-constrained future) to top everything off, build a deep pantry (and a deep garage, or basement, or other onsite storage) and to make any investments and improvements.

Your goals for your home (assuming it's "the place" where you plan to ride out the next years of your life) should be to make it as energy efficient as possible, fully maintained, and stocked up with spare *everything*. Whether you want to be more resilient or merely to beat inflation (because your money will buy less next year than this year), stocking up is the right move.

Cry Once

Have you ever noticed that yard sales and flea markets are filled with the same two types of stuff? There you will find decades-old tools and appliances that still work, and newer crap that doesn't work. The newer stuff is usually made cheaply and has been manufactured by the most inexpensive labor available at the time, often with planned obsolescence as the underlying corporate strategy. The older products, made with much more care and better materials, amazingly often have many years of useful life left in them.

There's an important lesson to be learned here.

When acquiring home capital, go for the highest-quality, best-built items you can afford. One of our longtime readers at Peak Prosperity, who knows the value of dependability from his years of wilderness and military training, has coined this the "cry once" philosophy.

Generally, the higher the quality of an item, the higher its purchase price. It can hurt to pay top dollar, hence the "cry" part. But then it may last a lifetime, so that's where the "once" comes in. My own experience confirms that if I buy cheaper items, which usually means at lower quality, I tend to cry more due to inferior usefulness, poor design, aggravating breakdowns, and shorter lifespan. Truly, poorly designed, cheap products bring out my monkey fist of anger. Who's got time for that?

Over many years of observation, I've calculated that it is much less costly in the long run to cry once and invest in well-designed, durable products. Once the initial tears dry, you won't have any further regrets and quite possibly a lot of satisfaction.

This strategy applies to nearly everything, from goods to services to relationships. Invest in quality to ensure they'll be there when you need to count on them most.

An adjunct strategy is to make sure you take the time and effort to take care of the products you buy and use. Grease is far cheaper than repairs.

This is especially important given a future defined by the Three Es. If you decide to buy cheap, what's to guarantee that replacement parts will still be available later on?

Health

If you have your health, you have a vital form of capital. It is the absence of health that often serves to make us realize how important our health really is to our happiness and contentment with life.

Being healthy makes sense in every era and under every circumstance, so it's really not a unique recommendation to make. What I'd like to add to the conversation is the idea that being in shape will be an essential element to successfully thriving in some future scenarios. It's possible that being out of shape reveals an underlying assumption that the future will be just as easy and benign as today, with the same comfortable lifestyles and easy access to medical care when and if needed. In my view, those are flawed assumptions.

What if the period of ease and stability we're in is a transient artifact of the age of petroleum, something that we know will be drawing to a close at some point? Given that, doesn't it make sense to begin acting as if it's already true, and that the best time to get in peak physical condition is right now?

Who knows? We all may be doing more physical labor in the future, walking and biking more, and being outside doing this and that. If you feel you could benefit from a similar path as we've taken, the most important elements to focus on are:

Nutrition—Everything rests on good nutrition. Not only does it deliver the essential nutrients your body needs to function properly, but it's also the key to weight loss. In addition, it's your most effective vehicle for reducing the inflammation and toxins responsible for aging, injury, and disease.

Eat poorly and it does not matter how much you exercise, you will still be unhealthy. The Standard American Diet (SAD) is really quite toxic, and the more you learn about the roles of sugars and seed oils in creating a lot of illness the more horrified you'll be.

Physical activity—Focus on developing strength, flexibility, endurance, and coordination. My fitness program currently consists of farming, but for non-farmers, programs like CrossFit promote high-intensity, varied exercises with supervised coaching and effective results. Whatever your preferred avenue, the key is regular daily exercise, even if that means just five minutes of situps and pushups between rounds at your computer.

Sleep—The benefits of sufficient sleep are many, and the cost of too little can range from chronic fatigue and lack of focus to weight gain, to greater risk of diabetes and heart attack. Sadly, over 75% of Americans experience some form of chronic sleep disorder. Fortunately, there are functional medicine experts who specialize in sleep disorders and are quite successful at helping problem sleepers become regular sleepers. The most important tip is to avoid blue screens (computers, smartphones, TVs) two hours before bedtime. If you can't, then use blue-blocking eyeglasses. They work like a charm!

Stress reduction—Stress is a killer, and our modern lifestyle is full of it. It weakens our immune systems, ages us, affects our weight, teeth, and temperament. Finding ways to minimize stress's ability to take root in our bodies and minds—with mindfulness, meditation, yoga, and so forth—is well worth the time invested.

All of these are important in your pursuit of better health. And improving one of them will usually help with improving the others, as well. But one of these is worth discussing further, as its impact on your health, body shape, performance and well-being is hard to overemphasize, and that's nutrition.

Science has finally caught up with nutrition, and we know you really are what you eat. Your body entirely replaces itself every two years. Your brain rebuilds itself in one year, your DNA renews itself every two months, your blood is entirely renewed every four months, and your body builds a whole new skeleton every three months. In just one year, your body is 98% replaced. New building blocks are brought in and old ones are flushed out. Obviously, this is a very complex process and having the right ingredients in place is essential.

Many modern foods are flat-out toxic to our bodies, and we now understand the biochemistry that makes them so. Sugars are inflammatory; their chemical nature makes them attack the lining of our blood vessels like water corrodes iron and living with daily low levels of inflammation leads to joint pain, low energy, circulatory problems, poor skin, and weight gain, too.

Sugars are added to an astonishing number of the foods we eat as companies exploit our innate attraction to sugars. We find it added to spaghetti sauce and tortillas, so-called healthy yogurts, and added to spicy hummus as well as our gourmet morning coffee. Once you begin reading package labels, it's astounding how hard it is to avoid refined sugars. Our strongest recommendation is to abandon the USDA guidelines, which are overly weighted toward carbohydrates, and avoid nearly everything found in the center aisles of your local grocery store in favor of healthy, living food. The heavily processed foods found in the center aisles are loaded with fructose and stripped of life. Sure, there are calories to be found there, but not much else.

You are what you eat, and it took your author a number of decades and his own chronic health issues to finally figure that out.

Nature Connection

In too many people's lives, a connection to the natural world has almost entirely disappeared. Daily contact with the outdoor world has been reduced to a scant few seconds between the car door and our front door. Because of this limited exposure, it's easy to forget that humans remain 100% dependent on natural systems for our survival.

Increasing amounts of research, and good old common sense, are telling us that it is vital that we get nature connection time. Being outside is a soothing remedy that activates some sort of primal switches inside of our DNA blueprints. Be sure you get plenty of outside time, if only for the UV and infrared light from the sun, which activate our Vitamin D and mitochondrial energy production, respectively.

Mastering Stress

More mentally resilient people share a number of common traits. At the top of this list is having a support system of friends and family who can share in the struggles.

Humans are a social species; we need each other. To enrich our lives. To lean on for help when we need it. Without the support of others—both physical and emotional—we're capable of much less.

Understanding how your body functions under stress will help you recognize when it threatens to derail you. In an agitated state, it's much harder for others to help you and for you to be open to receiving their efforts, let alone make good decisions.

When these moments arise, there are coping mechanisms you can use to defuse the anxiety. Here are the ones the Navy SEALs use (and those guys deal with a *lot* of stress!):

1. **Goal setting.** The ability to reason and plan helps to keep the stress and chaos at bay. No matter how bad the situation, always have a goal, even if that goal is simply taking one more breath.

2. **Mental rehearsal and visualization.** This aligns the body and mind so that stressful gaps between the two don't arise or are minimized. Mentally rehearsing scenarios allows things to unfold more effortlessly and naturally when they actually arise. So, you might rehearse what it would be like if you lost your job.

3. **Self-talk.** Self-talk, especially positive self-talk, has a powerful calming influence on the mind and body. *Okay, self, we're going to make it through this and have a great story for the campfire later . . .*

4. **Arousal control.** Slow, deep breathing delivers more oxygen to the brain and tells the body that everything is okay. After all, we're breathing long and slow, aren't we? This practice can enhance brain awareness and alertness.

The reason the Navy has a program to control the mind–body reactions is because they know that the emotional core of the brain (that pesky amygdala again!) is what takes over when things get dicey. It's nothing to be ashamed of, it's simply how we're wired neurologically. But often our culture demands that we act as if it doesn't exist.

Which is why, even if we're not in a panic-inducing crisis, the same low-grade anxiety-producing responses can be churning along, reducing our motivation, slowly inflaming our body, and ruining our daily joy and long-term health.

The Spiritual Side

For many people, a big part of emotional resilience is rooted in spiritual connection. This is tricky territory, so I'll begin by saying that it's not my intent here to elevate or malign any one religion over another. But I do wholeheartedly support the idea of developing spiritual purpose in whatever way is meaningful for you. Some find it in organized faith. Some find it in nature. Some find it in science. Some find it inside themselves.

We are all tested in life, by trials and tribulations and, ultimately, by confronting our mortality. If your emotional resilience is what helps you react well during these tests, it's your spiritual resilience that gives you the conviction to push through them.

Keeping the perspective that we are part of a bigger story arc allows us to understand that the world is not set against us personally, and there are larger processes in play for the universe, the planet, humanity, and our communities.

Each of us has a role to play, no matter how small, in each of these gigantic processes. Realizing this puts our personal egos and challenges into perspective. From this sense of humility, peace, compassion, and love result.

There's a great mystery to life and seeking meaning is a noble pursuit that has always been a part of being human. There are a great many spiritual teachers out there and if you have an open mind, there's something to be gained from listening to a range of them. Borrow the insights from each that resonate with you.

By combining a spiritual worldview with self-mastery, you will be able to better handle whatever life throws your way. Remember, it's not the insult that determines your fate, it's your reaction to it. The good news? That's something you can be 100% in control of.

Wealth

The time has come to *really* diversify, away from wealth being nearly entirely contained within and measured by the world of central bank fiat currencies. If all you have are dollars, or yen or euros or yuan, or even if you have a diversified holding of all of them, you are still 100% exposed to the poor decisions and ideologies of the money printers (central banks) and spenders (governments).

When you truly understand that what we call "money" (actually *fiat currency*, which often violates one or more features of real money) is just a claim on things, and further that debt is itself just a claim on future money, then you will appreciate why you must get out of those paper claims and into real things. Why? Because an ever-expanding set of claims—exponentially expanding, at that—assume the future economy of things will match it when the time comes. But the resources for that future of *more* simply don't exist. It's elementary math.

Let's look again at the expansion of fiat currency in response to Covid by the U.S. Federal Reserve in Figure 31.2 (which is the same as Figure 13.1). That expansion was both preposterous and revealing. Preposterous because who could ever think that expanding the money supply by 40% in just two years was a reasonable thing to do? Revealing because it shows that any and every crisis is yet one more reason to print with wild abandon. In other words, expect more of the same in the future.

The 40% rise was equal in size to all of the money that had been created throughout all of the United States' entire economic and political history up through 2006. Every war fought, every bridge built, every farm plowed, and every building built led to the creation of as many dollars as were created during two years of Covid.

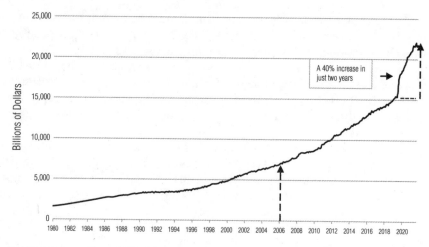

FIGURE 31.2 Broad (M2) Money Supply in the United States

What, exactly, was built and what new flood of products and services were introduced as a result of all that currency creation? Nothing, really, as the economy barely budged. The very predictable outcome was inflation, which the United States and Europe got good and hard beginning in 2022.

The Great Wealth Transfer

It's time to broaden the definition of "wealth" to include your money and money-like assets, your tangible physical assets, your skills, knowledge, *and* your time (meaning how well you are using your time here on earth to accomplish your soul's purpose). These periods of extreme currency printing are universally misrepresented in the press as periods of currency debasement, that is, inflation. "Oh goodness," the articles will exclaim, "things are getting more expensive!" Instead, we need to see these periods more properly for what they are; they are *wealth transfers*.

Those who hold excessive paper claims lose out, while those holding real, tangible assets win.

I've written extensively over the years about the coming wealth transfer. Now I am writing about the wealth transfer in the present tense because it's already here and has been happening for some time. The process is designed by very smart people who happen to be doing something quite dangerous and immoral: transferring wealth from the many to the few. The first part of the wealth transfer process has a name: *financial repression*.

Financial repression happens because governments always get themselves into a condition of too much debt and they have few politically acceptable ways of escaping that situation. The formula works like this:

Step 1: A government (or an entire nation) gets into trouble by borrowing too much.

Step 2: Rather than pay this debt down honestly via cutting spending (unpopular) or by defaulting (even more unpopular), the government conspires with the central bank to slowly liquidate the stack of obligations by forcing negative real interest rates on everyone—that is, when you get paid less in interest than the current rate of inflation. So, if you get 0% on your savings, but inflation is 5%, you lose.

Step 3: But there's a problem: Negative interest rates don't work if people can dodge financial repression by taking their money elsewhere, so a ring fence has to be built out of capital controls and explicit interest rate caps on and across the whole spectrum of interest-bearing securities. Nobody can have access to positive interest securities, and they may even need to have their cash taken away (this is what the war on cash is really about) if confronted with actual negative interest rates at the bank.

Step 4: Sit back and watch with glee as everyone with savings silently and steadily has their purchasing power transferred to the debtors, be those public or private entities.

This is theft, plain and simple; engineered theft of the highest order. It takes from the many. This is what Ben Bernanke, Janet Yellen, and then Jay Powell were carefully overseeing during their tenures at the Federal Reserve, and they didn't care one bit about you or the social pain and economic misery they inflicted on hundreds of millions of people (a.k.a. "not the 1%").

They might not actually be bad people, but they sure acted like sociopaths. The programmatic, policy-driven loss of income that their financial repression created harmed the elderly, pensioners, savers, and the young. All to benefit a government that has a spending problem and to pump up the profits of the big banks and portfolios of the wealthiest people. If it looks like a duck, walks like a duck, and quacks like a duck . . . it just might be a duck.

So, financial repression is Act I of the Great Wealth Transfer. It's happening and it will continue to happen for a very long time. The middle class will experience this as a steady erosion of their ability to feel financially secure. It's a drip, drip, drip style of torture. Eventually those drips morph into a final and rapid deluge. A final orgy of money printing is always the end of the story.

History is full of periods when well-meaning and self-interested leadership tried to cover up past mistakes with more money printing. We have loads of history to study on the matter and the only thing lacking here is general awareness of, and interest in, those lessons. Fortunately, it's all there to study.

Consider the Weimar Germany experience between the years 1918 and 1923. A set of bad decisions, a prior war, and a punitive reparations treaty all combined to create a period when printing more and more money made sense to those in power. And so, they did with much applause from seated politicians and much of the populace too, it should be noted.

At least for a while.

But you know how all that money printing turned out: Wheelbarrows of cash were used to buy loaves of bread, vast fortunes were lost, savings were entirely wiped out, and the moment is still referred to by many as a period of great wealth *destruction*. And, indeed, many experienced it that way.

But the truth is that true wealth was not destroyed, it was *transferred*. It passed from the unwary to the alert and it did so in enormous and magnificent amounts.

Real wealth, of course, is factories and farms, buildings and houses, raw land and minerals and water and food. There were just as many of these forms of wealth before the Weimar hyperinflation as there were afterward. That is, the amount of real wealth did not change as a consequence of all that money printing and subsequent monetary collapse.

But who owned that wealth changed. True wealth was not destroyed (the money was), it was transferred.

And this is the hidden part of money printing: The inevitable destructive events are always presented to us as if they were some form of natural disaster, unseen and unforeseeable, just an accident that happened. "Oh no!" the newspapers will cry out, "so much wealth has been destroyed!"

But now you will know that nothing of the sort will have happened at all. Real wealth remains, but who owns it is what defines the winners and losers of every wealth transfer era. To be on the right side of that line, presuming you'd rather be on the receiving than the donating side, you need to boost your ownership of real wealth.

The Scarcity Mindset

Often the first step for people is deprogramming the singular view that money (and only money) = wealth. Again, money is not true wealth; it is a *claim* on wealth. Paper money, and its electronic equivalents stored as ones and zeros on bank hard disks, has no actual value all by itself. You can't eat it, you can't wear it, and it won't massage your tired muscles after a hard day's work.

Yet relentless cultural and social reinforcement of the "money = wealth" view has led many to hold that myopic view. The problem? It can really lead one astray. Its core is a scarcity model based on the idea that there's never enough money in one's life. I've met billionaires who were terrified of losing their money, or at least of not having as much as the next billionaire. It seems crazy, but a fixation on money can create a powerful scarcity mindset even among those living amidst the grandest abundance ever seen in human history. There's never enough, for some reason. Everybody feels like they always need more.

Mental health and true personal liberty begin by setting the scarcity mindset aside. The gateway word to happiness (and contentment) is "enough." Do you have enough? Most people in developed countries have more than enough, by several orders of magnitude. At least by historical standards, or any reasonably objective standards. This is vital to do because we're about to enter a period where more wealth won't just magically emerge all around us as it has in the past—thanks to surplus energy provided by fossil fuels—but will instead be frustratingly harder and harder to come by. Those who haven't prepared, who haven't educated themselves and therefore don't understand the process, run the risk of being perpetually unhappy because they are facing what they experience as increasing scarcity, which can be terrifying.

Protecting Your Monetary Wealth

At the writing of this book (fall of 2022), inflation is at the highest it's been in at least four decades. And it's not contained to any one country but is rampant across the United States and Europe. The reasons include legitimate supply chain shortages such as in raw materials and energy, but the main culprit is money printing. My prediction is that we'll see lots more money printing all the way to the bitter end.

This is simply an extension of the trends already in play and playing the historical odds. Humans have always defaulted to money printing because it both (1) destroys the little people and (2) enriches the already wealthy people who—surprise!—make all the rules and important decisions.

So, to avoid those ill effects and to protect your monetary wealth, the idea is to move away whatever currency your country uses and into things like:

- Energy companies, specifically oil- and gas-producing companies.
- Gold, silver, and platinum.
- Arable land.
- Land with timber and firewood trees.
- Productive real estate, especially commercial buildings that are suited for manufacturing real things that people need.

- Homestead investments, including solar, better insulation, new windows and roof(s), and durable appliances.
- Deepening your inventory if you own a business.
- Copper, cobalt, and other industrial metals whose extraction costs will skyrocket once the peak oil predicament is more widely recognized.

Build Your Knowledge and Skills

Knowledge and skills are the most portable forms of your personal wealth. They go with you everywhere. If I was suddenly left adrift in a foreign country with only the clothes on my back, my knowledge and skills would be my most valuable form of capital. And they would be worth a lot because I have spent a lifetime accumulating new skills and knowledge.

I know how to ferment and distill alcohol, I understand medicine and its practice, I know how to garden and preserve food, I am a very good shot, I can play guitar and balance a company's books.

Knowledge really comes alive with the marriage of theory and practice. The degree of overlap between the two is important because it determines your level of mastery. And mastery is important because it's what you use to create value. The more mastery you have, the more value you can create to exchange for other desired resources (income, goods, services, etc.) or to enjoy directly yourself (entertainment, homestead improvements, social currency, etc.).

For the more empirically minded, think of this relationship as a set of equations:

$$\textbf{Information} + \textbf{Application} = \textbf{Mastery}$$

and

$$\textbf{Mastery} \times \left(\textbf{Effort} / \textbf{Time} \right) = \textbf{Value}$$

So, in order to produce value, you need to start with information and application. And you need to have both—they're equally important. Information without application is practically useless. Things hardly ever run in the real world in the same way they're predicted on the chalkboard—something all those early aeronauts who crashed before the Wright brothers' successful flight at Kitty Hawk learned the hard way.

Not only can pure "book smarts" be useless, but it can also be dangerous. The hubris of those who think they understand everything but don't have an on-the-ground perspective to counterbalance their judgment often leads to perfect logic that crumples when it slams into an imperfect reality. The current efforts of the Federal Reserve to sidestep the business cycle and manage the prices of all assets around the world using only the crude pairing of interest rates and the printing press is just one such example.

Application uninformed by information is equally futile. It's just blindly going through the motions without understanding the why or the how of something. Imagine the unskilled worker whose job is to pull a lever on his machine to complete a task. What if he needs the machine to increase output? What will he do if the machine stops? Or the lever breaks? Our worker is helpless to address questions like this outside of his own experience. Such blind adherence to "it's always been done this way" can be seen in our modern "Big Ag" factory-farming practices. They deplete our topsoil and require expensive and unhealthy inputs annually, ignoring the wellspring of new models demonstrating a better way to affordably farm the same foods organically and much more sustainably.

By increasing your knowledge and refining your skills into mastery, you are investing in yourself. Especially for younger people without a lot of monetary capital, the most important thing you could be doing is building your skills. Apprentice under a master and you'll get there quicker.

Use Time Wisely

Time is our most valuable asset, one we have less of with each passing moment.

Philosophers of days past kept skulls on their desks as a reminder that their time on earth was short and not to be wasted. While a bit macabre, this was an effective way to maintain the perspective that every moment is sacred and precious, and to be used to its fullest.

But you don't need a skull on your desk if you have children. Growing kids are an effective reminder that time is flying by and you're getting older. Like all good reminders of the fleeting nature of time, kids let us know that if we have life goals to accomplish, there's no time like the present.

As I've alluded to numerous times, each of the steps toward resilience takes time to accomplish, some more than others. For a number of them, it may take a year or more to make real progress.

As you look at the time you have to invest in improving your life—this week, this month, this year—ask yourself: "How much of it will I budget to spend developing resilience?" And knowing that there will always be more to do than you have available time, ask next: "Given that time budget, which steps will I prioritize?"

As should be crystal clear by now, our work with the Three Es in the Crash Course points toward huge changes headed our way. Our economic model is unsustainable and therefore has a crisis (or a set of crises) as part of its very design. In parallel with that, humans are headed toward a very large ecological crisis. Nobody knows exactly when these systems will veer off in a brand-new set of directions, but we have a lot of data to suggest that this will happen within the next two decades and, once it hits, the pace of collapse will speed up exponentially.

Nobody knows exactly when these changes will impact us personally. Because of this, and because we cannot know if the next big systemic shock will happen tonight or in 20 years, we should act as if it's going to be tonight.

When it comes to using my time on becoming resilient, my personal motto is *I'd rather be a year early than a day late.*

Community Capital

In 2015, authors Philip Haslam and Russell Lamberti published the book *When Money Destroys Nations: How Hyperinflation Ruined Zimbabwe, How Ordinary People Survived, and Warnings for Nations that Print Money.* After running through all the variables influencing why some people died, some merely survived, and others actually thrived, the one that stood out the most was an individual's personal community. Social capital is not how many people you know, but how many people you know who you can trust, and the depth of those bonds.

Of all the steps I've taken, I consider building my community the most important element of my resilience. Whatever the future holds, I'd rather face it surrounded by people I respect, admire, and love in my local community, people I trust and know I can count on. That's a form of true wealth.

As social creatures, with all of our gifts and flaws, strengths and weaknesses, the simple truth is we need each other. We rely on people in our community to do the things for us that we can't do well ourselves, but the biggest need is for the emotional nourishment that we receive from each other.

It's telling that one of the most punitive forms of punishment that humans have ever devised is prolonged solitary confinement. With enough time in isolation, some people are irretrievably damaged. What's also interesting is that we've never been so technologically connected yet so physically and emotionally isolated from each other. It's as if we've self-imposed a brutal solitary confinement on ourselves to the point that we could be in a crowded room yet feel all alone. The suicide statistics for the United States (including, especially, the deaths of despair logged in the fentanyl overdoses) confirm that many of us are actually desperately alone.

Our physical and emotional, intimate connections with each other nourish us in ways that are difficult to measure, but easy to detect. Touch and eye contact are wired into us as necessary elements of healthy living.

Deep interpersonal connections are what bring fulfillment and meaning to our lives. We all crave to be given the opportunity to bring our gifts into the world, and the reflections of caring people who really know us are essential to that process.

We want to be really seen, to mentor, to give and receive, to express our unique gifts, and to express those gifts in each of the roles we can fill as we age from infants to elders. At least, that's how it's supposed to work.

Seamless and joyous transitions through life's developmental stages happen best when we are part of a whole and intact community. While such communities are rare, and some readers may doubt they even exist, they are increasingly being sought out and created by people, especially younger people who have decided that there's more to life than an isolated consumer-driven lifestyle. They are seeking the more connected and authentic relationships for which we are all innately wired.

One of the very best realizations that can emerge from a wider perspective on the predicaments we face is that life is not to be wasted, present-day circumstances are demanding we bring our very best selves forward, and that our relationships are as essential to our own happiness as they are to the fate of the world.

Taken together, all of our relationships and experiences with the people around us form, over time, what is called *social capital*. With social capital, we can call in favors, anticipate needs, reach out to give and receive support, witness and participate in important life events, and weave the strands that become ropes of connection over time.

Most people intuitively understand the importance of social capital, but strangely, in our experience, it's quite often an underinvested area. Many people seriously underestimate the time and dedicated effort that is required to build true community. It's not something you can purchase and be "done" with, the way you can with food storage preparations or a solar installation. And it's not something you can immediately create for yourself, no matter how socially gifted you might be.

Here's a situation we've run into before. One person in a relationship will peer into the future, run a few mental calculations, and suddenly proclaim: "Honey, we need to move to the country!"

This person might think that they need to move really far out into the country, away from people, even the ones they already know, in order to be safe. This might make some tactical sense, at least under certain scenarios, but at a cost their partner is unwilling to bear.

What these people who seek safety at a distance are missing out on is the concept that social connections are as valuable as *any* other asset they might own. They are critically important not just to our happiness but also our potential future security. That is, one's community capital really matters. On this front, moving away sometimes makes sense; other times it really does not.

We each value different things in different ways. For the person who has always measured worth in dollars or personal accomplishments, the actual value of social capital can be an unfamiliar concept. Similarly, the person who wishes to protect their family by moving farther away may be undervaluing the strength and importance of the connections that their partner or children have already forged right where they live.

Social capital is a very real and highly valuable commodity, one that takes time to build no matter how motivated or gifted one may be at forming connections.

Local Culture Matters

You might have an ideal living arrangement and lots of nearby and strong social connections, yet still be in a bad situation if your local culture is either weak or hostile. You may judge your local culture to not be the right one for riding out the future, as it may be too violent already, or suffer from entrenched and terrible leadership, or lack any basic awareness of the true nature of the many predicaments we are facing.

Here's a good case study of how different cultures can behave very differently given the same situation.

New Orleans, 2005 Hurricane *Katrina* slammed into Louisiana on August 29, 2005, devastating the city. A general evacuation order was issued, but because the storm surge caused the failure of 53 levees, 80% of the city flooded, preventing many citizens from leaving.

In the immediate days that followed, bedlam reigned. Stores were looted (initially by those desperately seeking food and water), and soon more violent crimes like carjacking, murder, and rape were reported. Vigilantism spiked in response, as people sought to protect themselves and their property. The city police were soon joined by the National Guard to restore order, resulting in deadly clashes with the populace and rampant reports of law enforcement abuse and misconduct.

Relief supplies were abysmally long in arriving due to terrible mismanagement of the logistics by local authorities, Homeland Security, and FEMA. Deaths continued in the days following the hurricane from thirst, exhaustion, and violence that better coordination could have avoided. In the end, the shortcomings of its culture made the destruction in New Orleans much worse than it should have been. In some cases, neighborhoods that organized themselves for security would not allow people of certain races to pass through as they sought assistance. People unused to caring for themselves reacted angrily when their normal channels and systems broke down. Later, as politicians attempted to use the evacuation diaspora to their advantage, long-simmering race and class divisions within the city erupted again.

The levee system could have been engineered to withstand *Katrina*'s storm surge, but its repair and maintenance had been neglected over the preceding decades as politicians raided the budget for their pet projects. Moreover, a federal government that made itself immune to redress simply built the levees poorly while pretending they were not. The insular and territorial agencies responsible for responding to such an emergency clearly did not work in close enough partnership, before or during the tragedy.

Unfortunately, a city that normally pulled together during a normal hurricane situation literally fell apart when a new type of tragedy unfolded. New Orleans was simply very poor in the kind of cultural capital that would have helped it persevere through a crisis like *Katrina*. Yes, *Katrina* was a bad hurricane, and the subsequent flooding was the breaking point for a unique American tragedy, but the entire blame for the horrible aftermath rests with a failed culture at all levels, including too many people reliant on government to fix every problem.

Now, contrast this to another, even worse, natural disaster that occurred on the other side of the world just a few years later.

Japan, 2011   On Friday, March 11, 2011, a magnitude 9.0 earthquake struck of the Pacific coast of Tōhoku, Japan. This was the fourth-most-powerful earthquake in recorded history.

Felt all throughout Japan, the earthquake created tsunami waves over 100 feet high that flooded coastal regions, traveling as far as six miles inland. Over 15,000 people were killed (over seven times Hurricane *Katrina*'s death toll) and over a million buildings were damaged or destroyed. And, famously, three reactors at the Fukushima Daiichi nuclear power plant were destroyed, creating a radioactive crisis in the immediate aftermath of the disaster.

Yet while the loss of life and infrastructure was many times more severe than with *Katrina*, there were extremely few reports of looting, violence, or crimes of any kind. Police and military personnel were welcomed and provided frontline humanitarian relief. When government resources weren't available, locals banded together to provide for each other. Supplies and services made their way quickly to the many affected regions, and cleanup of the devastation happened remarkably quickly.

Much of this calm and effective response demonstrated by the people of Japan was due to values deeply rooted in the culture there. First off, whereas American culture is individualist, Japan's is collectivist—the needs of the group are considered more important than those of the individual. Concepts like *gamen* (enduring deprivation and making sacrifices) and *ganbare* (trying your best, no matter how hard the situation) guided the populace to work together and remain steadfast for the community's sake. A little more of this in New Orleans could have prevented a lot of the chaos that ensued after the levies failed.

We're not trying to glorify Japanese culture over American. Indeed, the passivity with which they accepted the government's media statements did not serve them well during the evasions the Japanese utility company TEPCO made as it scrambled to deal with the core meltdowns at Fukushima. But we do feel that it is valuable to demonstrate the extreme difference in response that different cultures can make to the same situation.

Consider the things you prioritize: career opportunity, living in balance with nature, safety and security—whatever they may be. Ask yourself if the culture where you currently live will serve you in your pursuit. If so, wonderful. If not, it may be time to consider taking action.

Finding a Culture That Serves You

If you conclude that the pervading culture where you live doesn't serve you well, you have two options: make the best of it, or relocate.

Relocating, obviously, is the more complex of the two and is not to be undertaken lightly. And for some reading this, it may not be feasible currently, given family, career, finances, or other obligations. But sometimes, it's the right decision.

It's my personal opinion that many cities are ill-equipped to face the coming future and will be terrible places to live if you value personal safety and freedom from the taxing grind of petty crime. What *Katrina* visited upon New Orleans, economics has brought down upon Detroit. If we're correct, then a similar fate awaits other major cities, and some of them are barely holding themselves to a civilized standard as it is.

The downslope of energy is going to be particularly vicious to cities that are simply gigantic sinks for energy, water, and other inputs and huge emitters of waste. Our 100-year experiment with concentrating more and more people into cities made a lot of sense when energy was plentiful but they will be impossible to maintain in their current arrangements during energy scarcity.

Conclusion

I hope this has inspired you, or motivated you, to begin the process of taking responsibility for your own resilience and future outcomes. The time of trusting our leadership to "do the right thing" has come and gone. It seems doubtful that they even know what the issues are, let alone have the capacity to offer constructive responses to our many predicaments.

Humanity has been here before, but always locally, never globally. Sure, the Romans collapsed, but Chinese dynasties had no clue about that fact until they were notified some time later. This time is different. There's nowhere to go that won't be affected. The human organism now spans the entire globe and we've scoured the entire planet for the best resources. Now we must quickly adjust and accept that the days of easy pickings are over, that growth is now our enemy and not our friend, and that we're going to have to live within much smaller financial, energy, and ecological budgets than in the past.

But all is not lost. Far from it. It's going to a turbulent period of time to be sure, and many people may die from the lack of foresight and planning (and you and I may well be among them; who knows?), but this is also when the new story gets written. To be in that game, to be a "signatory" on that new human contract, you have to be in the game.

Becoming resilient offers you not only the chance to be in that game, but to live a more meaningful, safe and happy life too.

Everything we think we know about the world is now changing; some for the worse, some for the better. Those in our Peak Prosperity tribe of resilient and prepared people are stacking the decks in their favor. Once the dust settles, the world will be rebuilt again, almost certainly under very different terms, and humanity will carry on. It always has, and it will again.

Along the way, we'll probably be reminded that *it didn't have to be this way.*

My sincere hope is that we'll use that regretful thought to do better next time, to be thoughtful, to use common sense, and to never again let careless and self-absorbed people anywhere near leadership positions.

Appendix

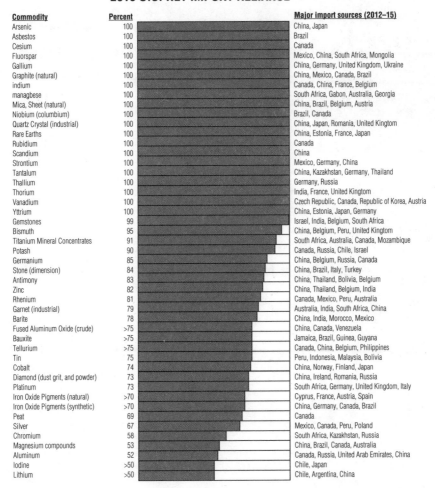

2016 U.S. NET IMPORT RELIANCE

Commodity	Percent	Major import sources (2012–15)
Arsenic	100	China, Japan
Asbestos	100	Brazil
Cesium	100	Canada
Fluorspar	100	Mexico, China, South Africa, Mongolia
Gallium	100	China, Germany, United Kingdom, Ukraine
Graphite (natural)	100	China, Mexico, Canada, Brazil
indium	100	Canada, China, France, Belgium
managbese	100	South Africa, Gabon, Australia, Georgia
Mica, Sheet (natural)	100	China, Brazil, Belgium, Austria
Niobium (columbium)	100	Brazil, Canada
Quartz Crystal (industrial)	100	China, Japan, Romania, United Kingtom
Rare Earths	100	China, Estonia, France, Japan
Rubidium	100	Canada
Scandium	100	China
Strontium	100	Mexico, Germany, China
Tantalum	100	China, Kazakhstan, Germany, Thailand
Thallium	100	Germany, Russia
Thorium	100	India, France, United Kingtom
Vanadium	100	Czech Republic, Canada, Republic of Korea, Austria
Yttrium	100	China, Estonia, Japan, Germany
Gemstones	99	Israel, India, Belgium, South Africa
Bismuth	95	China, Belgium, Peru, United Kingtom
Titanium Mineral Concentrates	91	South Africa, Australia, Canada, Mozambique
Potash	90	Canada, Russia, Chile, Israel
Germanium	85	China, Belgium, Russia, Canada
Stone (dimension)	84	China, Brazil, Italy, Turkey
Antimony	83	China, Thailand, Bolivia, Belgium
Zinc	82	China, Thailand, Belgium, India
Rhenium	81	Canada, Mexico, Peru, Australia
Garnet (industrial)	79	Australia, India, South Africa, China
Barite	78	China, India, Morocco, Mexico
Fused Aluminum Oxide (crude)	>75	China, Canada, Venezuela
Bauxite	>75	Jamaica, Brazil, Guinea, Guyana
Tellurium	>75	Canada, China, Belgium, Philippines
Tin	75	Peru, Indonesia, Malaysia, Bolivia
Cobalt	74	China, Norway, Finland, Japan
Diamond (dust grit, and powder)	73	China, Ireland, Romania, Russia
Platinum	73	South Africa, Germany, United Kingdom, Italy
Iron Oxide Pigments (natural)	>70	Cyprus, France, Austria, Spain
Iron Oxide Pigments (synthetic)	>70	China, Germany, Canada, Brazil
Peat	69	Canada
Silver	67	Mexico, Canada, Peru, Poland
Chromium	58	South Africa, Kazakhstan, Russia
Magnesium compounds	53	China, Brazil, Canada, Australia
Aluminum	52	Canada, Russia, United Arab Emirates, China
Iodine	>50	Chile, Japan
Lithium	>50	Chile, Argentina, China

FIGURE A.1   Minerals Fully or Partially Imported by the United States

Notes

Chapter 5: Dangerous Exponentials

1. Wisdom from Pakistan, "The World's Expected Carrying Capacity in a Post Industrial Agrarian Society," *Oil Drum: Europe*, November 1, 2007. **www.theoildrum.com/node/3090**.
2. Albert A. Bartlett, "Forgotten Fundamentals of the Energy Crisis," *American Journal of Physics* 46, no. 9 (1978): 876. **www.albartlett.org/articles/art_forgotten_fundamentals_overview.html**.
3. Albert A. Bartlett, "Arithmetic, Population, and Energy" (video). Last modified June 16, 2007. **www.youtube.com/watch?v=F-QA2rkpBSY**.
4. C. Bergsten and others, "Energy Implications of China's Growth," in *China's Rise: Challenges and Opportunities* (Washington, DC: Peterson Institute for International Economics, 2009), 137–168. **www.piie.com/publications/chapters_preview/4174/07iie4174.pdf**.
5. "China Energy Information," Enerdata. **https://www.enerdata.net/estore/energy-market/china/**.

Chapter 6: Problems and Predicaments

1. John Michael Greer, *The Long Descent: The User's Guide to the End of the Industrial Age* (Gabriola Island, British Columbia: New Society, 2008), 22.

Chapter 7: An Inconvenient Lie: The Truth about Growth

1. "Kenneth Boulding," *Wikiquotes*. **http://en.wikiquote.org/wiki/Kenneth_Boulding** (accessed September 7, 2010).
2. "Geithner Op-Ed: 'Welcome To The Recovery,'" press release, U.S. Department of the Treasury, August 3, 2010. **https://home.treasury.gov/news/press-releases/tg809**.
3. Julian L. Simon, "When Will We Run Out of Oil? Never!" *The Ultimate Resource II: People, Materials, Environment,* December 23, 1993. **www.juliansimon.com/writings/Ultimate_Resource/TCHAR11.txt**.

Chapter 8: Complex Systems

1. Explanation of economic equilibrium from: **https://www.econport.org/content/handbook/ADandS/Equilibrium/LongEquil.html**.
2. Eric Beinhocker, *Origin of Wealth: Evolution, Complexity, and the Radical Remaking of Economics* (Boston: Harvard Business School Press, 2006), 68.

Chapter 9: Our Money System

1. Justin Scheck, "Mackerel Economics in Prison Leads to Appreciation for Oily Fillets," *Wall Street Journal*, October 2, 2008. **http://online.wsj.com/article/ NA_WSJ_PUB:SB122290720439096481.html**.
2. John Kenneth Galbraith, *Money: Whence It Came, Where It Went* (New York: Houghton Mifflin, 1975), 18.
3. Michael McLeay, Amar Radia, and Ryland Thomas, "Money Creation in the Modern Economy, *Quarterly Bulletin 2014 Q1*, Bank of England, March 14, 2014. **https:// www.bankofengland.co.uk/quarterly-bulletin/2014/q1/money-creation-in- the-modern-economy**.
4. "The Story of the Federal Reserve System," Federal Reserve Bank of New York. **https:// www.newyorkfed.org/medialibrary/media/outreach-and-education/comic- books/NewYorkFed-StoryoftheFederalReserveSystem-WebColor.pdf**.
5. "Putting It Simply," Federal Reserve Bank of Boston, 1984.

Chapter 10: What Is Wealth? (Hint: It's Not Money)

1. Adam Smith, *The Wealth of Nations* (New York: Classic House Books, 2009), 1.

Chapter 11: Debt

1. Herbert Stein, "Herb Stein's Unfamiliar Quotations," *Slate*. **www.slate.com/id/2561** (accessed November 5, 2010).
2. Carmen M. Reinhart and Kenneth S. Rogoff, *This Time Is Different: Eight Centuries of Financial Folly* (Princeton: Princeton University Press, 2009).
3. Ibid.
4. "The Debt to the Penny and Who Holds It," *U.S. Treasury*. **https://fiscaldata.treasury .gov/datasets/debt-to-the-penny/debt-to-the-penny**.
5. John C. Goodman, "Kotlikoff: Real Federal Debt Is $239 Trillion," Goodman Institute, December 3, 2019. **https://www.goodmaninstitute.org/2019/12/03/kotlikoff-real- federal-debt-is-239-trillion/**.

Chapter 12: The Great Credit Bubble

1. "Predicting the Housing Future: Los Angeles and Orange Counties. Using the Case-Shiller Index to Find a Bottom," *Dr. Housing Bubble*, June 21, 2008. **www .doctorhousingbubble.com/predicting-the-housing-future-los-angeles- and-orange-counties-using-the-case-shiller-index-to-find-a-bottom**.
2. Jonathan Ping, "Median Housing Price to Income Ratios For Various Cities," *My Money Blog*, December 21, 2006. **www.mymoneyblog.com/median-housing-price-to- income-ratios-for-various-cities.html**.
3. "Update: Ratio Median House Price to Median Income," *Calculated Risk*, June 2008. **www.calculatedriskblog.com/2008/06/update-ratio-median-house- price-to.html**.
4. "The South Sea Company," *Wikipedia*. **http://en.wikipedia.org/wiki/South_Sea_ Company** (accessed September 7, 2010).

5. Jonathan McCarthy and Richard W. Peach, "Are Home Prices the Next 'Bubble?,'" *Economic Policy Review* 10, no. 3 (2004). **www.ny.frb.org/research/epr/04v10n3/ 0412mcca.html**.

6. Ludwig von Mises, "Interest, Credit Expansion, and the Trade Cycle: The Monetary or Circulation Credit Theory of the Trade Cycle," *Human Action: The Scholars Edition*. **http://mises.org/humanaction/chap20sec8.asp** (accessed October 25, 2010).

Chapter 13: Like a Moth to Flame: Our Destructive Tendency to Print

1. Chris Roush, "Fed Reporter da Costa Leaving WSJ," *Talking Biz News*, July 30, 2015. **https://talkingbiznews.com/they-talk-biz-news/fed-reporter-da-costa-leaving-wsj/**.

2. Alan Greenspan, "Gold and Economic Freedom," in *Capitalism: The Unknown Ideal*, ed. Ayn Rand (New York: Penguin Group, 1967), 101–108.

3. Carmen M. Reinhart and Kenneth S. Rogoff, *This Time Is Different: Eight Centuries of Financial Folly* (Princeton: Princeton University Press, 2009).

4. **https://research.stlouisfed.org/aggreg/swdata.html**.

Chapter 14: Fuzzy Numbers

1. Kevin Phillips, "Numbers Racket: Why the Economy Is Worse than We Know," *Harper's Magazine*, May 2008. **www.harpers.org/archive/2008/05/0082023**.

2. "Fed Luminaries Spar Over U.S. Inflation Target," *Wall Street Journal*, April 20, 2009. **http://online.wsj.com/article/SB124006652812232007.html**.

3. "Zimbabwean dollar," *Wikipedia*. **http://en.wikipedia.org/wiki/Zimbabwean_ dollar** (accessed September 7, 2010).

4. "Consumer Price Index: December 2007," Bureau of Labor Statistics. **www.bls .gov/news.release/History/cpi_01162008.txt** (accessed October 25, 2010).

5. "Retail Food Prices Up at Beginning of 2008," American Farm Bureau, March 27, 2008. **www.fb.org/index.php?fuseaction=newsroom.newsfocus&year =2008&file=nr0327.html** (accessed September 7, 2010; calculations were done manually by author).

6. Timothy Aeppel, "Accounting for Quality Change," in *Essentials of Economics*, ed. N. Gregory Mankiw (Mason, OH: Cengage Learning, 2008), 350.

7. John Williams, "Alternate Inflation Charts," Shadow Government Statistics. **www .shadowstats.com/alternate_data/inflation-charts** (accessed November 8, 2010).

8. Ibid.

9. Nicole Mayerhauser and Marshall Reinsdorf, "Housing Services in the National Economic Accounts," Bureau of Economic Analysis, 1. **www.bea.gov/papers/pdf/ RIPfactsheet.pdf** (accessed September 7, 2010).

10. Dylan G. Rassier, Bettina H. Aten, Eric B. Figueroa, Solomon Kublashvili, Brian J. Smith, and Jack York, "Improved Measures of Housing Services for the U.S. Economic Accounts," Bureau of Economic Analysis, May 5, 2021. **https://apps.bea .gov/scb/2021/05-may/0521-housing-services.htm**.

11. Ibid.

12. Phillips, "Numbers Racket."

Chapter 15: Crumbling Before Our Eyes: The Story of Concrete

1. "Investment," 2017 Infrastructure Report Card," **https://2017.infrastructurere-portcard.org/solutions/investment/**.
2. Dean McCartney, "The Problem with Reinforced Concrete," *The Conversation*, June 17, 2016. **https://theconversation.com/the-problem-with-reinforced-concrete-56078**.

Chapter 16: Energy and the Economy

1. Global GDP Data. **ourworldindata.org**.
2. Vaclav Smil, "Energy in the Twentieth Century: Resources, Conversions, Costs, Uses, and Consequences," *Annual Review of Energy and the Environment* 25:21–51. **https://www.annualreviews.org/doi/pdf/10.1146/annurev.energy.25.1.21**.
3. Thom Hartmann, *Last Hours of Ancient Sunlight, Revised and Updated: The Fate of the World and What We Can Do Before It's Too Late* (New York: Three Rivers Press, 2004): 12–13.
4. C. J. Cleveland, "Net Energy from Oil and Gas Extraction in the United States, 1954–1997," *Energy* 30 (2005): 769–782.
5. Nate Hagens, "Unconventional Oil: Tar Sands and Shale Oil—EROI on the Web, Part 3 of 6." *Oil Drum*, April 15, 2008. **www.theoildrum.com/node/3839**.
6. Cutler J. Cleveland and Peter O'Connor, "An Assessment of the Energy Return on Investment (EROI) of Oil Shale," Western Resource Advocates, June 2010. **www.westernresourceadvocates.org/wp-content/uploads/dlm_uploads/2015/07/oseroireport.pdf**.
7. Cutler J. Cleveland et al., "Energy and the U.S. Economy: A Biophysical Perspective," *Science* (New Series) 225: 4665 (August 31, 1984), 890–897.
8. Daniela Russi, "An Integrated Assessment of a Large-Scale Biodiesel Production in Italy: Killing Several Birds with One Stone?" *Energy Policy* 36 (2008): 1169–1180.
9. H. Shapouri et al., "The 2001 Net Energy Balance of Corn Ethanol," USDA Office of the Chief Economist, July 14, 2004. **www.brdisolutions.com/Site%20Docs/Net_Energy_Balance_of_Corn_Ethanol_Shapouri.pdf**.
10. D. Pimentel and Tad Patzek, "Ethanol Production Using Corn, Switchgrass, and Wood; Biodiesel Production Using Soybean and Sunflower," *Natural Resources Research* 14:1 (March 2005): 65–76.
11. "What Is the Energy Payback for PV?," *PV FAQs*, US Department of Energy Solar Energy Technologies Program, January 2004. **https://www.nrel.gov/docs/fy04osti/35489.pdf**.
12. Ida Kubiszewski et al., "Meta-Analysis of Net Energy Return for Wind Power Systems," *Renewable Energy* 35 (2010): 218–225.
13. 1 Gallon of Gas = 124,262 BTUs. *Source:* **www.eia.doe.gov/kids/energy.cfm?page=about_energy_conversion_calculator-basics**. 3,412 BTUs = 1 KWh. *Source:* U.S. Department of Energy, Bonneville Power Mgt. 1 gallon of gas = 36.4 KWh (124,262 BTUs in a gallon of gas divided by 3,412 BTUs in 1 KWh). Human work (sustained): 74 watts/hour (agricultural work) to 100 watts/hour (very fit individual). Therefore, 1 gallon of gas = 492–364 hours of human work output.

14. David Pimentel and Mario Giampietro, "Food, Land, Population and the U.S. Economy," *Carrying Capacity Network*, November 21, 1994. **http://dieoff.org/ page40.htm**.
15. Mark Cartwright, "The Household Staff in an English Medieval Castle," *World History Encyclopedia*, June 1, 2018. **https://www.worldhistory.org/article/ 1234/the-household-staff-in-an-english-medieval-castle/**.

Chapter 17: Peak Oil

1. Richard Heinberg, *The Party's Over*, 2nd ed. (Gabriola Island, British Columbia: New Society Publishers, 2005); Thom Hartmann, *The Last Hours of Ancient Sunlight* (New York: Three Rivers Press, 2004); James Howard Kunstler, *The Long Emergency* (New York: Atlantic Monthly Press, 2005); Matthew Simmons, *Twilight in the Desert* (Hoboken, NJ: John Wiley & Sons, Inc., 2005); Richard Heinberg, *Power Down* (New York: Oxford University Press, 2009); Kenneth S. Deffeyes, *Beyond Oil: The View from Hubbert's Peak* (New York: Hill and Wang, 2005).
2. Kevin Morrison and Steve Johnson, "UK Net Oil Importer for First Time in Decade," *Energy Bulletin—Post Carbon Institute,* August 11, 2004. **www.energybulletin .net/node/1604**.
3. Andrew McNamara, "Highway of Diamonds," *ASPO Australia*, March 4, 2008. **www.aspo-australia.org.au/general/highway-of-diamonds.html**.
4. "More Than 90% of Australia's Fuel Imported—Leaving Country Vulnerable to Shortages, Report Says," *The Guardian*, April 21, 2022. **https://www.theguardian .com/australia-news/2022/apr/21/over-90-of-australias-fuel-imported-leaving-country-vulnerable-to-shortages-report-says**.
5. Chris Martenson, "The Looming Energy Shock," *Peak Prosperity*, July 1, 2017. **https:// peakprosperity.com/the-looming-energy-shock/**.
6. "Export Land Model," *Wikipedia*. **http://en.wikipedia.org/wiki/Export_Land_ Model** (accessed November 5, 2010).

Chapter 18: Shale Oil

1. Collin Eaton, "Oil Frackers Brace for End of the U.S. Shale Boom," *Wall Street Journal*, February 3, 2022. **https://www.wsj.com/articles/fracking-oil-prices-shale-boom-11643824329**.
2. EIA Map of Shale Basins. **https://www.eia.gov/analysis/studies/worldshalegas/**.

Chapter 19: Necessary but Insufficient: Coal, Nuclear, and Alternatives

1. Julian Simon, "When Will We Run Out of Oil? Never!" *The Ultimate Resource II: People, Materials and Environment*. **www.juliansimon.com/writings/ Ultimate_Resource/TCHAR11.txt** (accessed October 30, 2010).
2. Associate Professor Simon Michaux, JKMRC Friday Seminars 2022 (video), **https://youtu.be/MBVmnKuBocc**.
3. Vaclav Smil, *Energy Transitions: History, Requirements, Prospects* (Westport, CT: Praeger, 2010).

4. National Research Council Committee on Assessment of Resource Needs for Fuel Cell and Hydrogen Technologies, "Plug-In Hybrid Vehicle Costs Likely to Remain High, Benefits Modest for Decades," *Transitions to Alternative Transportation Technologies—Plug-in Hybrid Electric Vehicles* (The National Academies Press, December 2009). **www8.nationalacademies.org/onpinews/newsitem .aspx?RecordID=12826**.

5. Tracy Hu, "Uranium Gains Momentum as China Recommits to Nuclear Power Development," S&P Global, March 21, 2021. **https://www.spglobal .com/marketintelligence/en/news-insights/latest-news-headlines/ uranium-gains-momentum-as-china-recommits-to-nuclear-power-development-63258723**.

6. "Uranium Mining," *Wikipedia*. **http://en.wikipedia.org/wiki/Uranium_mining** (accessed October 30, 2010).

7. "Uranium Resources and Nuclear Energy," Energy Watch Group, December 2006, 9. **www.energywatchgroup.org/fileadmin/global/pdf/EWG_Report_ Uranium_3-12-2006ms.pdf**.

8. "Fast Breeder Reactors," *Wikipedia*. **https://en.wikipedia.org/wiki/Breeder_ reactor#Development_and_notable_breeder_reactors**.

9. "World Uranium Reserves," World Nuclear Association. **https://world-nuclear .org/information-library/nuclear-fuel-cycle/uranium-resources/supply-of-uranium.aspx**.

10. "Clean Coal or Dirty Coal?" *Alternative Energy Blog*, October 3, 2006. **http://alt-e .blogspot.com/2006_10_01_archive.html**.

11. Smil, *Energy Transitions,* appendix 1.

12. Albert A. Bartlett, "Arithmetic, Population, and Energy" (video). Last modified June 16, 2007. **www.youtube.com/watch?v=F-QA2rkpBSY**.

13. T. W. Patzek and G. D. Croft, "A Global Coal Production Forecast with Multi-Hubbert Cycle Analysis," *Energy* 35:3109–3122.

14. Dennis Avery, "Biofuels, Food or Wildlife? The Massive Land Costs of U.S. Ethanol," Competitive Enterprise Institute, September 21, 2006. **https://www .cei.org/wp-content/uploads/2010/10/Dennis-Avery-Biofuels-Food-or-Wildlife-The-Massive-Land-Costs-of-US-Ethanol.pdf**.

15. "How the Palm Oil Industry Is Cooking the Climate," *Greenpeace International*, 2007. **www.greenpeace.org/raw/content/international/press/reports/palm-oil-cooking-the-climate.pdf**.

16. Suzanne Goldenberg, "US Navy Completes Successful Test on Boat Powered by Algae," *The Guardian,* October 27, 2010. **www.guardian.co.uk/environment/ 2010/oct/27/us-navy-biofuel-gunboat**.

17. Personal conversation with David Murphy, an EROEI researcher.

Chapter 20: Why Technology Can't Fix This

1. James Temple, "At This Rate, It's Going to Take Nearly 400 Years to Transform the Energy System," *MIT Technology Review*, March 14, 2008. **https://www .technologyreview.com/2018/03/14/67154/at-this-rate-its-going-to-take-nearly-400-years-to-transform-the-energy-system/**.

Chapter 21: Minerals: Gone with the Wind

1. "Cleopatra: (Late 69 BC–August 12, 30 BC)," Wikipedia. **http://en.wikipedia. org/wiki/Cleopatra_VII** (accessed November 5, 2010); "Cheops Pyramid: 2589– 2566 BC," Oracle Thinkquest. **http://library.thinkquest.org/J002037F/cheops_ pyramid.htm** (accessed November 5, 2010); "Space Shuttle Columbia," Wikipedia. **http://en.wikipedia.org/wiki/Space_Shuttle_Columbia** (accessed November 8, 2010).
2. Christine McLelland, "What Earth Materials Are in My Subaru?," **https://core .ac.uk/download/pdf/5213665.pdf**.

Chapter 22: Soil: Thin, Thinner, Gone

1. "How to Feed the World in 2050," Food and Agriculture Association of the United Nations, October 2009, 8. **www.fao.org/fileadmin/templates/wsfs/docs/expert_ paper/How_to_Feed_the_World_in_2050.pdf**.
2. Rob Avis, "The Story of Soil," Permaculture Research Institute, June 17, 2010. **http://permaculture.org.au/2010/06/17/the-story-of-soil**.
3. W. M. Stewart, "Fertilizer Contributions to Crop Yield," *News and Views*, Potash and Phosphate Institute and Potash and Phosphate Institute of Canada, May 2002.
4. Cheryl Long, "Industrially Farmed Foods Have Lower Nutritional Content," *Mother Earth News,* June/July 2009. **https://www.motherearthnews.com/sustainable- living/nature-and-environment/nutritional-content-zmaz09jjzraw/**.
5. James Elser and Stuart White, "Peak Phosphorus," *Foreign Policy*, April 20, 2010. **https://foreignpolicy.com/articles/2010/04/20/peak-phosphorus**.
6. Timothy Egan, *The Worst Hard Times* (New York: Mariner Books, 2006), 8.

Chapter 23: Parched: The Coming Water Wars

1. Lester R. Brown, *Plan B 4.0: Mobilizing to Save Civilization* (New York: W.W. Norton, 2009).
2. Brown, *Plan B*; and Sandra Postel, *Pillar of Sand: Can the Irrigation Miracle Last?* (New York: W.W. Norton, 1999).
3. Brown, *Plan B*.
4. Ibid.
5. David Seckler et al., "Water Scarcity in the Twenty First Century," Water Brief 1 (Colombo, Sri Lanka: International Water Management Institute, 1999).
6. Dale Allen Pfeiffer, "Eating Fossil Fuels," *The Wilderness Publications*, October 3, 2003. **www.organicconsumers.org/corp/fossil-fuels.cfm**.
7. P. Torcellini, N. Long, and R. Judkoff, "Consumptive Water Use for U.S. Power Production," National Renewable Energy Laboratory, December 2003. **www.nrel .gov/docs/fy04osti/33905.pdf**.

Chapter 24: All Fished Out

1. Ransom Myers and Boris Worm, "Rapid Worldwide Depletion of Predatory Fish Communities," *Nature* 423 (2003): 280–283. **www.nature.com/nature/journal/ v423/n6937/full/nature01610.html**.
2. Lester R. Brown, *Plan B 3.0: Mobilizing to Save Civilization* (New York: W.W. Norton, 2003).
3. M.L.D. Palomares et al., "Fishery Biomass Trends of Exploited Fish Populations in Marine Ecoregions, Climatic Zones and Ocean Basins," *Estuarine, Coastal and Shelf Science* 243 (September 30, 2020): 106896. **https://www.sciencedirect .com/science/article/pii/S0272771419307644#fig4**.
4. Arthur Max, "Toxins Found in Whales Bode Ill for Humans," *ABC News*, June 24, 2010. **https://phys.org/news/2010-06-toxins-whales-bode-ill-humans.html**.
5. John Roach, "Source of Half Earth's Oxygen Gets Little Credit," *National Geographic News*, June 7, 2004. **http://news.nationalgeographic.com/science/article/ source-of-half-earth-s-oxygen-gets-little-credit**.
6. Steve Connor, "The Dead Sea: Global Warming Blamed for 40 Percent Decline in the Ocean's Phytoplankton," *The Independent*, July 29, 2010. **www.independent .co.uk/environment/climate-change/the-dead-sea-global-warming- blamed-for-40-per-cent-decline-in-the-oceans-phytoplankton- 2038074.html**.
7. Watson W. Gregg and Margarita E. Conkright, "Decadal Changes in Global Ocean Chlorophyll," *Geophysical Research Letters* (2002) 29:15. **https://ntrs.nasa.gov/ api/citations/20010067778/downloads/20010067778.pdf**.
8. David Perlman, "Decline in Oceans' Phytoplankton Alarms Scientists," **SFGate .com**, October 6, 2003. **http://articles.sfgate.com/2003-10-06/news/17513683_ 1_plankton-ocean-plants-carbon-dioxide**.
9. Alastair Bland, "The Ocean's Mysterious Vitamin Deficiency," *Hakai Magazine*, January 28, 2021. **https://hakaimagazine.com/features/the-oceans- mysterious-vitamin-deficiency/**.
10. Ibid.

Chapter 27: The Bumpy Path to 2030

1. "Bank of England's Mervyn King Says HBOS and RBS Came within Hours of Collapse," *Telegraph*, September 24, 2009, **https://www.telegraph.co.uk/ finance/newsbysector/banksandfinance/6226238/Bank-of-Englands- Mervyn-King-says-HBOS-and-RBS-came-within-hours-of-collapse.html**.
2. Donella Meadows, *Limits to Growth* (New York: Signet, 1972).

Chapter 28: The Good News

1. H. E. Daly, *Steady-State Economics: The Economics of Biophysical Equilibrium and Moral Growth* (San Francisco: W. H. Freeman, 1977).
2. *Wissenschaftliche Selbstbiographie. Mit einem Bildnis und der von Max von Laue gehaltenen Traueransprache*, Johann Ambrosius Barth Verlag (Leipzig 1948), p. 22, as translated in Max Planck, *Scientific Autobiography and Other Papers*, trans. F. Gaynor (New York: Philosophical Library, 1949), pp. 33–34, as cited in T.S. Kuhn, *The Structure of Scientific Revolutions* (Chicago: University of Chicago Press, 1962).

3. "Local Exchange Trading Systems," *Wikipedia.* **http://en.wikipedia.org/wiki/ Local_Exchange_Trading_Systems** (accessed November 4, 2010).

4. "Demurrage(currency),"*Wikipedia.***http://en.wikipedia.org/wiki/Demurrage_ (currency)** (accessed November 7, 2010).

5. "Ecological Footprint," *Wikipedia.* **http://en.wikipedia.org/wiki/Ecological_ footprint** (accessed November 4, 2010).

Chapter 29: Closing the Book on Growth

1. Simon Michaux, "The Mining of Minerals and the Limits to Growth," Geological Survey of Finland Technical Report, March 2021. **https://www.researchgate.net/ profile/Simon-Michaux-2/publication/351712079_The_Mining_of_Minerals_ and_the_Limits_to_Growth/links/60a6273d45851505a0e4ddcf/The-Mining-of-Minerals-and-the-Limits-to-Growth.pdf**.

Index

Page numbers followed by *f* refer to figures.